Whe
Customers
think we
don't
care

ENDING

ACTIONS

THAT

SELF-DESTRUCT

COMPANIES,

CUSTOMER

SERVICE

AND JOBS

McGRAW-HILL BOOK COMPANY Sydney

New York San Francisco Auckland Bogotá
Caracas Lisbon London Madrid Mexico City
Milan New Delhi San Juan Singapore
Toronto Kuala Lumpur

McGraw·Hill Australia

A Division of The McGraw·Hill Companies

National Library of Australia Cataloguing-in-Publication data:

Buchanan, Richard W.
When customers think we don't care: ending actions that self-destruct companies, customer service and jobs.

ISBN 0 074 70930 5.

1. Customer relations. 2. Consumer satisfaction. 3. Customer services. 4. Success in business. I. Title.

658.812

Published in Australia by
McGraw-Hill Australia Pty Ltd
4 Barcoo Street, Roseville NSW 2069, Australia
Acquisitions Editor: Javier Dopico
Production Editor: Megan Stansfield
Editor: Joy Window
Proofreader: Tim Learner
Designer: Kimberley Talia
Cover Design: Norman Baptista
Illustrator: Jed Mahoney, Banshee Graphics
Typeset in Bembo by Banshee Graphics
Printed on 80 gsm woodfree by Prowell Productions Ltd, Hong Kong.

To Jenny and all our children

Contents

Preface

An appropriate opening for both this book and the times in which we live is an old Chinese curse:

May you be born in interesting times

The reason for this is we are going through some of the most 'interesting' times the world has ever known and this has taught us that such times can certainly feel like a curse. Interesting times are 'interesting' only because they are different from what has come before, and that difference will demand we do things differently than we used to. Not all of us are sure we will be up to it—particularly within our place of work.

Dealing with that change is what this book is all about—dealing with change that has affected your employment in the past, change that is impacting on it now, and change that will be asked of it in the future. Because of this focus, it is important to start with a few comments about change in general and how it can be dealt with.

Change knows no 'sides'

Failure to cope with change will be equally painful to all employees, whether they be owners, managers or workers. So, this book will not push any particular position. I want everyone to do well ... and this will happen only if all work together equally.

Change is often painful

Sometimes, people get hurt by change. Don't think I don't understand that—from all angles. Although I work at a university, I am not from an ivory tower. Past work on assembly lines, as a gardener and as a truck driver has given me a unique (for an academic) point of view—that of the real-world employees who must deal with the life change brings them. I am on their side, no matter what level this may be.

The way 'things are' is not always the way I would wish them to be

We don't live in an ideal world. I wish we did—and sometimes when I discuss the 'rules' by which the game of change facing your employer is played, I would do anything to have them some other way. But you and your fellow employees will be much better off knowing the way these rules are, so you can play them to your own advantage rather than sitting around complaining about things none of us can change.

Dealing with change will require new approaches

If doing things the 'old way' worked, you would have no problem, for there would be no change required. This is not the case, and this book presents a whole range of very changed thinking about employees and employers. Some of these ideas may be difficult to accept, but ask yourself, 'If all this book offered was the same old thing, what earthly good would it be?'

Indeed—what a good place to begin!

Turning cultures that can't into cultures that care

1

The enemy within that sabotages companies, customer service and jobs

HOW YOU'LL DRIVE AWAY THE SOURCE OF YOUR PAY—AND WHAT IT WILL TAKE TO STOP IT

Employers rarely have much to fear from outside forces—when any employer fails it is usually because its own people drive away the hands that feed them.

It happens everywhere ...

Whether corporate giant, corner store, non-profit/charity or government department, the process works like this.

Sally goes into a large department store and can't find what she wants. She sees two salespeople talking behind a counter and stands in front of them. They keep talking. Finally she works up the courage to ask one of them a question. The other snaps for everyone to hear:

Excuse me, can't you see we're talking!

Sally scurries out of the store, vowing never to return. The store eventually closes for good. The employees blame 'bad management'.

Francis drops into a small restaurant for lunch. She has been wanting to try this place for months, as she often buys her lunch out. Settling down with her meal, she notices that the music playing in the background is so loud she can't talk with her companions—or hear herself think! She sees other customers are having similar problems. So she politely asks a waiter if it can be turned down. His response:

3

> *No way, lady! The boss says he likes the music that way—*
> *cuz it adds to the ambience.*

Feeling a migraine developing, Francis runs from the building, knowing she will never come back. Months later the restaurant closes ... to be replaced by a fast food pizza place. She later hears 'the boss' figures 'people just don't appreciate real class'.

An appliance company spends a fortune to develop a 'fast toast' toaster, and even more millions advertising its existence to get people to buy it. Rich is a workaholic who hates waiting for anything, so goes out and tracks one down at a local appliance dealer. He finally finds an uninterested salesperson who points out where the toaster is to be found. Almost ready to buy, Rich asks a logical question: 'How fast is it?' To this the salesperson replies:

> *I don't know. I don't like toast.*

Rich leaves with his wallet untouched. A year later the appliance company withdraws the new model due to slow sales. They figure people just weren't interested in its features.

Even 'not-for-profits' and government departments do it.

Bill and Jenny are avid Christians, have moved to a new town and are looking for a church to join. Sunday morning they check the *Yellow Pages*, and find almost none of the churches have an ad—and those who do haven't mentioned when their services are. They eventually find one to visit, kind of like it and, hearing that the pastor is from their home area, request he give them a call. Nothing happens. When they call the church office on another issue and mention not having heard from the pastor, they are told, 'He's too busy to be calling people'. They figure a church that busy can't be for them.

They try again. One church has a sign (which got off the boat with Noah!), but from the faded paint they can see they offer an 8 o'clock service. They get up early and go—only to be greeted with closed doors. They hear later that church hasn't had an 8 a.m. service for 10 years! Bill and Jenny figure that if God *could* die, the church members in that area would be unplugging His life support system!

A government tax department was notorious for taking 20 rings to answer the phone, losing the caller when it did, and for workers who didn't return the stacks of messages on their desks. Tax returns were often lost, resulting in nasty letters from the department to harassed taxpayers, threatening them with all kinds of disaster.

Mistakes were an everyday thing, and the workers felt 'above it all'—as they had worked for the government for 20 years and more. Eventually, responding to an election almost lost over anger involving this department, those in charge farmed out most of the work to an outside accounting firm. The workers remaining were either sidelined into dead-end careers, released or forced into early retirement. 'Dirty politics' was said to be the cause of all this.

Even *you* do it!

How about a story which even *you* may do? You need to make an important call—and the person you are calling isn't in, but has a voice mailbox asking you to leave a message at the 'sound of the tone'. You quickly reel off, '[Beep] Hi, this is Rich at blah/blah/blah/blah/blah-blah, thanks' (done with the cadence of a submachine gun).

Unless the person being called has a wonderful memory, they probably won't get both your name and your number in one go. The human mind just can't take this much information in as fast as it is given. So they have to listen to your message ... and your name ... and your number several times in order to return your call. (*Moral*: If you want them to return your call quickly, state your name and phone number—including area code—at least twice ... very slowly.)

When things like this happen, those on the receiving end think, 'Golly, these people just don't care!', and act accordingly. Those who are on the 'giving' end of such bad service—if they knew how their customers were feeling—might be thinking, 'But they don't know the facts. This was a bad day ... we are so busy ... how dare they complain? ... actually it was me doing them a favour ... etc., etc.'.

That's true. The customers don't know—and they don't care. Why should they? It's them giving you their money, not vice versa. It's not their job to care ... that's what they pay people like you for. Yet these events happen millions of times a day—with devastating effects—in every country in the world. In fact, they are so common that a warning (similar to 'cigarettes can be harmful to your health') seems necessary:

Warning
Once you have read this book those of you with a low level of tolerance for frustration will be doomed to a lifetime of anger! For you will begin to notice these events much more often than before. And they will really begin to bug you!

When *you* experience them, have you ever wondered how the organisations (and people) who do it can survive? In fact, they can't. *All* organisational failures are caused by customer service disasters like these.

When this happens it's a tragedy for everyone. It is a tragedy for the customer, for they get angry, frustrated and hurt when they don't get what they expect. Sooner or later they will 'get even', and this becomes a tragedy for the employers involved, as they see precious dollars walking out the door. Finally, it will be a tragedy for the employees who do it, for they are the very ones who will find themselves without a job when their employers fail.

This is how customer service—all employers *and their employees*—self-destructs. Logic suggests this can't be true, for why would any employee deliberately take away from their own salary? Although logic suggests it can't happen, your own experience will convince you that it does. And you can see the results on a regular basis.

The end results aren't pretty …

Every day you read about another one. Some poor outfit is folding, and all their employees are out of work. You watch the legal notices, see pictures of the closed buildings and the bankruptcy-auctioned remains, and your heart goes out to the people involved.

At the same time it's hard not to feel a mixture of smugness and fear as you think to yourself, 'We must be better than "them"', and wonder if you really are. It's that second emotion—fearing that the same disaster could happen to you—that this book is all about. If you haven't ever felt it, you are either wealthy or a fool.

If you do worry about it, the message of this book may prove a double-edged blessing. On the one hand, be assured that no organisation (including yours) has ever been put out of business by an outsider. On the other, be prepared to 'get taken down a notch'. For the only way to keep from future disaster is to admit that:

- You and your own employees all have within you the seeds of your own destruction.
- The only thing keeping this from happening is that other employers have employees working *even harder* at their own destruction than yours!

The reason the preceding says 'employer' instead of 'business' is that this does not apply to profit-making firms alone. The same holds true for churches, charities, government departments, special interest groups, labour unions and anybody else with employees (or, in the case of clubs, members). The only difference is that the process may work a bit more slowly, but it will be even more shocking to those who find themselves helpless when the 'permanent gravy train' they think they have been on comes to a shrieking halt.

The people who do it are the ones most hurt.

Total meltdown resulting in bankruptcy is not the only concern. This book is mostly about the people involved—you, your employees, and those in your family who look to you for support. And, as far as workers are concerned, a 'failure' takes place any time any employer fails to take advantage of any opportunity such that any employee finds themselves disadvantaged in any way.

For whether every employee or just one person in your entire firm is out of work—or can't get enough work to make ends meet—usually makes little difference to the person involved. It feels pretty much the same.

Finally, the employee 'culprits' are not members of just one group. They may include anyone who depends financially in any way on an employer—the workers, their managers and even the owners or stock/shareholders who direct the business. All may be responsible for the destruction of the hand that feeds them.

But when the disaster of unemployment happens to the employees involved, how could anyone in their right mind believe they were the ones behind their own end? The lack of logic is staggering. This is precisely what has left the basic causes hidden for so long.

Employees have always been thought the victims of organisational failure, not the source of it. They have (quite rightfully) received large amounts of sympathy while 'experts' (if anybody was interested) went sifting through the ashes looking for the business equivalent of an in-flight recorder to tell them of the events just before the disaster.

These same 'experts' have filled countless books with explanations for these failures, covering such issues as finance, marketing, economics and all the others found in any business education. In doing so they have not been incorrect, only incomplete.

Figuring out failure ...

Of course, the problems revealed by any failure can have many labels. But in attaching these labels, those involved have been working on very complex problems while ignoring very basic facts about the situation—facts so basic they are almost invisible, but which provide unmistakable clues to the real cause of any failure. These are as follows.

Fact 1: Not all organisations fail at the same time.

Even during the worst of times most organisations survive. Looking at it from a global view, one can see that even depressions and violent changes in economic climate see only a relatively small number actually going down the drain. In fact, never in the history of humanity has everyone been unemployed simultaneously!

Somebody always makes a go of it, no matter how tough the times, and some others usually do quite well, thank you. Why? Are they like the 'used car lot' in San Francisco that has this sign on it?

We pay the highest prices for the cars we buy ...
We charge the lowest prices for the cars we sell ...

... How do we stay in business?
WE'RE LUCKY!

No, it's far from likely that the survivors are just 'lucky'. Nor have they discovered some timeless secret of success denied others.

Fact 2: *There is no universal formula for business success.*

Business writers and researchers have been looking for an underlying secret of success almost as long as others have been searching for the Holy Grail! Countless books have hinted at having actually found some universal secret of success. However, if any of these are foolish enough to name real-live employers as 'better than the best', it generally is the 'kiss of death'. No sooner does the ink dry on such a list than some find themselves also featuring in bankruptcy proceedings!

Nor are these exceptions to the rule. Despite centuries of study on all the causes of/cures for failure, it is still hard to find many employers that are much more than 100 years old. And, when one does, such an exception is almost never thought a leader in its field. Most often it tends to be considered an isolated event, rather than the product of any conscious effort.

Based upon historical evidence, it appears clear there has never been *any* formula for success that has been everlasting. But this does not mean the reverse is also true. Although there has never been any single formula for employer success, simple logic reveals that there has always been one *universal factor of failure*. And, to the extent that avoiding failure is the same as getting success, it is useful to see what this might be.

Fact 3: *Employees are the* only *'universal factor of failure'.*

If one searches for similarities surrounding all organisational failure, they will find there is only one that has been around at the collapse of every employer in history—employees.

This is undeniable, as without employees there can be no employer. Wave a magic wand in front of Ford, GM, the Catholic Church, any charity or every government department, and eliminate all their employees. Do these organisations still exist? Of course not, for we have not yet reached the stage of having robots that can think as well as work. We still need somebody to 'push the buttons'.

This is not a trivial fact. It is a vital part of the riddle of failure. If we know employers cannot exist without employees, we also know that every organisation that ever failed had employees working away within it. They were present during the lead-up to the failure, and at the time that failure resulted in the loss of their jobs. This is inescapable.

So the question is not, 'Did they have employees', but rather, 'What were these people *doing* during the death throes of the hand which fed them'? Asking the employees is hardly going to result in an accurate answer. For, if one was at the helm of a ship when it went down, one is hardly dead keen to come forward and claim blame.

However, there is one group who always knows what happened, because they were around at the time of the disaster, had a hand in it and will be around long after. Who are these most knowledgeable of people? Simple—they are the customers of the failed employer, and they never totally disappear.

Fact 4: *The customers of failed organisations do not die with them.*

When anybody fails, their customers do not do the decent thing—go out, hide under a bush, and die with them! No, their customers always survive, and there is a good reason for this. The reason is what makes a person a customer to begin with:

> A customer is someone with a problem they are willing to pay someone else to solve for them.

Make no mistake about it, nobody gives anything away for nothing. People don't buy products; they *solve problems* by buying products. And people don't buy services; they *solve problems* by buying services. Even people who go to church are exchanging their time, efforts (if they serve within the church) and (eventually) money in return for solving some sort of problem.

The people who have the ability to choose *who* gets to solve their problems are what we know as 'customers'. Most commonly they are those who pay for products and services. In not-for-profit organisations and charities these people are often called 'donors', 'sponsors' or some other term. In some other cases the 'customer' is a bit harder to see, but is still there.

For instance, even the police have 'customers' in that they serve the general public—who don't directly purchase their services but certainly do elect the politicians—who comprise the committees that split up the taxpayer funds—that eventually become the salaries of the police—who serve the public by (hopefully) solving police-related problems. So it is with all government departments.

Seen in this way, there is no employer that does not have 'customers' of some sort. And, no matter what happens to whomever they used to give their money to solve their problems, these customers will always remain. For the problems needing to be solved never go away—so the customers attached to them won't either.

Therefore, the customers are always there to tell you exactly what happened when somebody failed. If asked, they always give the same summary—it's fact 5.

Fact 5: *The customers of failed firms have always taken their 'business' elsewhere.*

If customers are asked what this really means they will answer:

Oh, I found somebody else to give my money to for solving these problems.

For products and services this will mean finding somebody else from which to purchase. For charities it will mean choosing to make donations to another charity. For churches it may mean going to another church (or possibly none at all, and so donating their time and money to football or something similar). And for government departments it may mean either outsourcing a former government department (and the jobs it represents) or letting some other department do the work.

However, what is most useful about the thoughts of former customers is why they saw fit to take such a drastic action. It is always for the same reason: fact 6.

Fact 6: *Customers went to another supplier because they think they got a better deal.*

This must be true; customers would never go where they got a worse deal—this defies human nature. When pressed as to what represented this better deal, customers will always reply, 'We got ... a better product/service, cheaper price, more convenient place to buy, or more information about why I should buy'.

The same thing happens with charities/churches and government departments. When one of these non-business employers folds, it is because somebody else found a better way to solve their customers' problems—through a more convincing advertising campaign, a more attractive form of worship, better service, superior location and so on.

'Reality' may not have much to do with it.

It is important to point out why the word 'think' was stressed in fact 6. This was done to make an important point:

> If customers think they got a better deal and vote with their feet, whether or not they *actually* got a better deal is *totally unimportant*! Perception is much more important than reality when it comes to survival.

The reason this is worth pointing out will be easier to see if one remembers that customers are always people with problems that need solving. Often, people who make their living from solving them (particularly if they have been doing it for some time or have taken large amounts of formal education in order to do it) begin to believe they have a 'divine right' to tell others the best way to solve these problems.

When this happens, established suppliers often miss what amounts to a major competitive threat by saying, 'Well, [piff, piff], it's not really a better deal', and go on their merry way to disaster. For, if customers think it's a better deal and are willing to put their money where their mouth is—by voting with their feet—as far as those who stand to lose/gain jobs are concerned, it *is* a better deal.

A good case of this is doctors who deliver babies. At one time they had this 'business' totally to themselves. Along came midwives who offered home birth. And the doctors responded, 'Well, [piff, piff], the midwives don't have the sanitation of a hospital, they lack some of the monitoring devices, they don't have the immediate operating room back-up that we do. It's not really a better deal [piff, piff]'. But the expectant mothers didn't care. The entire midwifery profession owes its survival to this short-sighted kind of idiocy.

The point for everybody to learn is this. Whatever you, the problem-solver, think is a 'good deal' is almost totally unimportant. The key is perception, not 'reality' (whatever that is). Your biggest threats will not go away just because you think they should.

Of course, the reverse is also true for new organisations that never 'get off the ground'. Ask those expected to support the new venture why they didn't, and they will say, 'Oh, the old organisation offered me something I thought was better than the new'. Or, 'the new offered me nothing better than the old. There seemed no reason to change'. A whole lot of 'dot.com disasters' learned this the hard way.

'Conclusive' evidence for why failure happens ...

If we put all of this together, a very interesting conclusion about failure can be reached. The process would sound like this if we asked the people involved:

Q1 Now, when the old supplier died, you (the customer) didn't disappear, you just went elsewhere. Right?

A1 Right.

Q2 And you went elsewhere because you thought you were getting a 'better deal'. Right?

A2 Right.

Q3 And this 'better deal' was with regard to the products/services, prices, promotion, or availability the 'winning' competitor offered. Right?

A3 Right.

Q4 Well, what about the people who worked for the 'losing' competitor. Couldn't they see what was happening?

A4 I guess so ... nothing ever remains invisible for long.

Q5 If they saw what was happening, couldn't these people have changed what they were offering, so there was no reason for you to go?

A5 Probably; anything is possible with money.

Q6 Then why didn't these silly souls who saw their customers walking out the door—with their *jobs* attached—*change* so that there was no reason for you to leave?

A6 That is a very good question indeed, and one this book will answer. However, the inescapable fact is:

> Every employer that has ever failed has been put out of business by its own people who produced barriers which pushed those they served elsewhere!

Moral: a life-giving word change

One way the preceding can have immediate value for you—and all with whom you work—is to resolve to make a personal change in the words used in the work place. The reason this would be useful is that words are important—they tell people how to *feel* about something—and through this tell them *what to do* about something. This has a major impact on survival.

For example, during the Vietnam war conflict a set of words became so popular, powerful and dangerous they became a court-martial level offence for those found using them. What were these words? 'Somebody fragged the lieutenant.'

For those not up on their Vietnam-era military jargon, what 'fragging' meant was deliberately causing the death of one's commanding officer by shooting, bayoneting, or tossing a hand grenade at them. It was a major problem during 'Nam, as it became an 'in' joke. The problem was that while some were laughing ... others were dying.

So the command came down, 'You use these words, and we will see you in the stockade'. What words did the army insist be used instead? Why, the truth: 'Somebody murdered the lieutenant'. You see, when someone used the right words, it caused them to think about what was happening ... and maybe it wouldn't happen so often.

There are a similarly dangerous set of words which get used in every employer in the world. They are trotted out when one of two very common events happens. These events are:

- somebody who *used to deal* with your employer either partially or totally quits; or
- somebody who *could have dealt* with your employer either doesn't even consider you or (worse still) does consider you, but still goes elsewhere.

When this happens most employees will respond with the most dangerous workplace words ever said:

> Well, I guess we lost that customer. (The most dangerous workplace words ever used)

These words are so dangerous because they take away from both the importance and the cause of what has happened. They are said in a joking vein. And they give the impression that, ' ... nothing we [the employees] did had anything to do with what has happened. There is nothing we could have done to keep it from happening. It was probably God's will (and who are we to argue with God?)'.

So nothing will change. And it will probably happen again—with all the personal disaster that implies. If this sounds worth preventing, just make the following changes in your workplace words.

> Don't ever say:
>   I guess we lost that customer.
> Say:
>   **We drove them away!**

For this is what really happened. And it causes much more useful questions to be asked—questions like 'How?' and 'Why?' and 'How can we keep it from happening again?'

Why employees do dumb things

With regard to 'How?', it happens through those events that rob from the salaries of those who do them. They represent 'the enemy within'. Why do employees do them? It's not because they are stupid but because they don't know any better. Employees do self-destructive (dumb) things because:

- They have been told to do them by a management that doesn't know any better.
- They deliberately want to hurt their employer, because they don't know any better.
- They do so without realising what they are doing—because they don't know any better.

The common element of 'they don't know any better' is both the cause of the problem and a clue as to how to fix it. If one could only find out what it is that the employees (including the owners/managers) don't know, one would hold the key to a solution for this universal source of failure.

Fixing it is not as easy as it looks.

For many plagued by customer service/marketing failures like those featured in this book, the solution seems remarkably easy. It is rather like noticing that a home one has just purchased has chipped paint on a second-storey window ... and all that will be required is to paint over it. Since what a customer-service failure really represents is a failure to do something the customer wants done, the 'painting over' approach will be to run some kind of customer service seminar explaining to employees how to do the things not getting done ... and asking them to do better. This may help a bit, but only rarely will it be enough to totally solve the problem.

The reason 'painting over' the problem will not be enough to do the job is because of a little-recognised fact. Although the goal of all marketing—improved customer service—is one of those 'sacred cows' right up there with all else that is good and true:

> There is no logical reason for most employees to *want* to give better customer service!

The great unanswered questions of marketing and customer service

Face facts. There are three questions most customer service training leaves unanswered. They are:

1 Improved customer service always involves some employee(s) somewhere ... somehow doing more than they are already doing. Why should they *want* to make this extra effort?

2 The objective of improved customer service is always more business (of some sort). To the employees involved this will always mean more work! Why should they *want* this?

3 Customer service failures serious enough to merit attention are not isolated events, nor are they accidents. They take place within a culture of people who can't help making them happen. Why should the culture *want* to change?

Failure to address the preceding issues means that after a flurry of surface activity the real improvements secured by any customer service program may not amount to much. Like putting good paint over chipped, the rot will soon return.

The secret is a culture change.

The only way to really fix a customer service problem is to change the culture in which it happens so completely that it cannot happen again—because the culture doesn't *want* it to. This requires not just painting over a window, not just painting the second floor, not even just painting the 'house'. What it really takes is pulling the whole thing down to the foundation and starting over again.

Starting over from the foundation

Doing this will require unravelling a number of what are at best myths and at worst outright lies that everybody knows but no one believes. 'Everyone knowing but no one believing' means there are a number of 'facts' surrounding employers which everyone 'knows' and which are just not true! In fact, they are so obviously false that few who have worked for a living haven't had their own doubts about them.

Because they are universally popular, and state what most wish to hear, no one follows up on these doubts by saying, 'The emperor has no clothes' and questioning these 'facts', let alone the flawed conclusions they produce.

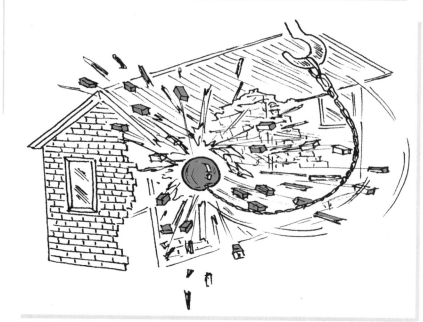

Figure 1.1 The house of marketing and customer service—starting over from the foundation

Yet if these 'facts' are pulled apart and exposed for the lies they are, an entirely different view of the workplace world is gained. This is one not totally at odds with what has gone before, but based on an entirely different logic that produces astonishingly different answers about the real causes of/cures for employer failure—and one which allows people to operate with a great deal more clues about what is really happening and about how to change it.

Four 'facts' that force failure

Although there are only four of these 'facts', their explanation and interaction are so tightly woven together that unravelling them (and showing how to set them straight) will take up most of this book.

Lie 1: *People are basically noble.*

Employers are made up of people (as is any 'customer' base), and until one reaches some understanding of 'what makes people tick' it will be impossible to do anything about controlling (let alone changing) any outcomes. Unfortunately, the basic premise of virtually everything that passes for 'modern management', 'scientific marketing' and psychology is based on the assumption that people are basically good—and always motivated towards the best interests of others.

Does this make sense to you? Despite what you might wish to believe, does your experience with others suggest that they will usually do what is best for you—or for them? Suppose we have it wrong. Suppose the basic motivation of virtually all human behaviour *is* selfishness. If it is, missing this basic fact produces all kinds of mischief.

The most basic problem it causes is that it hides the motivations of everyone involved. In theory, there are a large number of reasons why employees shouldn't produce barriers, and even more why the barriers should not be a problem to potential customers—if everyone were as noble as we are led to believe.

But if these 'reasons' why barriers shouldn't exist come from a view of human nature that is flawed from the beginning, then these same 'reasons' can't help us—and our belief in them keeps us from seeing facts needed to fix the situation. This is particularly so as it relates to the motives of the workforce.

Lie 2: *Employees care about their employer.*

This has got to be number one on the 'hit parade' of myths employers most want to believe. Do a 'SWOT' (strengths, weaknesses, opportunities, threats) analysis—ask any manager what is his or her organisation's greatest 'strength', and they will reply, 'Our employees'. Talk to them and you get the impression that everybody at 'Good Old Amalgamated Feeblefeltzer' is out there just waiting to die for their employer. Employees usually don't openly challenge this belief.

If this myth were true it would totally eliminate the problem of barriers; employees would never want to harm any organisation they loved this much. But, if people are basically selfish, ask, 'Why *should* employees love their employer?' Are those concerned better-paid/less over-worked/given better work conditions than they could get elsewhere? If not, why should they have any warm feelings about their workplace?

Beyond that, insisting that employees are not selfish blinds employers to what are some of the most powerful driving forces behind humans—motivations which the workers won't discuss openly with their employers because these are selfish, and therefore unmentionable.

Unfortunately, neither will employers discuss how their employees' desires relate to the employer, its motives, and what the employer is really likely to do to its people, and why. This is because these employer motives are also selfish (and likewise unmentionable).

This leads to lie number three.

Lie 3: *Employers care about their employees.*

It is very much in vogue for employers to beat their corporate breasts and proclaim to employees, 'We care—at Amalgamated Feeblefeltzer. We care about you—the individual—so much. Oh golly, how we care!'

Many employers probably do. But if people (including employers) are basically selfish, this can be true only to a very limited extent. If employees believe the full measure of this rubbish (and are themselves selfish), the main danger is they will take it to an extreme it was never intended to go to. They will hear what was never said but what they wanted to hear—namely that the organisation 'cares' about its employees more than it cares about the organisation.

It follows, then, that employees have no good reason to stop self-destructive barriers; they have been told that some kindly 'other' will keep on taking care of them—no matter what they do to 'customers'. As a matter of fact, under this 'cloud' driving a customer away is a really good idea—for it will mean less work for the employee to do, with no ill consequences.

On the other hand—and no better—if the employee doesn't believe this propaganda, then it becomes just one more mis-truth covering up what the employee believes are hidden wildly selfish employer motivations. This does little to foster cooperation; it encourages, at best, cynicism and, at worst, outright rebellion.

Mix all of this in with one last big lie and you have a complete picture of why every organisation fails because of its own people.

Lie 4 (the big lie): *Marketing can make people buy things.*

This is a whopper that all but a few rare marketers are afraid to state. Nevertheless it is implied by the very nature of what they do. For, if marketing—through advertising/salesmanship/public relations—cannot make people buy things, then of what earthly good is it?

The problem this introduces happens in two areas, which produce results that link together. On one side, asserting the thought that 'marketing is magic' tends to limit its influence to the promotional (advertising/salesmanship/public relations) areas most closely associated with marketing, in which marketers are supposed to be all-powerful in 'making the suckers buy'. The other side of the problem is that people outside the marketing area see absolutely no reason to stop producing their barriers if *their* jobs are not a direct part of the marketing department. For marketing is something 'they' (the marketers) do 'over there', and 'what I do in *my* job is none of their concern'.

Thus the entire organisation may believe that, no matter how awful their behaviour is to their customers, marketing will be able to fix all this with just the right advertising campaign, clever public relations gimmick, or sales device. Therefore, don't worry!

Putting it all together—why customers think you don't care

So what we have is a world where everyone acts on an assumption that no one is selfish, even though most people have a personal suspicion they may be. Employers behave as though their employees are totally behind them, even though there is ample proof to the contrary. And employers assert a 'caring' for employees that deprives workers of any motivation to look after their employer. Finally, the people down in marketing are from a profession that suggests they can 'fix anything', thereby giving others a strong reason to believe they can get away with anything—no matter how diabolical.

Small wonder then that the people highlighted at the beginning—and virtually every other employee—are all working so hard to put themselves out of business. Why shouldn't they? They have no reason not to—*especially since nobody is going to tell anybody what they need to know to want to do better.*

That is what this book is all about—exploring why employees shouldn't do this kind of thing from their own perspective, and what they need to be told in order to stop it happening. Finding out what this means will take us on a voyage of discovery that will pass through a number of almost unexplored areas of thought, including the nature of humanity, self-destructive acts from all perspectives and a whole new approach to business—post-modernist marketing.

In the process it will approach the whole marketing/customer service/self-destruction debate from a fresh, but more powerful viewpoint—namely, what's in it for those whose lives are most damaged by what happens 'when customers think we don't care'.

A look ahead

At the end of each chapter an action summary will suggest the kinds of things that need to be known in order to change a customer-service culture. This will be followed by *The bottom line*, a short summary of how the insights of the chapter can be applied to one's own workplace. There will also be an action exercise which will show how to pass valuable knowledge on to employees in a workshop format.

In most cases the action exercise will assume that your employees will have read the chapter of this book that precedes the exercise.

ACTION SUMMARY

Who are the enemy? The enemy are us!

Regardless of their type, organisations do not fail because of outsiders. They are always put out of business by their own people who produce barriers that drive their 'customers' away.

Why employees drive customers away

Employees drive customers away because they don't know any better. The problem is rarely that employees don't know what to do, but rather because the real culture in the workplace gives workers no personal reason for so doing. Simply holding a customer service seminar will not fix this, for it doesn't touch the 'hearts and minds' cultural issue at the centre of what amounts to asking people to do more in the future than they have in the past.

How to change a 'customer-killing' culture

Changing a culture in a positive direction requires sorting out four popular myths-cum-lies: (1) people are basically noble; (2) employees care about their employer; (3) employers care about their employees; and (4) marketing can 'make' people buy. So doing will help direct the hearts and minds of all employees towards more complete devotion to the needs of their 'customers'—for their own good.

It's all about people.

The approach taken by this book to achieve this will be that of finding some way to show employees something most have never seen before—*what's in it for them.*

THE BOTTOM LINE

You never lose a customer; you drive them away! Whenever any customer of your employer goes elsewhere, always ask, 'What did *we* do that made this happen?'

ACTION EXERCISE 1.1

How bad barriers can feel ... to you!

For: Employees at all levels   **Format**: 4–8-person groups
Materials required: Pencils and instructions
Objective: To show how widespread are the events by which employees literally drive away their jobs and salaries

Instructions

In this chapter we saw that employees can literally drive away their jobs and their salaries. Hasn't this happened to you as a customer? After forming into groups you will be discussing similar experiences.

Form into groups ... then:

In the first 15 minutes you are asked to come up with at least two similar personal experiences per group in which someone literally tried to drive you and your money away. Once you have these in mind we want you to:

1 Briefly describe what happened.
2 Tell us how the event made you feel as a customer (e.g. angry, upset, annoyed).
3 Tell us if you plan to do business with the subject firm again. If not, tell how you now satisfy the same needs (e.g. not buy the product/service again, take your 'business' elsewhere). If you do plan to stay with the same firm, explain both why you are willing to put up with such treatment, and whether you would put up with it were a better 'deal' to be made available from somebody else (e.g. is there nobody else to do it, has the firm 'made amends', and would you like to go elsewhere?).
4 In light of the above, what do you think is going to happen (in the long run) to the employees of the organisation who did this to you if what happened is typical of them (e.g. be fired, lose their jobs when firm goes out of business)?
5 Without naming any specifics, do you believe that our organisation is guilty of the same sort of thing from time to time?

Then be prepared to share your answers with us in the time remaining.

2

Where it all *starts* to go wrong—human nature

WHAT MOTHER NEVER TOLD YOU—HOW SELF-DESTRUCTION IS PLANTED IN ALL OF US

Something most of us learned from birth, and then had reinforced by 'science' and society, has been wrong from the beginning. Unless this mis-truth is corrected, there is no hope of creating an effective marketing/customer-service culture.

You can't deal with people without understanding human nature.

Here's how it works. Marketing and customer-service are all about people. Whether these people are customers, or those serving them, it is necessary to have a firm grip on a basic issue most ignore—what is the nature of 'human nature'? What makes this so vital is that most effective human activity is based upon a firm understanding of how others will react to whatever we do. This in turn is based upon what we *think* 'makes others tick'.

For instance, when we are driving down a highway, see another car approaching and keep to our side of the road, we are predicting the other driver will do the same. Or if we are having breakfast and ask somebody to 'pass the sugar', we are predicting that the other person will do so to keep from offending us. Then again, if we are an employer and pay somebody more than other employers will, we expect that these workers will be loyal and work hard.

Most of us never think about this much further. But if one does, it will become clear that every one of our own actions with others is based upon an underlying set of beliefs about other people, and how they will react to any situation. Putting this all together, one has 'human nature'. Our understanding of this nature helps us decide what to do in any situation.

We all have a personal opinion about human nature, whether we go to the extent of thinking it through formally, or whether it is just there driving what we do without much conscious thought. These opinions represent what many scientists would call a *theory*. All any theory represents is an opinion about how something works.

Everybody has an underlying theory, formal or not, about human nature—what it is and how it works. Some of these theories come from our own experiences, some were taught to us by our parents, and some come from 'science'. Unfortunately, two of these three sources of knowledge are usually wrong!

Most have it 'right' in terms of experience.

The most accurate theories of human behaviour usually come from personal experiences. These experiences normally cause us to develop theories centred upon what economists have long called 'the economic man [now person]' approach. This has sometimes been described as the 'rational person' approach. Unfortunately, the use of the word 'rational' or 'economic' can carry with it a meaning that—depending on the situation—some may not think is an accurate description of what is taking place. (In other words, what is 'rational' or 'economic' behaviour? It may look pretty bizarre to an observer.)

This is similar to the difference between 'reality' and 'perception' discussed in the first chapter. This one will be settled the same way by stressing the word *think* in the definition that follows. If someone 'thinks' their action is 'rational' or 'economic', it *is* for them. Keeping this in mind, the 'economic/rational' person theory can be summarised as follows:

> People will usually do what they *think* is best for themselves (overall) at the time.

It's hard to argue with this. All it says is what our own experiences teach—people generally will look after their own best interests. And we can make a good guess about their behaviour in any situation by (perhaps cynically) thinking through what they will *think* is good for them, and assuming they will do it. One doesn't go very wrong this way, and if human knowledge had been left at this, there wouldn't be much of a problem. Unfortunately it wasn't.

Our upbringing hasn't helped.

Ever since we were old enough to listen, most of us have heard from our parents a theory of human behaviour which—though not totally inaccurate—is usually incomplete and misleading. We were taught this whenever they slapped us up the side of the head and yelled:

> *You rotten little kid. Look at what you just did to your brother/sister.*
> *You're so selfish! Now you go off and think about what you have done.*

Most of us did slink off somewhere—usually wondering what they were on about, as the action(s) for which we were being punished seemed to make sense to our own 'economic person'. In other words, we had done what seemed best for us at the time.

Through these experiences most of us added a new word to our personal theory of human behaviour—'selfishness'. And we learned it was bad—real bad—in *all* cases. Although 'selfishness' seemed to consist of the same self-centred actions our experience had taught us worked, we learned we should despise it wherever we might find it.

This wasn't the worst thing which could happen to us, for uncontrolled selfishness *on our own part* is usually disastrous. However, what we also learned in the bargain was to reject all forms of selfishness *found in others—and to keep our own selfishness hidden* (lest we get clobbered for it). Unfortunately, what was lacking in our learning was any kind of balance.

Nobody ever told us that it is humanly impossible to eliminate *all* forms of selfishness, and failure to recognise this leaves a large hole in what passes for everybody's theory of human nature. This can make for decisions that are at best foolish and at worst outright stupid.

But failure to recognise basic truths about selfishness is exactly what has produced the sort of thinking described in the previous chapter, where it is assumed employees will *naturally* want to give better customer service when there is no *selfish* reason for them to do it. If we somehow have gotten the 'natural' aspects of selfishness wrong, the reason why this won't work would be obvious from the start. Unfortunately, the 'scholarly' approach (which normally challenges incorrect thinking) hasn't been much help.

'Scholars' have it even 'wronger'.

Places of higher learning have not been absent from the debate about human nature. Particularly in the 'social sciences', which deal with human aspects of life (like psychology, sociology, education ... and business), scholars have had to develop a platform of 'the way people tick' from which to base their thinking.

Since the beginning of time a battle has raged over the basic nature of people—with one side saying it is 'good' and the other just as loudly yelling that people are 'bad'. Lately the 'goods' have been outstripping the 'bads'—by large numbers.

This is particularly easy to see in modern approaches to business. Every new student of management is usually told that there are two basic theories about employees, both of which have something to say about human nature—*Theory 'X'* and *Theory 'Y'*. Theory 'X' pictures people as being lazy, selfish and uncooperative. The only things thought useful for motivating them are punishment and reward (heavy on the punishment!).

Theory 'Y' is the basis of today's 'enlightened management'. It assumes that people are basically good, always interested in others, naturally cooperative, and totally lacking in selfishness. Theory 'Y' suggests that the best way to get work out of people is to let them know what you want them to do—then get out of the way.

With the exception of the work related to something called behaviour modification, Theory Y (and its assumptions of human nobility) is the only one that has received much attention, research or use for the last 30 years. This is probably because it represents a view about people (in general) which each of us wishes to believe (about ourselves).

We want to believe good things about ourselves, and are willing to accept no less. There is nothing wrong with this, for it is the beginning of a sense of self-worth, which is the foundation for sound mental health. This done, most are also willing to (grudgingly) accept that perhaps other people are *also* basically good—thereby producing the assumption that people in general must be noble.

The danger in all this is that society has made any visible expression of selfishness a *deviation* from what is considered 'normal'. This deviation is so serious that (with the exception of discussions with one's psychiatrist) people are normally unwilling to admit personal selfishness, and they viciously attack—or refuse to cooperate with—any found hidden in others. This is exactly the same thing we learned from our parents—namely that 'selfishness is bad'—real bad!—*in all cases.*

This creates major problems, for it has meant that any commonly held view of behaviour based upon selfishness has largely been unexplored. People (whether scholars or 'just plain folks') rarely like to study something that might tear away at their own positive image of themselves.

But what if lack of thought about the issue of selfishness is wrong—and has been from the beginning? What this would mean is the theory of human nature most have—and upon which most actions are based—is wrong! So our thoughts about what it might take to get certain things to happen may *also* be wrong—or at least less effective than they might otherwise be.

What people don't know about human nature *can* hurt them.

An easy way to understand this is a simple scenario. Suppose one is going into business with a partner, and that person assumes their business partner is 'honest, good and true'. So they open their lives and their chequebooks to this other person. If this assumption about the other person's nature is incorrect, how harmful it will be! On the other hand, imagine how different our innocent partner's actions would have been if they had known from the beginning their new associate was dishonest, immoral and (probably) fattening!

Another good illustration can be found in that most basic of human partnerships, love. How many people do you know (including you) who have taken unfortunate risks based upon a rosy-hued image of their new 'beloved's' basic nature, only to find later that: (1) that image was wrong; (2) their real nature was much worse than you thought; and (3) you wish you had known that from the beginning—if you had, you wouldn't have done much of what you did.

The point to be found in all of this is simple. It is absolutely essential to have an accurate picture of what people are like before building any structures related to much of anything, let alone marketing and customer service. For, if we've got this 'nature of human nature' wrong, everything based upon that incorrect foundation will be a 'castle based on sand'.

It's not about whether people are 'bad' or 'good'—it's something which has been missed.

The intention of this book is not to change anybody's opinion about whether people are basically good or bad. (For what it's worth, this author thinks most *want* to be 'good'.)

Rather, it will explore an issue the 'nature of humanity' debate has missed, namely the 'badness' of selfishness—which has kept any ideas based on that issue from further thought. It will do this by exploring the idea that the basic nature of humanity is *always* selfish, but because of that universal presence selfishness is not as 'bad' as we have been led to believe, by both scholars and upbringing. And we should include it in any equation involving people.

This idea isn't totally new. Psychologists have for years tried to get people to accept that ideas/actions that might be considered 'selfish' are not 'bad'. But even this has largely been an attempt to deal with expressions of selfishness as a *thing apart*—rather than as *a part of* humanity. They have almost totally left the matter there. And almost no student of business has ever considered what might be learned by thinking through, 'What if the unthinkable were true?'

A new foundation ...

This book will consider the unthinkable. It will do so by starting out with many ideas ignored, overlooked or forgotten until now. This will produce many new insights useful to employers and employees alike. The first of these is the foundation upon which this book will be based.

> The basic motivation of virtually all human behaviour is selfishness.

The reason for the use of the word 'virtually' is that there is a small exception (called the 'sainthood factor') which might apply to a small group of people a small part of the time. However, because this is such a small exception, it won't be discussed here—but those who are curious or don't like the *personal* implications of admitting universal selfishness may contact the author if they are interested (details on p. 287). For most of us the assumption of personal selfishness can safely be made for most of our actions.

Accepting new realities about people may not be easy.

Some people exhibit an almost knee-jerk reaction to this foundation statement; it so completely opposes what they *wish* to believe. Their opposition and its form is so predictable it is worth discussing, thereby further exploring the truths connected to a flat assertion of universal selfishness.

Reality: *There are no human behaviours which are not selfish—*
at some point.

This book defines selfishness as any behaviour intended to be satisfying to one's self, whether that satisfaction is 'rational' or not. This is really no more than another way to state what the already discussed 'economic person' says.

Other definitions of 'selfishness' have been rather more limiting. They imply that selfishness means (only) situations in which an individual *unreasonably* obtains *personal benefit* at the *expense* of *someone else*. This is pretty tough to determine, for it involves so many unknowns.

For example, eating a piece of candy is not necessarily selfish behaviour unless the act of doing so means that:

- others cannot;
- these others want to eat it themselves; and
- the denial of these others is out of whack with some social concept of what is 'fair'.

This is rubbish on several counts. One is that it assumes that sometimes there is an endless supply of resources (where such selfishness *couldn't* exist), and in others there isn't (where it *could*). This book admits that sometimes it may *seem* that resources are infinite, but in fact—on a planet without endless resources—eventually food for one (for example) is food someone else doesn't get.

This is something that those who study global ecology are just beginning to understand. Humanity used to believe that individual actions affected only those doing them, but now it is becoming clear that such is not the case. For instance, when village people in Brazil help cut down the rainforest it may mean that global weather patterns change, and there could be a drought that wasn't there before over the whole continent. In another case, people in North America might use aerosols excessively, and eventually destroy the ozone layer—thereby producing skin cancer elsewhere. Truly, 'no man is an island' any more.

Beyond that, the classical approaches to defining selfishness also require knowledge of how *both* parties feel. The actions of one party must negatively affect the other party. Not only must one person *want* the single piece of candy, but the other person must *also* desire it at the same time. And not being able to have it must be an *unreasonable* situation for somebody (in the opinion of society).

How does one determine that? This is impossible to determine or measure from the outside, and could change from minute to minute. Trying to sort it out requires an infinite sense of truth that none of us has.

Isn't it rather easier to simply assume that (1) if a behaviour were *not* selfish no one would do it (e.g. the 'economic person' approach), and (2) *all* behaviours are therefore selfish to *some* extent on the part of those who do them?

For those who might cry 'circular reasoning', this book replies that all labels we use as language rely on circular reasoning. For instance, a 'table' is a 'table' because we decide that it is a 'table', and not a chair. There are no absolutes that tell us from the outside what is/is not a 'table' or anything else. We just decide to call it that—and everybody else agrees.

How people avoid admitting the obvious.

Doing the same thing for the term 'selfishness' causes no real harm, but whenever this is done some say, 'Oh, you don't mean "selfishness" do you? You *really* mean:

- goal-oriented;
- self-serving;
- focused;
- assertive'

or any other of the million-and-one labels we have come up with to hide good old personal selfishness. Most people are more comfortable with these terms than the word 'selfishness' because they are newer and no one has told us they are 'bad' (quite the contrary in today's 'politically correct' world!). However if one pulls these apart they still describe the kind of self-serving behaviour that is the hallmark of the 'economic person' ... and what we also know as 'selfishness'.

So it must be said that, 'No, these other labels are not what is meant—though they mean the same thing'. The term 'selfishness' has been deliberately chosen for this book because it is the most emotional term for what is meant—and is the trait we have all been taught to attack. But the desire to call it by another name indicates a second reality for it.

Reality: Most selfishness is hidden.

Because selfishness is commonly seen as being 'bad', it is normally hidden from both ourselves and others. Because it is so well disguised, the universal nature of human selfishness is also kept from view. This perpetuates the nobleness myth.

How well selfishness is hidden can be seen by a cynical examination of a few acts that probably others (and the one doing them) might not see as being selfish. Further analysis always reveals that they are. For example, a husband gives his wife a cookbook for Christmas. How sweet! How loving! The only thing more transparent would be a set of sexy nightwear! Truly the gift that keeps on giving! Cynics might suggest that the husband wanted better food, different food, wanted the cookbook for himself, wanted to keep his wife 'barefoot, pregnant and in the kitchen'. Or, as a particularly honest husband once put it, 'It was Christmas, I had to give her something, and it was on sale!'

Actually, it's impossible to get away from selfishness, no matter what is assumed. Even if the wife involved loved cookbooks, wanted *that* one, and the husband gave it to her just to make her happy, there is still a selfish pay-off for him.

This can easily be appreciated by anyone who has ever given someone a present that they thought would 'blow their socks off', but were startled to hear,

'My, that's interesting!' The crushing feeling of disappointment this brings the giver is prime evidence of a selfish pay-off expected, but not received.

Another example: somebody makes a large donation to the Heart Fund. Here it's even easier. Perhaps the donor has a bad heart and hopes for a cure, wants a tax write-off, or likes being seen as generous. Maybe they have been a 'rotten person' all their life and are buying what is called 'celestial life insurance' by doing something good at the last minute—in a mistaken belief this will buy their way into heaven.

Or somebody chooses not to steal some money even though 'no one would know'. Isn't this fun? Perhaps the person has a large conscience which they don't wish to provoke, or has a secret fear that someone *might* find out. Maybe they like the one-upmanship derived from feeling superior to petty thieves. Maybe the amount of money involved isn't worth stealing (e.g. you can trust me with five dollars—but not five thousand!), or maybe the person involved is just honest. What this usually means is they have had ingrained in them principles of honesty which are so strong it would take more effort to override them than to ignore the temptation.

Whatever the case, if almost any human act is examined deeply enough it is impossible to know for certain whether some selfish motive (conscious or unconscious) is—or is not—involved. However, one thing is certain. If the act didn't make sense to the person doing it at the time they did it, they wouldn't have done it (the 'economic person' again!).

This is pretty shocking stuff, but a more complete study of human selfishness has even more uncomfortable things in store.

Giving people 'everything they want' may slow up—but doesn't stop—human nature.

One approach to dealing with human selfishness consists of trying to overcome it with whatever it demands, on the basis that then it will go away. Neville Chamberlain tried this before World War II by letting the Nazis have whatever they wanted. It didn't work then ... neither will it work on any lower level of human want due to another reality.

Reality: Human selfishness is insatiable.

This means that not only are humans selfish, but no matter how good a deal they are given, they can always find a way it *could* be better. And they will always find it. They are, therefore, never satisfied.

A good example of this can be found in the tale of a grandmother walking her grandson along a deserted beach. Suddenly a freak wave crashes over him and washes him out to sea. She stands there, staring at where he had just stood, looks heavenwards, and begins to argue with God. Wagging a finger accusingly in the air she cries:

Why did you do that? He was a nice little boy, never argued with his parents, and never smarted off at nobody. You put him right back safe and sound.

The next moment a second wave crashes ashore and *does* deposit him safely on the sand. But is she happy? No, she looks heavenward and shouts:

He had a hat ... what happened to that?

Her response is typical. Leading psychologists have also expressed this thought. One of the most prominent of these, A. H. Maslow, came up with what he called a 'need hierarchy'. This states that people first serve their basic needs (for food, shelter and clothing) until they are more or less satisfied. They then move upwards to needs for safety until they are mostly happy with this issue, and then on to the next need.

Reading between the lines this means that humans are *never* happy for long. They just keep on extending what they want. This has serious implications for customer service. It puts an end to any hope of getting away from selfishness by giving people 'everything they want'. This won't work, because what people want always keeps extending outwards—like the farmer who said all he wanted was his own land ... and all the land around it (think about it).

It's not all bad news ... Lest this sound too negative, let us move quickly towards more comforting thoughts.

Reality: Selfishness is not necessarily 'bad'—in all cases.

Once human selfishness is seen as being something of a 'private part' which we *all* have, but keep hidden away from view, it begins to look much less awful than before—particularly when one considers that there *are* some forms of selfishness that *can* be good for all concerned. For instance, a desire to be a good parent can be good for the child (who benefits directly) *and* the parent (who feels good about being that way). It still has a selfish origin; it just doesn't cause any harm.

Besides, there are only three ways something can be 'bad'. First, something is bad if it is bad for the individual involved. For instance, selfishly eating too much leads to being fat, which can lead to heart attacks. But this is something that only the individual can determine; it is not for others to decide.

Second, something is bad if it is bad for others. But in the case of selfishness this is something we human beings work out among ourselves by being 'fair' (more about that in a later chapter).

The third way something is 'bad' is if it deviates from what is 'normal'. 'Normal' is something we determine by 'taking a vote'. If everybody had one eye, having two would be 'bad' because it wasn't 'normal'. We have been taught that selfishness is bad because it isn't 'normal'.

But if *all* human beings (and all human actions) are selfish, it becomes impossible to label any one individual as 'bad' just because he or she is thought to display some element of that *universal* characteristic. In other words, how can some characteristic be singled out for individual attention as being 'bad' when everyone has it? This is as dumb as saying someone is 'bad' because they have to eat ... or drink ... or breathe. We all must, in order to survive.

And (surprise, surprise) just like these basics of life, we all *do* have to be selfish (to some extent) in order to survive. This is what the next reality is all about.

Reality: All humans must be selfish (to some extent) in order to survive.

You may not have ever considered it, but our selfishness is what keeps all of us from being robots. If we weren't personally selfish someone could order, 'Go jump off a bridge'—and we would. We would do anything asked if we didn't all have our selfish nature that asks, 'Why should I? What's in it for me? Why don't you do it?'

All of this makes for a conclusion that takes away *any* possibility of being judgmental about just *finding* selfishness. For, seen in this light, saying 'You're so selfish' becomes a non-event like saying 'You're a human'. The response quickly becomes, 'So what else is new?', implying, 'Why do you even bother bringing this up?'

This is not to say that all forms of selfishness are desirable. But just finding selfishness in others—or admitting it about ourselves—does not mean that *anybody* is immediately beneath contempt. Neither does it require that such selfishness must be criticised, ignored or attacked without further consideration.

Seeing selfishness 'the way it is' avoids many problems before they start.

Getting employees to adopt this point of view is absolutely essential due to an important reality concerning the link between selfishness and employment.

Reality: All employers run on selfishness.

All forms of enterprise are definitely selfish activities (at some point). This is easiest to see for businesses, as they always have the goal of increasing *somebody's* wealth. When this is realised by employees, they often exhibit an instinctive reaction against being a part of this process. They do so with statements like:

*So why should I make him or her [the owners/directors/board members/
managers/whatever] more wealthy than they already are? They're so selfish!
They make enough money now!*

Similar (and sometimes worse) problems can afflict 'non-profit' charities and
government departments—because achieving some organisational goal usually
will lead to the advancement of *somebody's* selfish wellbeing. Depending on their
prior training (those from non-business backgrounds tend to be particularly
touchy about such things), these workers are likely to respond even *more*
negatively to the thought of participating in what they view as hypocritical
behaviour. They do so with comments like:

*You don't really love these [old people/poor people/trees/ whatever] the way I do. You
just selfishly want a big promotion/raise/etc. So, why should I help you?*

Managers are no better, for when they sense selfishness in workers they are
likely to lose respect and patience—and express it with criticisms like:

*These rotten selfish [employees/volunteers/civil servants/whatever]! All they want is
more money and less work. Why should I be interested in listening to them?*

The one thing that all of these employees can usually agree on is that the
people supplying the money that becomes their salary are no better—and
probably worse. Private comments like these are common:

*These lousy [customers/voters/parishioners/donors/members/whatever]! No matter
what we do they aren't satisfied. They're so selfish. Why bother listening to them? All
they will want is more.*

> The important thing to recognise is that all of the preceding
> statements are *absolutely true*—and *all* of them apply to *every
> employer* in the world.

What causes problems is that employees don't know that the selfishness they
find is not unique to them. They feel like:

*Mine's defective [my workforce/management/owners/customers]. They're so selfish—
and this is wrong. I must do something about this.*

Unfortunately, the 'something which is done' is usually to either passively (or
actively) resist cooperating with 'them' and their goals while simultaneously
hiding personal motivations. This does not represent an attitude helpful to
customer service. It makes things far worse.

When managers, workers and owners respond to conflict by either attacking
personal selfishness in others or denying/hiding *their own* nature they can become

'three ticks fighting over a dead dog'. They put so much effort into fighting each other that the hand that feeds them quietly goes elsewhere.

A good instance of this happened in a labour dispute recently. Both workers and management came to loggerheads over a number of issues that any outsider would have considered petty—on both sides. Neither would give an inch, and the plant faced a strike that went on for 2 months ... 3 months ... 6 months ... a year. Still, neither wanted to give in and 'lose face'.

Eventually the plant's customers found new suppliers elsewhere. The whole company went bankrupt, all the workers (and managers) lost their jobs, and the owners lost a fortune. But nobody gave in to anybody else's selfishness!

In another instance a company had a good year. And their directors awarded the top executives (only) a big pay increase. Unfortunately, these same executives saw no reason to 'share the wealth' with the rest of the firm—and even tried to give a zero increase to the 'rank and file'. Soon after this a strike action was called by a normally cooperative union—the anger of which the executives could not understand! It almost brought the whole house down.

What both these cases show is what happens if the issue of universal human selfishness is overlooked or assumed not to be present. The actions taken will range from foolish to suicidal.

How to make the 'nature of human nature' work for all

Because of this reality, this book will suggest an entirely new approach to human nature. It is summed up as follows:

> Employees of all organisations must *stop fighting* selfishness when they find it *in others* and *admit it about themselves*. Instead they should *assume* it is a natural part of humanity, *accept it, understand it*, and *use it* to everyone's benefit.

This is not to suggest that anyone should allow anybody to be taken advantage of. All that it says is that selfishness should not be ignored, dismissed, attacked or hidden. Rather, it should be brought into the open and used to mutual advantage.

Once people assume selfishness in everyone—and the first step of *acceptance* is in place—everybody can sit down in a setting which is much more real. All that comes from ignoring this is a feeling of trying to play a game in which one doesn't know the rules.

For, as shall be shown later, simply changing a view about the 'real' nature of human nature reorganises so much thinking as to create a totally different approach to marketing/customer service. IBM put this nicely when it coined the phrase 'garbage in—garbage out'. In other words, the outcome of any situation can be no better than its weakest point. If the idea of selfless human nobility is garbage, so is most of what stems from it.

Accepting that everyone is selfish is not easy—why it's worth it

The idea that people are basically selfish has given this author more headaches than any other idea in his last book. People just don't want to believe this: it is so different than what we *think* we know—and what we *want* to know. So why is this insistence upon selfishness still the basis of this book? There are several reasons.

It squares well with reality.

Think of your own experience. Regardless of what you might wish to believe, does the idea that most people are selfish come closer to describing how others have treated you than the opposite view?

It doesn't mean that you or anyone else is 'worthless'.

In fact, the opposite is true. For one thing, the reality that we are on a planet in which resources are limited—and we have to protect our own interests—is not 'our fault'. We didn't ask to be born into a situation where we must (to some degree) be selfish in order to survive. This may be comforting.

Beyond that, what most often causes us to think someone is worthless happens when they (or we) do something selfish. Once one gets the idea that this behaviour comes from a universal base, it is very hard to be judgmental towards anyone. In fact, having lived with this knowledge for 20 years, I can say it causes one to be much more accepting—and happy.

For what is disappointing about most lives is continually finding that those whom we most expect to be selfless—aren't. Whenever a business associate, employer, employee or life partner is found to have 'feet of clay', the tendency is to assume the 'mine's defective' position discussed earlier ... and either attack or set off looking for someone who won't be. This is a fruitless quest.

Bette Midler summed this up in a song within the classic movie *The Rose* when, after an unhappy love experience, she said she was going ' ... to find me a new man, a true man, a blue man—someone who will love me ... '. If we know everybody's selfish, seeing their true nature is not as upsetting ... or destructive. We figure (sigh) we might as well work with 'the devil we know than the devil we don't'.

It fits well into one of the world's great religions.

Whether or not one considers oneself 'religious', it is always easier to accept something if it seems to be in line with something else perceived to be 'good'. At least in terms of logic, the idea of universal human selfishness fits well within the teachings of Christianity.

The basis of Christian teaching is that God in heaven is perfect; humanity—no matter how 'good' it tries to be—is imperfect (even if in thought); God and heaven cannot accept anything which is imperfect without also becoming less than perfect (e.g. put one drop of red paint in white paint ... and it can never be white again), so God sacrificed His son to make those who believe in Him perfect—and acceptable to heaven. And this acceptance is based only upon the belief it is so—rather than on any number of 'good works' (which could have feet of clay!). It isn't hard to see how the idea of universal human selfishness could work into this structure.

It is also worth mentioning that the prior chain of thinking is probably the only way known to resolve an issue plaguing scientists of humanity since the beginning of mankind—and at the heart of this chapter. This is the tension between the nature of humanity and the worth of humanity.

If it is assumed all human activity is 'good' then all human acts (including genocide/murder/rape/theft) must *also* be good, but this doesn't make sense. However, if it is believed that everybody is flawed to some degree (selfish?), but God sacrificed his son to make up for this, then humanity must be of infinite worth—or God wouldn't have bothered.

It makes people much more productive than they otherwise would be.

The reason this is so is that accepting that people are selfish causes us to be more open about our own motives, and more likely to try to get them to line up with the selfish needs of others—which these others will feel more comfortable about revealing. So people can work together, rather than at cross purposes. Failure to recognise and act on selfishness (which will always be there anyway) causes decisions to be made within a cloud of 'human nobility' which really fogs up any decision making.

A good example of this happens regularly between our executive MBA students and their partners. Our program offers a 2-year Master's Degree In Business—meeting from 8:00 a.m. to 6:00 p.m. every third Saturday and Sunday for 2 years—while the students are working full time somewhere else. Not only are these students leaders—and therefore very busy people—*before* they start the program, but also (besides the time spent in class) the program usually demands another 20 to 30 hours per week outside of class. It isn't long before the time demands take their toll, and trouble begins within the students' relationships.

The standard approach taken by these students (and most others facing work-related conflicts) is to feel most hard done by, believe their partner is incredibly selfish, and try to slip off the hook by asserting, 'Well, honey, I'm doing this for us'. This almost never works, for 'honey' now must not only deal with a partner who is grumpy, stressed and never there for them, but one who also expects them to appear grateful in the bargain! The results are predictable—and devastating.

A good way to challenge this nobility is to ask:

If 'honey' didn't exist, would you probably do this anyway?

or:

Even if 'honey' were to run off with a vacuum cleaner salesperson(!),
would you still willingly give 'honey' 50% of the extra income this activity
on your part will create—forever?

If the answer to the first question is, 'Is the Pope Catholic?' and the second is, 'When Hades freezes over!' you aren't doing this for them! Although there may be some elements of self-sacrifice involved, don't expect people to believe them—and they are probably not the major reason you are doing whatever you are. You are doing this for you! The world won't end if you admit this.

It makes a lot more sense to say, 'Well, honey, I hope this has benefits for both of us—but I must admit I am doing *most* of this for me. Now, what can I do for you in return (e.g. fund a degree for you, have another child, do up the house, go on a world tour)?' What is wanted in return is not important—as long as those from whom one expects cooperation want it, and see getting it connected to whatever their counterparts want.

A good example of this in business was a rest home struggling with occupancy levels. No matter what they did, they never seemed to be more than 85% full. The management finally went to the workers and appealed for their help. Management admitted that raising the occupancy rate would help profitability, but added that if 95% occupancy were attained, it would be possible to spend a lump sum on whatever the employees wanted. And the managers asked the staff what this might be.

The staff went away and huddled. They surprised the managers by not asking for it to be paid to them personally, but instead put into a giant screen (50 inch) TV for the residents' lobby. Management agreed—thinking the desired occupancy would never happen. Imagine their surprise when within 3 months the facility was full, and the residents had their TV. Everybody was happy.

Accepting selfishness makes for better decisions.

In all cases what admitting personal selfishness in one's self—and accepting it in others—does is to lead to better decisions. For these decisions are not based upon a theory of humanity which is wrong to begin with. And they can be made with greater information than was there before. So decisions satisfying to both (and therefore more likely to be supported) can be made in a non-threatening environment. This approach means each and every decision is more likely to be successful than it would otherwise be—in absolute terms.

Things look even brighter when these 'better decisions' are viewed in comparison with those produced by other views of human nature. Besides not making people's motives clear, these rosy-hued approaches produce entire employers full of people unwilling to 'give in' to (or even work with) real or suspected selfishness in others—which they have been taught from birth to fight and despise. So those employers full of 'selfishness police' get very little done, while competitors smart enough to recognise the way things really are 'make hay while the sun shines'.

So, doesn't this all make sense to you? If you find yourself still resisting the basic thoughts of this chapter, ask yourself a very interesting question:

Are you *really* interested in learning something new and useful?

Every other marketing/customer service book you are likely to have read will have had an underlying belief in human nobility. As such, after a while all they can do is rehash the same old thoughts.

This one starts out with an assumption of human selfishness. And that very basic belief will produce astonishingly different approaches. (To see how different, skip ahead for a moment to page 254.) These approaches are bound to be new, for they come from a different starting point, and are supplied with more information before decisions are made. It can't hurt to at least listen, can it? And if these new tools really are closer to reality, you will be better armed than those who haven't thought through, 'What if the impossible were true?'

The remainder of this book is concerned with looking at the forms of selfishness that are most destructive to employers and employees. It will clearly 'call a spade a spade' and reveal what all sides of any customer service problem usually keep hidden.

The book will then indicate what to do about it. This should provide many new ideas which can ensure survival of your organisation—and keep it from too many times when your customers think you don't care.

ACTION SUMMARY

It starts with human nature.

In order to improve any situation where 'customers think we don't care', an accurate view of human nature (that of both customers and employees) is required. For it is from this platform that we form our own response to any problem by predicting how other people will react to what we do.

What we have learned about human nature is mostly wrong.

What most people believe about human nature comes from their experiences, their up-bringing and 'science'. Both parents and science err in teaching that 'people are noble', and that all forms of selfishness are therefore 'bad' ... and must be kept hidden. This position is well established, has never been challenged and causes endless problems. For it provides a basis of understanding which is incomplete, and actions that are likely to be ineffective are then launched from this platform.

The foundation of this book

The position this book will take is that people are basically selfish, but this selfishness, though hidden, is present in all human activity (particularly employers), is necessary in order to survive and is not automatically 'bad'. This is hard for most to accept even though it is what their own experiences teach them, does not detract from basic human worth, squares well with one of the world's great religions, and makes people who must work with others much more productive.

Being different can be better.

The reason for this greater productivity is that all parties to any problem who truly understand selfishness can work with more complete information. For all sides will be more open about their own motives—and more accepting of others' desires—so actions satisfying to all can be undertaken. This is bound to make these actions much more successful, particularly when other employers are so busy 'fighting against selfishness' that their customers quietly go elsewhere.

Do you want to learn something new?

Because assuming human selfishness is so unique, this book can make a promise few can. It can guarantee that it will not, like so many others, rehash thoughts everyone already knows. Rather, it will start from its unique foundation to build an understanding which turns out very differently from other books about business.

THE BOTTOM LINE

Selfishness is not automatically 'bad' and shouldn't need to be hidden. Learning to accept, understand and use personal selfishness for the welfare of all is the best foundation on which to base an effective marketing/customer service culture.

ACTION EXERCISE 2.1

Who's selfish? Not me ... or am I?

For: Employees at all levels   **Format:** Small groups
Materials required: Pencils and instructions
Objective: To show how universal selfishness is in all of us

Instructions

In this chapter it was said that there are very few actions which are *not* selfish. The following list contains a number of things someone might do that others (and probably the person doing them) might not consider selfish. One of these will be assigned to your group.

Form into groups ... then:

In the first 15 minutes draw up a list of all the reasons why what is described *could* be regarded as selfish:

1   Someone buys their partner flowers/candy/whatever.
2   Someone gives in to another in an argument even though the one who gives in 'knows they're right'.
3   Someone does a good job of whatever they are paid to do.
4   Someone decides to 'serve humanity' by becoming a nurse, social worker, (you fill it in) instead of making 'big' money.

Then be prepared to discuss your findings. What do they show about human nature?

Conclusion

There is almost nothing anyone (even you) can do for which someone else can't come up with some 'selfish' motive. As such, doesn't it make sense to stop attacking selfishness in others? We all have *some* selfishness in us, so why make such a big deal out of it? We can all be better off by accepting, understanding, and using selfishness in ourselves and others to promote the survival of our own employer.

3

How self-destruction works in workers—and how to stop it

WORDS WORKERS WON'T SAY—BUT EMPLOYERS SHOULD HEAR

Once the false veil of human nobility is lifted—and trust established—people can feel free to reveal how they *really* are. This is what employees would tell their employers—if they could. This chapter tells how employers could use this knowledge for the welfare of all.

Not everybody is on your side.

One of the most dangerous things any employer can believe is that barriers leading to its self-destruction are unlikely to be a problem—because *its* employees care about their employer too much to allow it to happen. In fact not all employees don't care—some clearly do—but rarely are they in the majority, and almost never do even *most* of them realise the most important (selfish) reasons for caring. Usually this is because they are never told them—mostly because management doesn't understand why it should.

The all-important reason for caring can be learned by asking what makes any person an 'employee'. In most cases the only thing required for someone to be an employee of an organisation is they draw an income from it. This means that owners, managers *and* workers are all employees in the sense meant in this book, so all that follows *could* be said of each category.

However, the insights of this chapter most often apply to lower-level staff, who usually don't have much of an ability to 'come clean' about their needs with their managers (except through confrontational unions).

In the old days the idea that workers were dependent on an employer for survival was seen as the only means of getting them to work (Theory 'X' again). In these more 'enlightened' times, stressing that employment is the means to a living is seen as old-fashioned and harsh.

Modern management theory has replaced the motive of 'making a living' with new ones such as 'personal development', 'job enrichment' or 'job satisfaction'. The current management focus on these items has caused a number of basic truths to be ignored for so long that they can almost be termed 'forgotten facts'—the most basic of which is as follows.

Forgotten fact: The most basic (and powerful) reason why most people work is to make a living.

There can be no argument that all the modern management ideas are parts of today's workplace. However, the truth is *they have no meaning in the absence of the ability to make a living.* In other words, it is impossible to either have—or not have—personal development, job enrichment and so on without *first* being able to make a living. Without this basis, the others simply don't exist for any but the rare rich who don't have to work but choose to do so.

Because this need to make a living is the most basic, it also stands to reason it is the most powerful. Despite this, it is one of the motivators least talked about with workers until the day when they receive their dismissal notice. By then it is too late.

On the other hand, some employers go 'off the deep end' in another direction by assuming that their workers will automatically be motivated to greater effort by a desire to keep their jobs. Wrong again!

The connection between employer and employee survival is not often clear to workers.

A factor linked to this one is caused by modern management practice. Many employers have grown so big and complicated that people forget their dependence on their employer.

Forgotten fact: People don't work for an organisation; they are the organisation. What happens to the employer will happen to employees. And what is said about the employer is said about employees.

Ask anyone who they work for and they will quickly reply, 'I work *for* Ford, General Motors, World Vision, the Army, etc.' Although this use of language is correct, it is also misleading, as it gives the impression that the employer and worker are *separate* from each other.

This prevents the worker from seeing any relationship between the employer's survival and his or her own. This problem is compounded by the sheer size of many employers, which denies any possibility of the worker feeling that he or she is an important part of it.

The worker may thus develop an attitude similar to that of a story told about a little old man sitting quietly on a deck chair of the *Titanic* while it sank slowly into the sea. Although others were running hither and yon, he seemed strangely calm. When a terrified passenger noticed this and asked how he could stay so cool in the midst of such danger he replied:

So why should I worry? It's not my ship!

Workers can ill afford to feel the same way. They need to know that if their employer fails, *their* source of livelihood goes too. The organisation also needs to remember that without its employees it too ceases to exist. They are all passengers in the same very leaky boat!

Thus it can truly be said that workers don't just work *for* an employer, they *are* the employer. What happens to the employer happens to them, and what is said about the employer also applies to them.

This second issue—that of whatever is said about an employer *is also said* about their employees—often escapes many. This can be seen any time workers gossip or openly complain about what happens at work, without realising there are many ears waiting to harm the workers' own best interests with what they themselves have said.

For example, a group of employees working for an ambulance company loosened up at a bar and regaled all who would listen with a 'hilarious' story about carrying a 300 pound woman down a flight of steps. People could hardly control their mirth as they told about losing their grip, letting go and watching the poor lady bounce down five flights to the floor. Too bad at least three people within hearing of their group decided, 'I'll never call that bunch', and one other was a health department inspector who decided he would! They were shut down the next day—and all lost their jobs.

Students of a nursing school fared a little better. Halfway through their program a flap broke out about some teaching-related issue, and the students were determined to run to the newspapers with it. One of the nurses' fathers quietly said, 'You could, but it wouldn't be wise'. To this the daughter replied,

'But this is awful ... the world must know ... we must do something!' Her father again quietly responded, 'You could, but it wouldn't be wise'.

The daughter blithered on for awhile, but finally recognised her father wasn't giving in, and asked, 'Okay, so why wouldn't it be wise?' The father replied that in one year the student was going to be looking for a job ... and would go out to the local hospital. When they asked from where the student graduated and learned it was the local nursing school, they were likely to reply:

> *Oh yeah, I heard about that one. They're no darned good, are they—*
> *I read about it in the paper.*

At this point the public side of the protest died, and the students (with their educators) sorted the situation out privately—which is what all should do (if possible). For whatever brush any employer is tarred with will also rub off on employees.

This sort of knowledge could go a long way towards motivating workers to protect their employer. However, workers usually aren't told this in any meaningful way. It seems so threatening. Beyond that, just how powerful a motivator this may be depends upon how much the worker values his or her job. Some care a great deal more than others. But don't make the mistake of believing that the desire to keep one's job will always be enough to make for great customer service.

Not every employee cares about keeping their job.

One can never assume everybody working for anybody is totally committed to their employer. And even if they seem to be, don't expect this to be for selfless reasons. Some employees will be committed to their employer for their own reasons, others will not really care either way, and some will actively wish to destroy it. These groups are called (respectively) 'stainless steel neurotics', 'members of the apathetic army', and 'suicidal employees'. Let's look at what makes each of them tick.

A minority of employees really care—but only because they value something their work provides.

Those who care the most about their employer may be called 'stainless steel neurotics'. These are people warped in a useful direction (!). They love what they do, who they do it for or how they do it so much that if they couldn't do it, they would grieve. These people remind one of a duo of little old ladies who worked for a pharmaceutical company making narcotic capsules during the early days of the last century.

These grey-haired grandmothers made their products by scooping morphine dust into the split halves of capsules, and then storing them away. What no one knew during these early days was that the dust kicked up by this process would filter into their nasal passages and produce for them an addictive 'monkey on their back' the size of a gorilla! However, it is reported of them that up until the time of their retirement they were always happy, never missed a day of work, and worked holidays and weekends without wages—truly every employer's dream!

Not all stainless steel neurotics need such artificial encouragement. In most organisations some will be found who are the result of a skilful matching of workers' talents and the jobs they do, resulting in the 'ideal' situation for each. For this author university level teaching is a bit like that. He loves it so much he would almost do it 'for free'—if this weren't so close to being the situation, anyway!

One *does* occasionally find entire firms full of people who act like stainless steel neurotics, but usually this is because for some reason the employers are able to treat their workers relatively better than the norm. And the employees know it.

Sometimes the advantage of treating workers better than alternatives is obvious. A good example of this is another pharmaceutical firm which is known for never firing anyone, marvellous working conditions, and salaries about 20% higher than most others. Of course, it is well able to be generous—having one product selling to the wholesaler for $12 a hundred, when it has a cost of 55 cents (including the bottle). With margins like this it has little trouble being good to its employees while still (as one dim-witted executive put it) making 'our 6% gross profit'!

In the above situation any moron could see why the workers would love their employer. They *think* they are getting a 'better deal'. The reasons why 'think' has been highlighted here are pretty much the same as they were in the first chapter. Whether or not employees are *actually* getting a better deal is anybody's guess (and not very important).

If they think they are or aren't—and this motivates them accordingly—is all that matters. Again, perception is more important than reality. So if the situation is less obvious to workers (or they don't trust it), don't assume it will help. For what the workers don't see (and believe) can't motivate them.

An example of this was an investment firm who expected a great deal out of its employees. When asked why, the CEO proudly pointed to an employee stock option plan. When asked how long it took to produce 'spendable' benefits, the CEO responded, 'Oh, about 20 years'. When asked how simple it was to understand he blurted out, 'Heck, even I don't understand it!' How this can be expected to produce any kind of results is anybody's guess. At a minimum, the firm would have been better off had their stock option's benefits been more immediate, obvious and understandable. The key is to make sure employees see positive outcomes for their employer result in positive (selfish) outcomes for them.

To solve that type of problem one employer stated their 'mission statement' as:

> *... to increase the wealth of owners and employees by being the best appliance dealer in the region.*

The key here is that the mission statement includes *employees*—while most don't. Satisfying both owners and employees won't be an easy goal to reach. But this mission statement does indicate that the firm at least understands that selfishness in their workers must be recognised from the beginning. If they can carry out the aims of the mission statement, it should help with their survival.

One way to accomplish such a goal is to have a financial structure so lush that better treatment is not very expensive for the employing firm. Unfortunately, few organisations enjoy this state. More often their resources are pretty much identical to those of competing employers.

Therefore, their treatment of workers leaves those workers with few reasons to develop warm feelings towards their employers. There is a way to help with this, but it requires recognition of another seldom-said truth.

Caring for employees can be overdone.

There *are* situations where the many concepts put forward by modern management can prove really useful. Job enrichment, better salaries, more desirable working conditions, personal fulfilment and all the others *can* go a long way towards giving workers reasons to be loyal to their employer.

Unfortunately, through the years, they and the human resource managers (previously known as 'personnel managers') who administer them have taken on a life of their own. Instead of creating better satisfaction intended to be the *means* to an end (i.e. better workers), the giving of employee satisfaction has sometimes become a goal in itself.

Often one gets the idea that the spreaders of all this happiness would have been parish priests if the pay had been better! Seldom is the connection made clear to employees that all their better treatment *cannot be continued* if it is *not paid for* by better performance. Therefore, workers can hardly be blamed if they are not stainless steel neurotics because of what is being done for them. They usually just figure, 'Enjoy it while it lasts'. Fixing this requires remembering another 'forgotten fact'.

Forgotten fact: The only purpose of modern management tools is to create a situation in which employees will be more productive for their employer.

The lesson to be learned here is to make sure that employees understand that what can be done for them is limited by what they do for their employer. Just as employers can forget to 'share the wealth' with employees, so can the employees forget the same about those for whom they work. And, no matter how much is done for them, some employees will still not care.

In many parts of the world we have built a society so secure that—for some workers—losing their job is not the worst thing they can think of, and is not the motivator it might otherwise be. In fact, other than the 'neurotics', worker loyalty in most organisations runs the range from lukewarm indifference to outright hatred.

Most workers think 'this is just a job'.

For most firms the majority of workers would be made up (at best) of what is 'the apathetic army'. Despite what they may tell their employers, for these people their job is really just a means to a living.

No matter how much effort is put into them, they become like the worker who was working on a cathedral destined to become an architectural masterpiece. Some art critic noticed what was happening and ran over to commend the labourer. When asked by the breathless critic, 'Son, what are you making?', the answer was, 'Ten bucks an hour'!

Lest you feel too superior about your own motivations, just take a simple test guaranteed to identify soldiers in the apathetic army. Ask yourself whether, if someone were to offer *you* a job identical to your own in every respect *except* that it paid 50% more, you would accept it. If the answer is, 'Does paint dry?', you know where to pick up your uniform!

The simple truth is most people think their job is 'just a job' and they develop almost no warm feelings either for it or their employer. At best they feel friendly indifference. But even for these people there can be a strong motivation to keep *this* job, because they don't know:

- whether or not they could come up with another job;
- whether this *other* job would start soon enough to do them any good; and
- if this *other* job would pay as well as their current one.

If they knew all the answers to these questions to be 'yes', they *would be* in the *other* job. So the possibility of losing their current job could be a powerful motivator—if they were consciously aware that it could happen. They are almost never made aware of this possibility. If they were, the outcome might be very different.

An example of this was a family-owned firm which was eventually sold to a larger one. When someone explained that the reason the family sold was the lack of profitability, their former employees were in tears. Their question was, 'Why didn't somebody tell us? Perhaps we could have done something'. Perhaps they could have—their response indicates that it least some would have liked to have tried. This is not always the case.

Some employees not only don't 'care', they actually *want* to destroy their employer.

Hidden within most organisations is another more dangerous set of employees— sinister ones about which little is written in 'scientific management' literature (admitting they exist would challenge the myth of universal nobility!). But most can recognise (and name!) people who fit this description in their own workforce.

These are people who are warped in a negative direction. They *hate* what they do, who they do it for, or how they do it so much that (perhaps subconsciously) they would like to see their employers go down the drain. These are what I call 'suicidal employees'.

Suicidal employees represent the biggest challenge with regard to barriers. Not only do they not want to have *fewer* barriers, in their heart of hearts they really want *more*. They are like the worker in an auto plant who was so angry with his employers he decided to sabotage them.

His actions were not noticed until the proud owner of a new car discovered its dome light would not go on. Desperately, his dealer searched for the solution to the problem. The wires running into the headlining, the switch, the bulb and the socket were all checked and found to be faultless. Finally, in desperation, the mechanics decided to take down the headlining (having avoided this until now because of the work involved).

They followed the wire up the pillar into the headlining and found a short gap between it and the wire going into the socket. Between the two ends was a note taped to the roof saying:

Congratulations, you smart son of a gun. You found it!

Similar to this was an airline attendant who was being extremely pleasant to a particularly nasty customer who cursed her and finally huffed off with his boarding pass. Someone standing behind him had noticed this scene and asked the attendant how she could listen to all this and remain smiling. She happily replied:

He is going to London … his bags are going to Japan!

Despite the fact that some of these cases seemed richly to deserve what they were getting (or in some cases not getting), this is not always the situation. More often it is that the customer is just the unlucky 'winner' in some worker's anger lottery.

These workers are mad at the world in general, and their lot in particular. They feel they have a right to take it out on anything that moves—and they do. The deeper their hatred, the more outrageous their behaviour. They are almost like mass murderers who deliberately provoke police into killing them.

. Unfortunately this option is not open to employers! Even though they know perfectly well who is a suicidal employee, they may not be able to do anything about it. The workers may not *quite* be bad enough to fire, or things like legal issues, unions, family ties (the worker may be married to the boss!) and even the affection of their co-workers can stop the employer cutting out what amounts to a cancer which will spread if left unattended.

These 'cancers' spread through:
* undermining management programs;
* constant complaining about minor problems; and
* bad work habits—all of which may be copied by other workers.

This possibility of spreading is where the greatest danger lies. Although most organisations have a small number of suicidal employees, on their own they may represent an acceptable level of risk. They are much like the margin for error tolerated by some firms who employ quality control.

Nobody's perfect, so a *few* such grumps can usually be shunted off to some area where they can't hurt anybody. But if these employees are allowed to *spread* their attitude among their workmates, the *entire workforce* can become 'suicidal'. And there is no question that—at critical times—such people can do a great deal of damage (even as individuals). It is important to get them either to leave of their own accord, or be isolated by their peers. This can be accomplished if employers keep one fact in mind.

Suicidal employees may be crazy, but they aren't stupid.

Many (but not all) suicidal employees will either change or leave if they see it is in their best interest. The easiest way to accomplish this is to get these people to determine what they so despise about their current job, then encourage them to see if they can find a job elsewhere which overall will suit them better. It is important not to do it in a threatening manner for the suicidal employee—or anyone else.

Indeed, every employer should be quite willing to let their employees investigate other options. This costs nothing, as employees who wish to pursue this will do so anyway, whether employers encourage them to or not.

Being nasty about it means that:

- employees assume something *must* be wrong (or Gestapo tactics wouldn't be needed), and this increases the likelihood that they *will* look elsewhere;
- employee departures that were going to take place anyway may happen without much advance notice;
- employers may find out that something is wrong with *them* only when it has become really serious (see below); and
- suicidal employees will have one more reason for *not* leaving.

If such workers find a better job they should be encouraged to take it. (Some employers have even gone so far as to help set them up in their own business!) An owner of a bike shop twice named 'The Best Bicycle Shop in the Country' found this most effective.

When asked how he got to be so good, he replied that the first thing he did was to sit down and interview all his employees. To his astonishment he found that about one-third of them didn't like bicycles! He helped these people find employment elsewhere—and in one case set them up their own business. So there was no reason for anyone to be bitter.

The remainder (who were mostly 'bike nuts') were retained, and matched with new employees who also loved bicycles. Hey presto! Instant fantastic customer service!

Although the preceding was an inspiring case, whenever anybody (even suicidal employees) is allowed to openly pursue what is (selfishly) best for them, it is likely to also be best for the employer.

If a suicidal employee leaves there will be a big party, everyone (particularly the employees who remain) will be happy, and with any luck the suicidal ones will go to work for a competitor! But if they don't find a better job it is just possible they may conclude that there is something wrong with *them*, and change their attitude.

One odd exception to this rule may occur when some employee suffers from what is called 'golden handcuffs'. Such a person may have a skill so specialised (for instance managing a post office) that no other employer is willing to pay as much as the current one.

However, in such an instance marvels can sometimes occur if it is asked of the employee, 'If your current employer is willing to pay you more than others seem to think you are worth, is this something to be angry about, or grateful for?' This is almost never said—but should be.

On the other hand, maybe it is not the workers who are wrong, but the employer. Should this be the case, it is to the employer's benefit to listen and change so that it is at least no worse than the alternative—otherwise it will lose all its good people, and those who remain will be so bitter or untalented as to guarantee the doom of the entire organisation.

If none of the above will work, then it may be best for everybody if the suicidal employee changes jobs. Unfortunately, this is usually not easy for managers to bring about. If it was, somebody would have done something long before. Why they haven't often relates to the ruckus it would cause with the employee's co-workers. However, this needn't represent an impossible problem.

If a suicidal employee won't leave, their co-workers may help with the situation.

Often the thing that most protects suicidal employees is their standing with their co-workers. And, assuming these co-workers are not themselves suicidal, this standing is usually based on a *mis*-understanding of the facts surrounding the workplace. Usually the co-workers have absolutely no idea of why the suicidal one is a threat to the entire workforce and must be removed for the good of all—unless somebody tells them.

The basis of this threat is that a suicidal employee is (at best) a half-hearted employee. And given this fact, the employer needs *two* of them to represent one decent worker. This gets expensive for the employer.

But the way suicidal employees get around this and attract sympathy from their co-workers is by wrapping themselves in a 'red robe of righteousness' and uttering the ultimate modern-day curse:

All this outfit cares about is making money!

... which implies that *this* employee is drawn to a higher calling! In a way this is another verse in the 'You're so selfish—I'm not' theme of the previous chapter. For most employers, trying to deny some sort of emphasis on money defies credibility, and further strengthens the suicidal employee's case.

It is much wiser not to deny an emphasis on money, but rather to shift the focus of this emphasis to the employee by asking, 'Do you draw a salary?' When the inevitable 'yes' answer is given, ask, 'How's it paid?' and 'Would you work without it?'

When again the worker responds in ways betraying his or her *own* focus on money, it can be shown that the worker values it just as much as the employer. The problem may be a matter of how far this focus goes, but its basis is *not* the importance of money.

Trying to say it is somehow 'different' for the employer represents hypocrisy similar to that involving a story of a young couple parked beside a lake one night watching the submerged submarine races (!). One was hustling the other and enquired, 'If I had a million dollars right here ... would you ... kiss me?' (cleaned up for G-rated audiences!). The second responded, 'I guess so'.

Whereupon the first dug in a pocket, came up with a 50 cent piece, and said, 'Well, then, how about for this coin?' To which the second replied, 'My goodness no, what kind of a person do you think I am?' The answer, of course, is:

We've already established that. Now we're just haggling about the price!

Whenever anyone takes money for a salary, they pretty well give up their ability to find fault with others for finding money important too. But, besides cheating their employer, suicidal employees also cheat the customers they serve—and their co-workers.

Suicidal employees cheat those for whom they work.

Their salary goes into the selling price of whatever they provide, and if they are not productive their customers are getting ripped off—just like their employer. Sometimes this can be an effective issue for workers who really love their 'customers' (e.g. nurses in a hospital).

Suicidal employees threaten the survival of their co-workers.

Beyond this, it can also be shown that a suicidal employee puts his or her co-workers at a risk only slightly less than if they were waving around a loaded .357 Magnum! As has already been discussed, suicidal employees are expensive. At some level this can threaten the survival of an entire employer. But even if it isn't this serious, sooner or later management will sense an unnecessary expense and lightning will strike.

Unfortunately, for various reasons, it may not get the right person. It may catch the worker next door—who *was* trying to do a good job but got caught in the crossfire. Understanding this can sometimes make the suicidal worker look decidedly less noble to those around them.

Suicidal employees drive their co-workers crazy.

Finally, suicidal employees often are deeply resented by their co-workers. For not only are they known to not be pulling their weight, but also their rotten attitudes can cause harm of their own. This point was made in a customer service seminar directed at a group of port workers. When the issue of suicidal employees was brought up the whole room erupted! After a while it became clear that, far from being sympathetic, these people *hated* their suicidal peers. This was summed up by one dock worker who blurted out:

I wish you would get rid of these people. We have had it up to here with their constant moaning, complaining, and outright b _ _ ching [rhymes with witching] that makes us miserable by giving us things to worry about we wouldn't have thought of on our own!

Most people can identify with this. We all know some co-worker we go to see when we need a new reason to slit our wrist! If we haven't already thought of it, they have—and will tell us, whether or not we want to hear it.

So seeing a suicidal employee depart may be presented as something not totally negative to that employee's co-workers. Add to this the fact that it may be best for the suicidal one, and the whole workplace has a chance to heal.

Sometimes losing one's job is best for the (suicidal) one losing it.

Last, but not least, it may be helpful to point out that the person most hurt by a suicidal employee is not someone else, but that very employee. A suicidal employee sticks to a job because of a forlorn belief he or she couldn't do as well elsewhere. What this means is that, in exchange for the salary represented, suicidal employees are telling themselves a lie. This lie says, 'I like this job', when they know inside they don't.

Industrial psychologists now know how to spot the stress this causes by looking for workers who hate their work so much it means they never enjoy their recreation periods. Although most people start looking forward to a weekend on Monday, suicidal employees go beyond this by dreading going back to work, starting with Friday evening. They worry and fret all weekend, so much that by the following Monday they are not rested. And therefore they get even worse. As they spiral downwards, their stress builds up like steam inside a kettle. It mounts up and eventually rattles the lid until it sneaks out and burns somebody. How it sneaks out will be determined by the employee's own individual weaknesses. They will eat too much, drink too much, smoke too much, be a swine to live with (or a combination of all four—and more), but the stress will come out and burn many innocent people in the process.

When it does, they *never will* enjoy the 'extra' money they make from staying in the hopeless job. For they will wind up spending it to fix problems they wouldn't have had if they hadn't stayed in the job. In this regard it is very much like an old definition of a marriage partner—somebody who helps you to share the troubles you wouldn't have had if you hadn't married in the first place!

If none of this forces an exit, the situation may still not be hopeless.

And so it can be seen that the suicidal employee is a menace to not only his or her employer, but also to customers, fellow workers and (most importantly) themselves. Sometimes when all of this is pointed out, suicidal employees may solve the problem by removing themselves. But, even if they don't, their co-workers may still render them harmless by isolating them—if these same co-workers understand how much damage suicidal employees can do to those around them.

An example of this was a busload of employees who were one day ferried in to hear a motivation speaker who explained about suicidal employees. On the way back the speaker was discussed, and the suicidal employee within the group snarled, 'Obviously it's more of the same old company s_ _ t'.

However, he was stopped dead by another popular employee who told him off by stating:

I think you are a suicidal employee just like the speaker said. You idiot, this is my job you're messing with, and I think you should shut up!

Apparently you could have heard a pin drop all the way back! Unfortunately, this kind of thing rarely gets said because co-workers aren't told *why* they should feel this way.

If the contents of this chapter both shock you and make you realise that a great deal of helpful information is not being made available to workers, you have a good understanding of two basic—but related—problems present in most customer service cultures.

The most obvious is that workers can't or won't level about their own (selfish) motivations. So no one thinks of telling them what employees need to know to stop their own self-destruction. A mirror image to this problem is that managers also can't or won't reveal employer motives—and what will happen if these aren't served. So the whole problem becomes even worse.

How this works will be discussed in the next chapter.

ACTION SUMMARY

Workers won't tell you ...

Because nobody wants to admit they are selfish, managers aren't told a great deal about their employees. If they were, they would understand the following.

Nobody is selflessly devoted to their employer.

Workers can be divided into three groups, none of whom really care about their employer, except with regard to how their jobs meet the worker's *selfish* needs. The most devoted—stainless steel neurotics—are a very small minority who 'love' their work only because they think it gives them more than they could get elsewhere. The vast majority—the apathetic army—don't consciously care about their employer, but do want their jobs to continue, as they are not sure they could get equal ones quickly. Suicidal employees hate their work so much they consciously or subconsciously try to destroy their employer.

Employees need to know 'what's in it for them'.

Employers *can* minimise barriers produced by any of these groups through using a long-neglected employee motivator, the desire to keep one's job. This can work directly with both the neurotics and the apathetic. And it can be used indirectly with these two groups to isolate suicidal employees if they cannot be removed, retrained or encouraged to leave.

However, the only way 'keeping your job' will be a motivator is if employees see their jobs as worth keeping. And if they understand how their jobs can be lost through their own actions.

To tell employees *all* of 'what's in it for them' employers will have to open up as well.

This will require that employees be given information which is usually withheld from them by managers who, like the employees, don't want to look selfish. How this can work will be covered in the next chapter.

THE BOTTOM LINE

Employees will be behind their employer only to the extent they see this as benefiting their own (selfish) interests. Make sure there are plenty that do, as otherwise any attempts to create an effective marketing/customer service culture will be totally ineffective.

ACTION EXERCISE 3.1

Understanding 'suicidal' employees

For: Employees at all levels   **Format:** Small groups
Materials required: Pencils and instructions
Objective: To gain an understanding of how 'suicidal employees' feel

Instructions

In this chapter we heard about the suicidal employee. This is a worker who hates his or her job so much that they get to the point of being self-destructive. Without naming any names, do you believe that our organisation has some of these?

Most workers who have been working for any length of time have gone through at least one 'suicidal' employment experience. Today we will discuss how this feels.

Form into groups ... then:

In the first 15 minutes try to find someone in your group who has been through a situation like that—one in which they used to have a job they absolutely hated to the point it began to affect their personality. See if they are comfortable sharing with their group how they felt about it at the time. If they are, discuss:

1 What did the job involve doing?
2 What was there about it they hated so much?
3 Did the worker's hatred of the job begin to 'get at them' in other ways after a while, and what were these (e.g. did they start smoking too much, eating too much, being grumpy with family, etc.)?
4 How did they solve this problem (e.g. by quitting, getting fired, etc.)?
5 How did they feel after the problem was 'solved'? Did they feel much better, wish they had left sooner, etc.?

Conclusion

Suicidal employees represent a danger to themselves, the employer for whom they work, and their fellow employees. They should be given as much support as possible. But, for the good of all, the situation should not be allowed to go on forever.

4

How self-destruction works in management

WHY CLOSE-MOUTHED MANAGERS MANGLE EVERYONE'S CHANCES

Because of their own motivations, managers never feel free to tell employees what they most need to know. This is what managers would say if they could—and how it would help the situation.

It's like watching an accident happen— you feel powerless to stop.

Managers often watch with horror as they see their employees taking actions they know will not be good for anyone. They understand full well a number of realities which, if known, could be used by employees to protect themselves. Unfortunately, these are rarely said until it's too late. Most managers wish (from the bottom of their heart) that these realities weren't a part of the life around which all must revolve. Nevertheless, by *not* saying them more harm is done than good.

What needs to be heard is as follows.

The *real* authorities running most employers aren't the managers.

Within most employers the workers see the managers they report to as being the ones in charge of their welfare. Unless the manager is some sort of owner-operator this is rarely so. The real 'power behind the throne' belongs to whoever owns an organisation. But managers rarely tell employees this (it makes them look so powerless!)—nor do they tell their workers how it affects what must be done.

The *real* authorities running most employers don't *really* care about employees.

These owners don't work with the employees on a day-by-day basis, don't know most (if any) of them, and have no real reason to be interested in employee welfare. They didn't buy into an investment in order to give money away—they bought a business to make some, *now!*

The reason for stressing 'now' is because money made in the future generally has little value to most owners, for nothing spends harder than a 'tomorrow' dollar (e.g. how many people do you know who are happy to get paid for today's efforts sometime in the future—if things work out?).

This is particularly true in the so-called corporates which are owned by people who have bought shares of stock. The only value these shares have is provided by whether the firms they represent are making money in the short run which will either be returned immediately to the owners or cause the prices of their shares to go up quickly so they can sell them. So the idea of building a happy profitable workforce (for the future) is likely to fall on deaf ears, as is any interest in the welfare of employees other than as immediate money makers.

The *real* authorities running most employers care only about making money.

This is easier for employees to understand if they are asked about their own investing, for instance when they put their money in a bank which will lend it out to somebody else to run a business. Do the people who have banked their money know about the people who work for the businesses to which their money has been lent? Do they care? Of course not!

All the people putting money in a bank care about is whether or not they get it back—with interest! In other words, the only interest owners have is their *own* interest. At some level—depending upon how much distance there is between owners and employees—identical feelings are present for all employers.

This is easy to see for government departments. The voters who ultimately own them are not much interested in the employees who work for them—as long as they are productive enough to lower taxes! The same even holds true for the directors of charities who often see themselves as stewards of the funds they control—and want to make sure these are used as efficiently as those of 'for-profits'.

What this means is the employers who 'beat their breasts' and proclaim an infinite caring for their workforce know their message has a hollow ring. Employers are run by managers who have their masters—and these masters are mostly interested in money. So how much 'caring' can be done definitely has its limits. However, what this means to employees is rarely said.

Making money puts a limit on how much 'caring' can be done.

Employees who believe their employers' 'we care about you' message—to the point that they think they can keep on making barriers without consequences—are unaware of what they most need to know. What workers need to hear about is the 'four-letter word'—with more than four letters.

In business there is clearly such a four-letter word (with more than four letters). It must be a four-letter word—as it is almost never talked about by managers. Workers are never told it is one of the major motivating forces of all employers, and rarely is it mentioned above a whisper that this 'activity' is going on during working hours. In light of this it is hardly surprising that workers try as hard as possible to keep any of it from happening!

What is this four-letter word with more than four letters? 'Profit'! What few workers know is that profit (of some sort) is the number one motivation behind all organisational activity (even that of government departments and so-called 'not-for-profits'). *And the need to make some sort of profit is more important than caring about employee desires.* The reason workers don't know this is their managers have not told them.

Because the whole issue of profit—and what happens if it is not made—is bound up with owners, there might be some reason to point the finger at them for this problem. But it is managers (whether they are or are not owners as well) who normally are closest to workers, and managers *do* know the facts about the situation. They make the decisions about what to tell or not tell their employees.

Managers withhold this information about profit because of a number of 'rotten reasons'. One of these is a belief that employees won't understand it.

This one could be true, but more often it is a case of managerial arrogance. Many figure that the accounting used to determine profit is too complicated for the 'poor workers' affected by it, so it is never mentioned to them. This is ridiculous.

True, accounting is complicated—it is complication that keeps accountants in work! The basic nature of profit, however, is not. It is a concept that can be expressed most simply as:

$$profit = income - outgo$$

Profit is very much like a pocket. Money is put in the pocket (income). Money is taken out of the pocket (outgo). Everyone understands that more money cannot come out of a pocket than what went into it (unless of course you are the US Government!). What this means is there must be an end (sometime) to the amount of 'caring' that employers can do for workers.

Workers often sense this—and managers (sooner or later) demonstrate it is true. But this doesn't keep them from 'shouting to the roof-tops' an endless caring—when *they know* there is a limit to how far they can really go. Not admitting this causes similar problems for other types of employers, even though their workers don't realise it.

Even 'not-for-profits' have money-related limits.

There is one group of employees who hear particularly little about their organisation's finances. This is because they are thought to be 'different'—even though they aren't. Many people believe that so-called 'not-for-profits' and their government-department cousins can ignore the need to make ends meet. They think that these 'non-profits' are somehow different. But this is never true.

Surprise! Surprise! These 'non-profits' buy their business stationery from the same printing supply shop as the for-profits. The for-profit employers always have an income statement at the bottom of which it says, 'profit/loss'.

The not-for-profits have the self-same forms to fill out. The only difference is at the bottom of theirs it says something high-sounding like, 'excess of revenues over expenses', 'capital replenishment', or the ever-popular 'surplus'. But what the 'bottom line' is and what it does are always the same.

All organisations (even not-for-profits and government departments) simply *must* make more money than they pay out, or employee pay cheques will come back marked 'Firestone'—for they will have bounced higher than a rubber ball!

This point was once made by a Catholic priest who attended a marketing seminar for rest homes. He was asked why he was there ... after all, he ran a 'non-profit'. To this he replied as he lit his pipe:

My employees don't think they are doing the Lord's work unless they lose money [puff], and the Lord can't afford a whole lot more of that kind of work to be done [puff], so I'm here trying to keep the Lord from going bankrupt [puff]!'

This 'confession' is always true. No organisation can ever survive if it pays out more than it takes in ... and none ever sits on bottomless resources. Because of this it can truly be said all employees work for a for-profit employer.

If employees also knew the exact limits the need to make a profit introduces, what financial issues produce it and what happens to workers if financial targets are not met, everyone would benefit. This would happen as workers felt a desire to meet financial goals based upon *their own* welfare. Unfortunately, the workers are unlikely to even learn that a profit is even being made ... let alone how much.

Managers fear revealing *too* much.

One thing managers don't like to admit is that their own welfare is frequently linked to financial targets. If the employer does well, they do well. But telling workers this seems self-centred, so they generally keep their mouths shut about it. And there is an even bigger reason to keep quiet about profit-related issues.

Many managers make profit the 'great unmentionable' out of a mistaken fear that, if their workers knew *any* money was being made, they would 'pillage the village' and make impossible demands at salary discussion time. So this topic is kept 'safely out of their sight'.

This never makes sense. Why it doesn't can be determined by asking such a manager, 'Do you file financial statements?' When they answer, 'Yes', ask, 'Who types them?' When they answer, 'Some sort of secretary or clerk', ask, 'Have you cut their tongue out?' They will reply:

Uh, no, we lost that in the strike of '47!

All this suggests is that workers do know money is being made. But what they know is the most dangerous thing to know about any topic. They know half the story.

Workers generally know about income. This is obvious for anyone who has ever listened in on workers in any organisation, and heard someone say:

*Do you know that last year Amalgamated Feeblefeltzer made
10 million dollars?—and I'm making a lousy 10 bucks an hour. I tell you somebody
is getting rich off of our backs. Something's not right—
we got to do something about this!*

Workers always know how much money is coming into their employer. They learn it from financial reports, gossip, rumour or whatever. What they usually don't know is where it comes from ... and where it goes to.

That employees don't know where it comes from (or goes to) can easily be proven by asking, 'Where does your pay cheque come from?' The vast majority will reply, 'The payroll office'.

Unless their employer has a printing press in the basement in which the authorities would be very interested, almost never can this be true. Only after great prodding do employees reluctantly think through that *every penny their organisation receives comes from customers of some sort.* Once this is done the second thing employees need to know is where all this money goes.

Normally, most of every dollar that comes into an organisation (sometimes all of it) goes whizzing back out on some sort of 'outgo'. For most employers many of these 'outgoes' cannot be quickly changed without shutting down the organisation.

For instance, imagine that someone's power bill was $2000, and they called up the power company to object by saying, 'We don't feel like paying the bill this month—it's too high'. The power company will respond by saying, 'That's fine', and throw the switch, cutting off all power ... and the organisation stops as well.

For most employers there is little they can quickly do to cut down outflows without stopping or reducing production. But for all organisations there is one outgo that is the biggest category they can do something about without stopping the organisation. For all employers this is wages and salaries.

Employees need to know this, for once they do an old saying makes a lot more sense and should be knitted by artists on samplers to be hung in employee rec-rooms. It goes:

If your income doesn't equal your outgo, your upkeep will be your downfall.

With some education most employees will grudgingly admit that their employer must at least make enough profit to cover all expenses—including their salaries. I mean, let's not mess about with essentials! From there they will go on to decide that making a profit in the sense of covering expenses (particularly their salary) is not really wrong—it's just that their employer wants to make *too much* money (e.g. more than breaking even) that has them all wound up. For most employers and employees this has to be straightened out. This may require admitting some further hard truths.

Employers not only have to make a profit, it must be a *'fair'* profit.

As already mentioned, workers *do* generally have some idea that money is being made. And, even after subtracting expenses, what's left over can seem a fortune for anyone on an hourly wage. Leaving the impression that huge 'ill-gotten' gains are being enjoyed by someone lays the ground work for tremendous ill feeling. This is tragic—particularly when there is no reason for it.

At the centre of this issue is determining what for everyone involved is a 'fair' profit. And this requires unravelling the meaning of the word 'fair' (which must have a terrific press agent because it sounds so much more noble than it really is).

Although the concept of 'fairness' is considered to be one of the most lofty values of a civilised society, what it really means is not nearly so positive. Unravelling 'fair' from the righteous cloud that surrounds it reveals this:

Fair means selfishness held equal.

Think about it. A fair situation is one in which everyone is allowed to be equally selfish, as determined by his or her own value system.

As an example, imagine a parent with one piece of cake and two kids, both wanting it. It is a wise parent who lets one kid cut the cake and the other choose which piece they want. Assuming both kids are playing with a full deck, each will consider this 'fair', and the situation will not be heard of again.

Incidentally, I did this once and it worked! I let one kid cut the cake—and no brain surgeon ever did a better job of laying a fine line! I let the other choose which piece—and she got out her jeweller's eye-glass to examine them more closely, laid each on a scales, and sent them both off to a chemical lab for analysis to determine which had more icing! I never heard another whimper from either of them again because they both thought the situation 'fair'. Does this not mean that in their heart-of-hearts they were not both selfish little brats who would have been more than happy to do their brother or sister out of the cake had I let them? Of course not—they take after their father! But because they were allowed to be equally selfish (e.g. they were treated 'fairly'), they were both happy.

Keeping this definition of 'fair' in mind goes a long way to determining what is a 'fair' profit. It will mean that somebody believes they are being allowed to be 'equally selfish' as others.

That raises the next issue, 'Who gets to determine what is a "fair" profit for any organisation?' Logically, few will argue that the owners are the ones entitled to this decision.

What represents a 'fair' profit is determined by issues far from any manager's control.

Explaining that owners (the 'real authorities') are investors provides a good platform for explaining what employees need to know about how a 'fair' profit is determined. Although this term brings to mind pictures of complicated market transactions, there is nothing complex about what is involved. Investors are just 'rent-a-bucks' who momentarily have a few dollars available that they are willing to rent to someone (in this case to run a business).

Framing it in this manner can do a lot to help employees to identify with the situation, particularly as most of them have been investors too. They were an investor when they had a few extra dollars they were willing to put into a bank, some other financial institution or some instrument such as a bond.

When they did this, did they do it just to share their excess funds with their fellow humans out of the goodness of their own hearts? They did not. They expected some form of rent for their funds. And they normally received this rent in the form of interest.

Asking employees, 'How much interest do you want?' brings them full circle with other owners/investors. For the expected answer is, 'How much interest could I get?' Just like any Wall Street banker, employees want the maximum return for their funds.

They want what is called either the premium rate or the prime rate. In simple terms all this means is the banking community's best guess as to what the minimum return on funds should be. This is usually an outside benchmark determined by groups far away from any individual employer.

Sometimes looking it up for employees may be useful but, whether or not this is done, all can understand that this rate (whatever it might be) produces a benchmark of financial performance. They can readily identify with a rule saying that if they can't get this rate, or close to it, they would be better off moving their money to where they can.

This principle of moving one's money to the maximum return is a useful one, as it also shows employees what might be the selfish motivations of those owners of a business who run it on their own money.

These owners can be 'direct' (meaning they put up all the money necessary to run the business), or they may be 'non-direct' (meaning they have pitched in to buy shares of a business too big for them to afford on their own).

Either way they are no less selfish than those who have their money in banks. They want to receive rent too, although how it comes may be a bit messier. Their rent comes in the form of appreciation, which means the business becomes worth more in the future than it was in the past, or they may receive dividends, which act very much like interest paid back to the owner. Perhaps they may receive both.

Whatever the case, in the long run this rent from ownership will generally settle down and equal what is called 'ROI'. This ROI (return on investment) should eventually equal the profit made by the business divided by what the business is worth (however that is calculated).

But this return on investment had better be equal to the premium/prime rate or better. *If it is not, the owner will not be receiving what is considered a 'fair profit'.*

And this owner would be selfishly better off putting his or her money in a bank where there is no risk.

Discussing with employees how much profit is made, what the business is worth, calculating the ROI and comparing this with the premium rate rarely does any harm. Usually the ROI is considerably less than the owner might wish. In such cases the workers see the 'king's ransom' of profit they thought being made off the sweat of their brows shrunken down to a reasonable size. And they may eventually appreciate the reason they should try to make it bigger. One additional point worth making is that this advice about explaining to employees how much profit *should* be made in order to get an adequate return on investment now even applies to 'not-for-profits' and government departments.

Not-for-profits and government departments don't escape the 'long arm' of ROI.

In the 'good old days' it may have been enough for not-for-profits and government departments to scrape along by just breaking even—no more! Both charities and governments are increasingly looking at their income-producing assets as a possible way to raise funds. And if these assets would make better money by being sold off and the money invested in financial markets, they may very well be looked at quite harshly. Employees of these types of organisations definitely need these 'facts of life' explained to them, lest they sail on unknowingly to what may be a personal disaster.

An example is a major religious organisation that owns a chain of rest homes for the elderly. The organisers came to the conclusion that some of these were not just a ministry, but actually could be used to *make money* to be passed on to some other need elsewhere. So some of the rest homes had profit targets assigned. If these targets were not met, the same consequences as apply to for-profits (see what follows) were likely to happen.

Governments are following the same pattern. For instance, many electricity suppliers used to be owned by governments and run as departments. Increasingly these units are either set up as profit-making organisations to decrease tax burdens elsewhere, or they will be sold off to the highest bidder. This isn't the only worry government employees may face.

Political 'ROI' may be different.

One little wrinkle government departments often add to all of this is something not exactly like ROI, but that works in a manner similar to it. Sometimes there are government departments (for instance social welfare agencies) who don't actually turn a profit but perform some sort of service that can have a major bearing on the popularity of the politicians in power (just see what sort of uproar being late with welfare benefits can cause!).

What politicians do in these cases is to compare the costs/benefits of having such a service done under government control with the costs/benefits of having somebody else do it. If there comes a time when it looks like somebody else could do the service more cheaply—without enough political backlash to offset the money being saved—governments may respond like a disappointed investor.

In this case the measure used by politicians to calculate these costs/benefits may be called a 'satisfaction survey' if done formally. Or it just may be some personal compilation of the number of embarrassing incidents catalogued in the recent past. For the employees involved, these may literally be just as crucial as money in the bank.

Whatever the type of employer, the odds definitely favour discussing both the issue and size of profits/ROI (both financial and political) with employees in a free and open manner. The alternative is to allow them to become jealous of profits and ignorant of the role they play in keeping their jobs.

Even if financial profits are unusually high, revealing this to employees is no less than they would probably find on their own anyway. And if it both helps make sure employers 'share the wealth' with their employees—and can be seen to help those same workers avoid the consequences of failing to make a 'fair profit'—the outcome will be positive for everyone. This is particularly so when one knows what is actually driving most employers.

Unfortunately, this all-important profitability can vary wildly from time period to time period.

'Little bits' mean *a lot* of profit.

One other item managers rarely tell employees is how finely balanced profitability can be—and why losing (or gaining) relatively small 'bits' of business can have such a major impact on survival. Employees just don't see why it is such a 'big deal' to lose a customer or two—I mean, they only represent a few per cent of sales. And the goods/services they represent 'not getting sold' won't eat any hay!—will they? Oh yes they will!

Understanding why is made easier by going back and looking at the 'profit equals income minus outgo' equation. What is not shown by this formula is that outgo comes in two 'flavours', variable and fixed.

Variable costs are things like raw materials that do tend to increase (in total) directly with whatever represents 'sales' for an employer. (For instance, if one widget costs $2 in raw materials to make, two widgets will cost $4, three will cost $6, etc.)

Fixed outgoes are costs that, over a reasonable range, do not increase (in total) directly with the number of units processed through an organisation. Good examples are insurance, electricity and property tax or rates. For example, imagine that whatever is 'sales' for your employer go down this year by 10% and the city decides 'your fair share' of property taxes is $10 000. So you go to the tax assessor's office and plead:

> *Au contraire, kind sir, surely you must be mistaken. Last year our taxes were also $10 000, but this year our sales are down by 10% … so we don't owe you any 10 grand. I mean, fair's fair, isn't it?*

Do you know how much chance this type of appeal will have with the city tax assessor? Do the terms 'slim' and 'none' mean anything to you? The city tax assessor (and quite a few other people who cost your employer money) don't have any relationship between what they charge and what you sell.

On the other hand, once these items are paid off for the year, they don't normally go up if your sales increase—even by a small amount. For example, if you have a good year and sell even $10 more than last, normally some of that extra 10 bucks would go whizzing out to pay both fixed and variable costs. But if the fixed costs have already been paid off, do you know what happens to the part of income which would have gone to pay for them? Right, it becomes profit, straight profit! So an increase of only 5% in whatever represents 'sales' for an employer can produce as much as a 10% to 30% increase in profit.

Unfortunately, the reverse is also true. The sword cuts both ways. Losing even 5% in 'sales' for most employers can decrease profits by 10% to 30%. The net effect of this is that not only are all customers important, but some are *very* important.

Profit means all customers are *not* 'created equal'.

Obviously, given the knife-edge on which profits are balanced, any increase or decrease in 'sales' from *any* customer is important. However, for most employers some *big* customers can do more harm than others.

What is called the '80/20' rule frequently prevails. What this means is that 80% of most employers' total sales will come from only 20% of their customers. The loss of someone within these 'top 20' is often disastrous, for not only does it mean a big loss in volume, but often that huge volume is more profitable than the same thing broken up into many smaller bits. However, employees who don't know this will frequently not only *not* give these 'big wigs' *better* service, they will actually give them *worse* service.

They may do this out of ignorance, or it may be quite deliberate. For some staff may figure they must represent 'democracy in action' and treat everybody alike, or at the working level these big customers may have staff who become quite well known to the working level staff of the provider. Such familiarity can bring with it very costly contempt that must be avoided at all costs.

As shall be shown, *any decrease* in profitability has serious consequences.

If a 'fair profit' is not made, what happens next will be painful!

Managers know this, but one of the strange things about modern management is that, by trying to be 'nice', managers are quite cruel. They do this by 'protecting' their employees from the painful truths of which the managers are all too aware. In doing so they allow the consequences of these facts to strike employees who—had they been aware of them—might have been able to stop them.

Although there *are* consequences of employee failure which might be good motivators because they are painful, they won't be told to those they would help the most—lest these people be somehow 'hurt'—and because employees don't like to hear about them. *This is despite the fact these painful consequences hurt much more when they do happen than when they are merely discussed.*

So these consequences become 'unmentionables' very much like death. Everybody knows it happens to everybody, but nobody wants to believe it will happen to *their* body! So nobody does much to keep it from happening at all.

We thus see the ridiculous outcome of managers taking a great deal of heat to 'protect' their employees from knowledge about consequences, when this knowledge could eventually result in every employee being better off. And when these consequences do result, some of these same employees are likely to turn around and attack the managers with the identical charge made by other employers who have failed:

Why didn't you tell us?

Why not, indeed? Just as the knowledge of the deadly consequences of smoking (for instance) can be a great reason to quit undesirable behaviour, so also can knowledge of the consequences of financial failure—if those who will suffer from them find out early enough. This is particularly so as rarely does any employer fail without having employees who individually or collectively knew how to stop it!

So what are these consequences which have become 'unmentionable' by managers and of which employers should be made aware? They are as follows.

Unmentionable consequence:
The organisation goes out of business.

Obviously if outgo is greater than income, sooner or later the well runs dry. Owners won't forever keep on throwing money into what looks a dry hole. When this happens the organisation will become bankrupt and die. This means that what the organisation did—as well as the *jobs* of those who did it—will end. (Charities work pretty much the same way with the same terminology as business, but for government departments 'going out of business' is usually described as either 'closing the department' or 'outsourcing' its job to private contractors.)

Any of these would seem a powerful motivator, but these issues are almost never discussed until it is too late. The first that most employees ever know about them is when they show up for work and find the doors locked. And generally the more trouble organisations are in, the less likely they are to tell employees about it.

The reason is a belief that these things needn't be discussed when the employer is doing well—why bother our employees when there isn't a problem, and doing so seems so threatening? What this means is that employer failure won't be discussed until it *is* a problem, and then it can't be mentioned. It can't be mentioned because it would alert everybody to the fact they *could* lose their jobs.

The problem then explodes because the good employees who can go elsewhere probably will, and will leave behind an organisation full of deadbeats, no-hopers and suicidal employees. The firm which *could* be in trouble most assuredly now *would* be in trouble.

So a situation very like the problem at the centre of a popular joke emerges. It is said that a moron had a leaking roof, but it never got fixed. For when it wasn't raining there seemed no need to do anything. And when it was raining one *couldn't* do anything!

The only way to beat this is to make sure that the *personal* consequences of total organisational failure comprise a topic which is always up for discussion. For best results this should be on a regular basis when there is no immediate cause for alarm.

An analogy between employer health and personal health/exercise seems a strong approach. Just as people should never be allowed to forget that the consequence of poor personal habits can be death, so employees should not be permitted to forget that poor work habits can lead to the same outcome for their employer.

However, employer 'death' is not the only consequence which needs to be discussed; there is another equally painful one that needs even more explaining, because some know so little about it. And far from fearing it, some employees actually *hope* for its happening. This is the possibility of their employer being taken over by someone else.

Unmentionable consequence: *The realities of being sold out/merged/taken over by someone else*

All of these are being treated in the same breath, for from an employee standpoint they all result in the same things. Often what amounts to an employer being sold off will be called a 'merger' because this seems so much less threatening. (Charities and governments are particularly fond of the term 'merging' because it means administrators/politicians won't have to admit something they control has failed, but rather can position it as some sort of 'improvement'.)

Supposedly the two merged employers will become 'one big happy' family that is a little bigger and a little happier than before, with no real changes. This is almost never true. The only reason for putting two employers together is a hope of a better outcome for the 'owners'. This 'better outcome' *always* requires changes, and these are usually threatening to at least some employees.

The really tragic fact about all this is that often any 'take-over' is welcomed with open arms by the employees involved. They are enthusiastic on the grounds that:

> Anything *is bound to be better than what we now have.*

A clear-headed examination shows why this almost never can be true. The most basic reason is that nobody sells a gold mine. The only reason most owners are willing to part with something is for reasons of health—the owner is worried to death about it! So the only employers normally up for 'sale' are those that are somehow 'weak'.

This usually also goes for strong non-profits/government departments. These are rarely up for grabs if not in trouble. The owners will figure, 'If it ain't broke, don't fix it'. And they don't.

Similarly, 'weak' employers usually can't afford to buy anyone else. They have enough problems just meeting their payroll. So normally, 'weak' employers are taken over by the strong. This applies equally to business, non-profits and government departments. But herein lies a seldom-mentioned 'rub'.

If someone else gains control of some employer because the other outfit was 'weak', who was really weak? Were the *desks* 'weak'? The trucks? The buildings? They might be but, as mentioned earlier, these are not what make up an employer in the most important sense. As emphasised in Chapter 3, employees don't work *for* their employer; they *are* their employer. And what is said about an employer is said about its employees.

If control of some employer is assumed by another because one was weak, it will be thought that it was because the *employees* of the one taken over were weak. The outcome is predictable. The new 'owner' comes in with a chip on the shoulder that says:

Look, turkeys! If you were dumb *enough that you were* weak *enough that we were* strong *enough to take you over (and not vice versa), then we must know something you don't. So from now on we are going to do things* our *way.*

Rarely is the new management foolish enough to come right out and say this. It is more likely that a meeting of the organisation taken over will be called by their new 'glorious leader', at which something soothing like this will be said:

… Ladies and gentlemen, we know that you are all worried about your future, but no one need be alarmed. We are now just one big happy family that is a little bigger and a little happier than we used to be, so no one need be afraid.

Then the new management walks out the door and the bloodbath begins. There will have to be some sort of 'bloodbath', because if the employer taken over was 'weak', it will pull down its new owner as well—if nothing changes. The situation is very much like some drowning swimmer pulling down the one meant to save her or him.

Beyond that, in many cases the new owner paid more for the employer taken over than the old owner thought it was worth (or else no exchange would have taken place). So the new management figures that by making some changes they should do even better. Where these changes will take place tends to be pretty predictable.

At the very least all 'IOU's will be cancelled. These IOUs are likely to come in two forms—formal and informal. Formal ones are conditions of employment or contract provisions that have been negotiated in the past. These may or may not transfer to the new owners and their employees.

More distressing are 'informal' IOUs. These things are never written down, but represent cases where employees figure they are owed something. They are most often expressed as:

I've given this outfit 20 of the best years of my life—they owe me.

This feeling is often quite true. If anybody has worked for anyone for any length of time, they inevitably do their employer favours—by working overtime that doesn't get paid, or cancelling a vacation to finish an assignment, and so on. And if the organisation has a brain in its head it will honour these IOUs in the future by saying, 'Joe (or Josephine) has been a good employee. Let's give them a break'.

The problem lies in *for whom* these favours have been done. Just as the organisation doesn't exist other than through its employees, this is also true here. These 'favours' were not done for the employer; they were really done for the managers of the employer.

Only if these managers are smart enough to recognise these IOUs—and if these managers don't change—will they be honoured. If the management *does* change, the new managers will neither know about nor care about these IOUs, as they weren't for them. As such they will not even be considered, let alone honoured.

Generally, employees (both workers and managers) *will* turn over. How much they will turn over varies from situation to situation. Normally, the top managers are the first to go, and none survive. At the middle management level about a third may make it. And, as little as 2 years later, only about a third of the original work force is likely to still be present.

What happens to all these people varies with the situation. Since employees are normally the biggest controllable cost, they will also be the first category picked over by the new management. Management will describe (not publicly) this process as clearing out 'dead wood'. Some of those cleared may not be as dead as others think, but the new managers and owners don't really care, as each 'hungry mouth' dismissed is one less to feed. And they figure they owe none of these people anything.

Beyond that, the new employer will also introduce some new systems (similar to their own) which it hopes will turn around whatever has been making the acquired organisation 'weak'. Some employees will be unable to cope with this and go suicidal, thereby leaving on their own. And those who remain are likely to find they have traded a *predictable* slave driver for an *unpredictable* slave driver!

What is meant here by 'predictable' and 'unpredictable' is that, over time, employees build up some knowledge of their owners/managers that makes their lives easier. They know what things set these people off—and how to get around them. (For instance, one manager may put a great deal of emphasis on personal grooming, another on being on time.) This makes employees feel better, for they can then control their own destiny (to some extent) by doing what managers like. They won't have this knowledge about anyone new—and this is bound to be scary.

However, the one thing that won't change is the reality of working for what employees feel is some sort of slave-driver. No manager of any organisation can ever escape the financial issues discussed in this and the previous chapter. They will be the same wherever one goes.

Beyond that, the new owners'/managers' desires are bound to be greater than those which existed before. Remember, they paid more for it than the old owner thought it was worth. So the new 'slave drivers' are not only likely to be unfamiliar, they may show even more *selfishness* than the old. Just like going out of business, these facts are almost never discussed with employees.

And, just like the case of going out of business, the best approach would seem to be not to discuss this consequence threateningly or when it looks inevitable. Rather, it should be treated as another organisational 'fact of life' over which the employees (through their work) may exercise considerable control.

In fact they do have at least *some* power over their future, for if they together create some unusually productive organisation:
- they make it less likely that they will be put 'up for grabs';
- even if taken over by someone else they may remain relatively untouched (as the new owner is 'afraid to mess up a good thing').

Either way they may keep still another consequence (discussed below) from happening.

Unmentionable consequence: *Unreasonable cost cutting*

Whenever either a new or an old owner gets into trouble, they are both likely to respond in the same way. Most frequently 'trouble' as used here means some sort of inadequate profit. Few employees really understand the chain of events this kicks off.

The first thing that normally happens is that managers will try to 'market' their way out of the problem by increasing the 'income' side of the profit formula. What this will mean is predictable. Large amounts of money will be thrown at advertising, public relations, and the sales force will be called on for greater efforts. This usually not only doesn't work, it may leave the employer even *worse* off!

Normally the money spent on promotion in this way vanishes into thin air. The only way to get it back is either to raise prices or cut costs. Raising prices doesn't look good when 'they aren't selling' anyway. So managers *will* turn to 'outgo'. This is because it can be changed with the flick of a pen—and produces the immediate results owners want.

Unfortunately, as discussed earlier, the biggest category of outgo which *can* be changed without shutting down the organisation is employee costs—and it is to this category that most pressures will be directed. What this will mean is cutting into employee numbers, conditions of employment/contract provisions, and so on. And it may also mean that those left behind work under miserable conditions in which every paper clip must be counted, and every pencil used forever.

Initially this may not be without cause. It is often true that if an organisation has somehow escaped unreasonable cost cutting, as much as one-third of their budget can be withdrawn without affecting very much.

But sooner or later something 'snaps' and an organisation is faced with having fewer employees serving as many customers as (or more customers than) in the past. This can't go on forever, and eventually the organisation stops delivering the quality of customer service that it did in the past.

Finding where this 'snap' occurs is difficult because it tends to be different for each employer. Also it takes a while for the customers to recognise what has happened. Glitches, foul-ups, and outright defects will be seen as untypical at first, but eventually customers *will* figure it out. When they do, they will stop bringing their income into the organisation.

When this happens the managers will, in knee-jerk fashion, once again cut costs (the biggest of which is still employees) ... and service will deteriorate still further ... so customers keep leaving ... and costs get cut further ... etc. ... etc. ... etc. Ultimately a downward spiral of income and outgo is begun which becomes almost impossible to stop.

The only way to halt it is either for management to put service levels back the way they were—this means increasing costs/prices, which it is unlikely to have the courage to do—or for someone to invest more money, which is also unlikely. Few owners will 'throw good money after bad' as they see some outfit heading downhill. The only way the spiral can *really* halt is either through bankruptcy or some sort of take-over, with all its consequences.

Although the causes producing this consequence may be different, the ideal treatment is the same. Along with every other threat to employee welfare, the reality that ignoring customers causes eventual undue emphasis on cost (the biggest of which is *employees*) should be treated as a 'fact of life'—a fact about which employees should be constantly made aware, particularly since managers are powerless to keep these dreadful things from happening.

Managers cannot keep the pain from happening.

It is too bad that most managers never make clear to their employees how powerless they are to keep the bad things from happening. If they did, perhaps the workers would be more energetic about protecting their own survival.

The way the process starts for any employer not making a 'fair profit' is this. The organisation's top manager will be called into the owner's office. It seems quite civilised. They may share some refreshments, and small-talk will be exchanged. But sooner or later the manager is told:

If this outfit doesn't make some more money fast I wouldn't make any permanent steps like buying a new home … I'd just rent *awhile and see how it works out—in case you should have to leave—if you catch my meaning!*

Once this is done the top manager will leave and call in the second-echelon managers who report to him or her. It will again be quite civilised. They may share refreshments and small-talk. But again sooner or later the top manager will have to say:

I've been told that if we don't make some more money my *head is going to roll … and ladies and gentlemen—before* my *head rolls*—yours *is going bouncing down the corridor.*

The message is loud and clear—'I would suggest we make some more money *fast*—if you know what's good for you'.

All through the management ranks the message will be the same: we want more money or we want your job. Faced with this choice the pressure on profits goes on, and produces the 'unmentionable' consequences already discussed. How long before this process of doom reaches each worker will depend upon the size of the employer. But it never takes more than a morning—*and it **will** get to each one.*

Although the outcomes of this chain of events may be harsh, it is important to understand two more things, which may help dealing with the whole process. The first has to do with a natural human response to want to find and strike out at the people causing the pain. The second has to do with how to avoid it altogether.

Although bad things may happen to good people, there are no 'bad guys' around.

Once the wraps of selfishness and secrecy are removed, it becomes very hard to find a villain anywhere in this piece. Owners are simply protecting their interests by looking after what their investment is doing, and both managers and employees from the top to the bottom are likewise only looking after their own jobs and welfare. These are just facts of life. The problem is that nobody is talking to each other, so they can't help each other to get what all of them want. And, at this point, the people don't understand a very comforting fact: it might not have to happen at all.

There *is* a better way.

Fortunately for employees there is *something*, which for them is normally 'the best game in town' because it doesn't come directly at worker expense (like all other alternatives). This 'something' is increasing income through marketing—not in the fruitless sense already discussed (and in which most believe) but in an all-new way which will involve every worker affected when 'customers think we don't care'. Explaining how this works will require some 'sorting out' of its own ... which will be covered in the next chapters.

ACTION SUMMARY

It's like watching an accident happen ...

Managers usually know the horrible consequences employee actions can bring, but often feel powerless to share them in any meaningful way, for this requires admitting hard truths most would rather gloss over or keep to themselves. Keeping these hidden is not in anyone's interest.

Hard truths must be shared.

The 'hard truths' which should be discussed with workers are as follows:

- The real authorities running most employers aren't the managers.
- The real authorities running most employers don't really care about employees.
- The real authorities running most employers care only about making money.
- Making money puts a limit on how much 'caring' can be done.
- Even 'not-for-profits' have profit-related limits.
- Managers fear revealing financial information to employees.
- Employers not only have to make a profit, it must be a 'fair profit'.
- What represents a 'fair' profit is determined by issues far from any manager's control.
- 'Little bits' mean a lot of profit.
- If a 'fair profit' is not made, what happens will be painful.
- Managers cannot keep the pain from happening.
- Although bad things may happen to good people, there are no 'bad guys' around.
- There is a better way.

How to do it

Setting this straight will require making an understanding of employer profit available to every worker who is interested. If an open and accepting atmosphere has been established, there should be no good reason for refusing to provide such information.

Why to do it

Once the preceding is done, it will be possible to explain to employees what should be their biggest single motivator for improved marketing/customer service—the personal consequences of employers not returning a 'fair' profit. It will also alert them to the benefits of seeking a course of action not likely to involve cutting costs (like them), but rather increasing income.

The best game in town

In other words, increasing income through marketing is 'the best game in town' for employees. But this cannot be of the traditional kind which probably got them into trouble in the first place.

THE BOTTOM LINE

Employees have as much to gain or lose from profit-related issues as their managers. As such they should know as much about it as the managers do, so they can act accordingly.

ACTION EXERCISE 4.1

What it costs to care for all of us

For: Employees at all levels   **Format:** Groups
Materials required: Pencils, instructions and financial information
Objective: To gain some understanding of what it costs to run your work unit

Instructions

In this chapter we were told that all employees work in a 'for-profit' situation in which the money coming in must at least equal the expenses paid out. Today we will see how big that cost is for us.

Form into groups ... then:

In the first 15 minutes you are asked to:

1   Develop a list of all the things on which your employer must spend money. (*Hint:* think of wages and salaries, rent, electricity, office supplies, the cost of the equipment we use.) Try to be as complete as possible and leave nothing out.
2   Once this list has been made, try to put down some estimate of how much is spent on each item (in total) per month.

Then be prepared to share your answers with others. We may try to get some sort of information from management to compare your answers with the 'real ones'.

Conclusion

There is an enormous amount of money that must be spent on a large number of things in order for us to do our jobs. If we don't bring in at least that amount we all face some terrible consequences, which will be discussed in the next chapter.

ACTION EXERCISE 4.2

The personal costs of failing financially

For: Employees at all levels   **Format:** Small groups
Materials required: Pencils and instructions
Objective: To understand the personal consequences of failing to reach financial goals.

Instructions

In this chapter a number of consequences of failing to meet financial targets were discussed. This is not to say that we are failing in any way. One of these is the possibility of being taken over by someone else because the one taken over is 'weak'.

Form into groups ... then:
In the first 15 minutes discuss what would happen if we were that 'weak':

1   For our department, business or work unit, what would being financially 'weak' mean? (*Hint*: Discuss income not covering expenses, being thought to spend 'too much' money, not bringing in enough money, etc.)

2   If our 'owners' got upset enough with us to allow us to be 'taken over', who might be our new 'owners'? (*Hint*: These may be other competitors who might like to do what we do, or have our equipment, etc.) Just give a name or two here.

3   Unless we were so strong when taken over that our new owners were afraid to 'mess around' with us lest they somehow 'break something that isn't broken', what might this mean for individuals? (*Hint*: Discuss coping with new managers, loss of any seniority, etc.)

Then be prepared to share your answers with us in the time remaining.

Conclusion

Generally, each of us as individuals is best off if we can make sure our employer meets or exceeds any financial targets it might have. What we have seen thus far is that *all* approaches (e.g. cost-cutting) that don't involve increasing our income can be painful to us. Therefore it is to our advantage to learn how to increase income. This means we must learn about marketing.

5

How self-destruction works in 'non-marketers', who want no part of it

WHY *EVERY* EMPLOYER *IS* 'THAT KIND OF OUTFIT'— THE TYPE THAT *MUST* MARKET

'Non-marketing' employees are responsible for a lot more customer service failures than 'marketers', but resist any attempt to change this. Here's why—and what needs to be learned in order to sort this situation out.

Don't expect marketing/customer service to be greeted with open arms.

It was said in Chapter 1 that 'customer service' programs presented to staff are rarely enough to solve any problems, for their objectives (more effort and more business) don't sit well within the culture of most employer–employee relationships. A further problem facing such training is that most employees (and their managers) see no reason why they should be included in it—so they aren't, or avoid going if they are!

There are three reasons for this:

1 Most employees think marketing/customer service has nothing to do with them because they work for an organisation they believe doesn't have to market, nor do they want it to. As such, they not only avoid any attempt to help them market themselves, they actively fight it.

2 Many others work in a 'non-marketing' area (like HRM, IT, accounting or anything which doesn't say 'sales/public relations/advertising'). So they assume they are not a part of it.

3 Still others *do* see themselves as a part of the marketing/customer service effort, but think they already know everything there is to know about it. So why learn any more?

This chapter deals mostly with the first of these problems, as well as how to correct them. The next two excuses for avoiding marketing/customer service training will be addressed in Chapters 6 and 7.

The 'toughest nuts to crack' are those who actively don't want to market.

Those who don't want marketing to be a part of their 'non-marketing' job feel this way for several reasons. Some are members of 'non-marketing' professions (e.g. lawyers, doctors, artists) or employers (non-profits/charities/government departments) who would rather die than admit they *had* to market.

Others are in 'non-marketing' areas (e.g. accounting, production, engineering), which fear and resent marketing setting foot onto 'their' turf. Whatever the case, the way these people avoid marketing is with statements like:

[sniff!] ... but surely we aren't that *kind of outfit [sniff! sniff!].*

This usually works. For it preys on the fears most people have about marketing. Slick used-car salesmen, false advertisers and other unethical marketers *have* burned most people at some time. These victims have a long memory, and what once happened to them leaves a taint that is hard to remove.

So many *do* think that marketing is the domain of sleaze-bags and scum. Surely our employer is not *that* kind of outfit—the sort that is a part of marketing. But it is!

Those who think they don't (and won't) ever market have a very small understanding of marketing. If they knew the truth about where marketing came from, and what it does, they would be much less reluctant to embrace it.

The only way to provide this truth is to start from the beginning, and produce insights about marketing from there. Once this is done, a new understanding about it can be gained, and this can then be taught to those who need it.

The first insight has to do with how marketing got started. Knowing where it began *does* give definite clues about its nature.

Marketing—in some form—has been around from the beginning.

Figure 5.1 shows the development of marketing. Most marketing historians will agree that marketing began somewhere in the beginning of time. This was

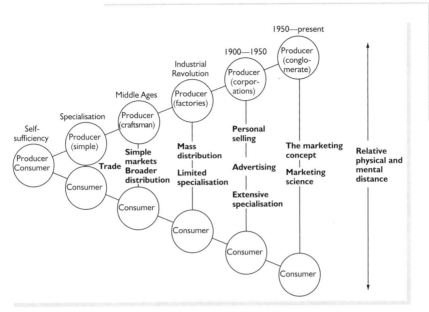

Figure 5.1 The evolution of marketing

when humankind was little more than apes swinging through the trees or people living in the Garden of Eden. Interestingly enough, both Genesis and Darwin work here.

Humans in these prehistoric times could be represented as the single circle labelled 'self-sufficiency'. At this point they were at once the producers and consumers of all they needed. If primitive humans were hungry they ripped a banana off a tree and ate it. Ripping the banana off the tree was *producing* it. Eating it was *consuming* it. Similarly, if these primitives were cold, they killed a sabre-tooth tiger for its fur and wore it. Killing the tiger for its fur was producing it. Wearing it was consuming it.

Although having a society that is totally self-reliant has a certain appeal to it, it also has a downside. Every society which is totally self-sufficient is doomed to be relatively unproductive, for everyone will be forced to spend most of their time at a job which they do not do well. This means that the most basic needs of humans to survive cannot be provided.

For instance, imagine a primitive (and self-limiting!) society consisting of only two individuals, caveman A and caveman B, who have only to do two tasks: farming (to get food) and hunting (to get animal skins for clothing). Assume also that their skills for so doing are not uniform. Caveman A (known as 'Green-fingers') is a terrific farmer. Everything he touches goes 'grow, grow, bloom, bloom' even if it was a weed to begin with. If he could spend his entire 18-hour working day farming (yes, they were unionised even then—International Brotherhood of Cavemen!), boy, would you have a lot of food!

Unfortunately, he can't. He must both farm and hunt ... and at hunting he is hopeless. He couldn't hit the broadside of a barn from the inside if the door were closed! So he blows off 17 of his 18 working hours trying to find some blind arthritic rabbit he can throttle into submission!

Luckily, across the street lives caveman B (known as 'Dead-eye') who is a terrific hunter. He is so good at hunting that when he walks through the forest the animals figure they might as well get it over with, so they run up and throw themselves on his spear. If caveman B could spend his entire 18-hour working day hunting, boy, would there be a lot of clothing! But he can't. He must both hunt and farm, but he is absolutely dreadful at farming (he once had a flowered apron and it died!). So he must waste 17 of his 18 working hours daily trying to get an alfalfa sprout to grow.

It all started with specialisation.

It didn't take long for these prehistoric citizens to get organised. What they did was to take the first step in the development of both civilisation and marketing—*specialisation*. That is, everybody decided to specialise in doing one thing to the exclusion of all others. Caveman A said, 'Look, I'll do all of the farming', and caveman B said, 'Terrific! I'll do all of the hunting'.

Unfortunately, this led to another problem. Caveman A would eventually have a huge stack of food (most of it mouldy), but suffer from frost-bite because he had no clothes. Caveman B would have a huge stack of clothes, but answer to the name of 'Slim' because he had no food. Again their (selfish) desires were not being served.

Specialisation produces trade.

In order to work all this out they had no alternative but to *trade* back and forth for what they respectively needed. The trade that took place recognised a major change that specialisation brought with it. The minute society decided to specialise, every individual in it formed into two groups: *producers* and *consumers*.

What is difficult to understand here is *we all are members of both groups* at the same time. But for any specific product or service we *have* to be one or the other. For instance, when it comes to customer service books, I am a *producer*. But when it comes to the food I eat, the clothes I wear, the cars I drive, I must be a *consumer*.

The same goes for you. You are a producer for whatever you do to make a living. You are a consumer of everything else. And in order to get this 'everything else' you must somehow *trade* with someone—and they with you. This is true for everyone.

All that this trade does is bridge something that wasn't there before specialisation—namely, distance.

Trade bridges physical and mental distance.

This distance comes in two separate forms: physical and mental. The easier one to see is *physical*. Under self-sufficiency the producer was literally in the same skin as the consumer. They were one and the same. There could be no distance between them. After specialisation, however, there have been two distinct groups. So there must be a physical distance between them.

This physical distance leads to a much more deadly one: *mental distance*. What is meant here can be seen by comparing the situation under self-sufficiency with that under specialisation.

Under self-sufficiency the mind of the producer was also the mind of the consumer. Since only a crazy person would produce something (for themselves) that they either didn't know about or want, there could be no problem.

But, under specialisation, the mind of the consumer is *different* from the mind of the consumer. There is always the chance that the consumer could somehow (selfishly) think differently about the item of interest than the producer does.

After specialisation producers could, for the first time, make an error that *couldn't* happen when self-sufficient. They could make something the intended consumer either didn't know about or want. Either of these would be deadly, because the producers would then be unable to trade for what *they* needed in order to survive.

The problem of 'distance' was not serious—at the beginning.

The likelihood of this happening was not much of a problem in the beginning. Back then the distance between producer and consumer was not very great. When producers and consumers lived beside each other it wasn't easy to go wrong. And, even if they did, it might not be very serious. Everybody was starving anyway, so nobody was too picky.

But humans weren't satisfied with the way things were. Like humans ever since, they wanted 'more'. The system found a way to give it to them—just like it always does.

Since the first attempts at specialisation, the relative distances (both physical and mental) have become greater. This is because the producers became more and more specialised and found ways to expand production, as they became:

- the craftsmen of the Middle Ages;
- the factories of the Industrial Revolution;
- the corporations of the 1950s;
- the conglomerates of modern times.

Depending upon the situation, these 'producers' would come to be known by many names. Some would become *businesses*, some *charities* or *not-for-profits*, and some *government departments*. Their 'consumers' would be labelled *customers*, *clients, donors, tax payers*, etc. However, regardless of what individual producers and consumers might be called, the problem caused by their growing apart through society's development would be the same.

Today's physical and mental distances are enormous.

Jumping forward to the present, we now have producers in factories located in Japan that supply ultra-sophisticated (picky) consumers who are oceans away (both physically and mentally) from them, and these consumers have choices—they can buy from any of many suppliers.

The likelihood of error (compared to primitive times) is very great. Under such circumstances it seems highly possible that some producer *will* make the basic mistake of producing a product or service either not known or unattractive to consumers. It is probably the danger of this error—and its consequences—that has led to what is now known as marketing.

Avoiding the possibility of error produced what is now called marketing.

In its most basic form marketing must avoid this error by bridging the gap created when specialisation split humanity up into producers and consumers.

This has always required doing the basic jobs of marketing, which are:

- to find out what consumers want;
- to produce what consumers want;
- in the place where they want it;
- at the price they want to pay for it; and
- use good promotion (advertising/sales/public relations) to tell consumers about it so these consumers can buy it.

The above is not new. It is the typical theme of modern marketing textbooks. One of the most popular marketing writers, E. Jerome McCarthy, summarised this in what has come to be known as the 'four Ps' of marketing. These assume that the job of marketing for every organisation is to make the following four decisions in a manner consistent with consumer needs:

1 Product—what product or service shall be made?
2 Price—at what price shall the above be sold?
3 Place—where and how shall it be sold?
4 Promotion—how will consumers be told about it?

Thinking about this process reveals some interesting things about marketing in general, and about those who want to consider themselves 'non-marketers' in particular. For such people (those in health care are prime examples) often go through a tremendous amount of agonising soul-searching when faced with the 'horrible' prospect of having to market. Comments like these are common:

Can *we market?* Should *we market? Oh dear, what will people think if we market?*

This self-doubt is all a waste of time! For the decision these people *think* they are trying to reach has already been made for them long before they took their jobs.

There has *never been* an organisation which *did not* 'market'.

As defined by the 'four Ps', every organisation has always marketed in *some* way. No matter how hard it may be to see, the selfishness of society means that employees will never be just given their salary. They always must exchange (or sell) some *product* or service for it—and that exchange must be satisfying or it will not continue. For companies, the product or service exchanged may be obvious. For charities or government departments it may be a bit harder to see, but it is a safe bet that nobody is going to give much to the 'John Q. Citizen Entertainment and Luxury Fund'. The charity or department must be seen to be doing something good or pockets won't open.

And for any exchanges like the above to take place some mutually agreeable *place of sale* must be decided upon, as such an exchange cannot take place in a vacuum. Of course, all the exchanges also require some sort of *price* in order to take place. This may be either in dollars or something valuable to both parties. Whatever the currency, something *does* usually get passed from one individual to another, whether what is passed goes between individuals, businesses, charities or government departments.

Finally, for this exchange to happen, some sort of *promotion* must be carried out by the producer so that the consumer knows the product or service is not only available, but also satisfying. Otherwise the producer might as well not exist (and probably won't).

A business may call this sort of activity 'advertising/public relations' or 'sales'; a charity (or art), 'informational materials'; and a government department, 'pamphlets'. However, what is going on is the same in all cases. As we can see from this, *everybody markets*. This insight helps reveal the truth of the next one.

Organisations can never decide *whether* they will market. They can only decide whether they will market *well*.

The 'four Ps' (or some equivalent) of marketing decisions *must* always be made in some manner, for a selfish society won't let the organisation exist without them. But without any kind of outside pressure—or marketing direction—*how* they get made can be very strange.

Without formal marketing input, *product* decisions are often made by people far removed from customers. Their choice of equipment may be based purely upon their own personal tastes, and without knowledge of the customer's needs. This equipment then churns out the only products or services it can—and the organisation *hopes* they will sell.

Without formal marketing input, *price* decisions are usually made by accountants, again far removed from customers. Their idea of 'marketing research' is to figure out what something costs, add a mark-up to it they think will pay the bills, and *hope* the price allows the thing to sell.

Without formal marketing input, *place* decisions are often a very mixed bag. Most frequently the organisation tries to make the place of sale convenient to themselves, and not necessarily to the customer. And they *hope* the consumer will go to the trouble of locating it.

For example, there once was a nursing home firm that chose site locations through its engineering department. Sites were chosen on the basis of having good solid rock underground (so the buildings wouldn't fall down). The firm then *hoped* there would be enough people needing its services around these locations so that its services would sell.

For many organisations, it is only after these three decisions are made that anything called 'marketing' is consulted. It is then *hoped* that some kind of *promotion* will fix any errors made in the other three areas.

So even organisations working like those described above can be said to be 'marketing'; after all, the 'four Ps' decisions are definitely being made by someone. But if it seems to you that a lot of 'hope' is involved here, you are absolutely right.

If it also seems that there is definitely some 'putting the horse before the cart' element here, you are right again. Any doubts you might have about the process are a clear indication that anyone could see this approach is far from marketing well.

Obviously it would work a whole lot better if all of the four decisions were made (from the beginning) in such a way as to be most pleasing to consumers—in other words, marketing *well*.

It is important to stress that the basic marketing decisions necessary for any organisation to survive cannot change. They must be made by *somebody* if the employer is to exist. Therefore, the only decision an organisation has to make about marketing is whether or not they will do it *well*. That is, will they do it in a manner that seems most likely to assist their survival?

Marketing practitioners (and academics) alike have traditionally made a 'big deal' out of the shift in thinking required. It really isn't all that significant.

For existing employers, marketing *well* means doing *formally* what at one time probably happened *accidentally*.

Any organisation that continues to exist has, at some point in the past, succeeded in getting the 'four Ps' relatively right. Although organisations don't like to admit it, their initial survival probably had more than an element of chance to it. As one Ford executive once stated:

> *All the planning in the world can't beat dumb luck.*

Usually what first gave any firm, charity, or government department the ability to survive was some highly fortunate set of circumstances. These meant that whatever they were doing in the 'four Ps' *was once acceptable* to their customers. Two things may cause problems after this.

The organisation's customers may change their minds about what they desire in each of these areas. If the employer continues merrily on its way without also making changes, it is doomed. A good example is the company making buggy whips in the 1800s. If it is not now making some other product it is likely to be in big trouble.

The other problem is that, once an organisation gets established, it begins to take on a life of its own. People within the functional areas (accounting, production, finance) far from the customer begin to lose touch. These 'non-marketers' settle down into their own little 'kingdoms' and make decisions based upon what they, the employees, want to do. Again, if these differ from what consumers want, the organisation is doomed.

This happens a great deal in the arts. Suppose that there is a local community theatre group who must survive by selling tickets to its productions. Often the director might have a very 'artsy' background, and wish to produce avant-garde productions. If the local public want musicals, the company will perish.

Avoiding these traps often only requires that the organisation *formally* adopt the same focus upon its customers that (by whatever process) *originally* allowed the employer to survive. This sounds easy. It isn't.

Many 'non-marketing' employees will resist any attempt to market well.

Far from being enthused about marketing well, many 'non-marketing' employees will fight tooth and nail against it. This may be hidden under a cloak of 'ethics', 'being professional', or some other 'noble' motive.

The real source of the resistance is usually much less selfless. It has to do with what marketing well will require of these people. At a minimum it will upset the power balance within the organisation. Marketing well usually means moving the source of decision making over some of the 'four Ps' to some area that the firm may label something resembling 'marketing'. (Some employers go to ridiculous measures to avoid admitting they have a marketing department, so these areas are given some noble title like 'outreach', 'liaison' or 'quality assurance'. But what they do is the same.)

Since all of these decisions were made by *somebody* in the past, any change usually implies at least two things:

1   displeasure with the efforts of whoever made them before; and/or
2   the rise of a new 'star' and the 'falling' of some other.

What this last issue means is that people with power won't like either the implied criticism or the giving up of their power 'real' marketing requires. For most employees, giving up power means less status, lower earnings and less likelihood of advancement.

As an example, suppose location decisions in the earlier nursing home case were shifted from engineering to 'marketing'. People in the engineering department would now be noticeably lower in the 'pecking order' than they once were. They won't like this. The second reason such changes will be fought is equally selfish. Marketing well will eventually make some employees' working conditions worse (e.g. 'They actually want us to build on a site which will require reinforcing, or be fully complete in less than 5 years, or use an architect, etc., etc.'). But this can't be avoided.

Marketing 'well' is not optional—unless jobs are.

Without some sort of intervention, the worsening of working conditions required by marketing well tends to happen sooner or later. The most basic reason is that any formal emphasis on customer needs places more importance upon what 'they' (the customers) want to consume and less upon what producers wish to provide. But this is not optional, unless jobs are.

This was well illustrated by a seminar given to a group of retailers who sold garage doors and equipment. When it was pointed out that their failure to be open on weekends (unlike their competitors who were open then) put them at a disadvantage, a tremendous flap began. The source of this anger was (as one noisy retailer put it):

> *Is marketing going to make us give up our weekends?*
> *I mean, we got to have a life!*

The answer, of course, was:

> *No, your customers will do this for you.*

Customers will do this by buying the equipment when and where it is most convenient to them, thereby putting the non-helpful retailers out of work. This didn't seem to occur to the retailers any more than it does to most employees.

When any kind of formal attempt to market well is begun it is common for the following remark to be made:

> *Since when did marketing start running this outfit?*

The truth of the matter is: it always did. It's just that nobody noticed it before, and no one called it 'marketing'. Still, this oh-so-typical reaction is what produces the last insight to be discussed.

Many existing organisations decide to market well only as a last resort.

For an existing organisation, any noticeable change towards the direction of marketing well is often the second most upsetting event in the life of the employer. The first was its establishment!

Havoc reigns as power structures are rearranged and long-standing working conditions are altered. Often the rank-and-file haven't got a clue as to why all this is happening, and they respond with deadly force to fight these infringements of their 'rights'.

What they don't know is their employer would never have begun this whole process if anything else had worked. Normally what has happened is a long process of erosion in whatever used to spell success. And this continual slide downhill is now signalled by the worsening of whatever amounts to 'sales' (how the employer gets its money).

The one exception seems to be when an organisation has a formal emphasis on marketing from the start. What this usually means is that those responsible for the employer's formation realised early on that they faced a situation so hostile they couldn't survive without it.

This is often the only way to get those in 'non-marketing' areas (accounting, production and so on) to accept leadership from another area. Otherwise they would be none too keen to accept the lessening of status and the deterioration of working conditions such leadership implies (more about this in Chapter 9). Thus, their 'first resort' was really a 'last resort' faced at the beginning.

The most important conclusion to be gained from all of this is that since all employers and employees *do* market in some way—and some day will be *forced* to market *well*—they might as well *start sooner rather than later*.

ACTION SUMMARY
Don't expect marketing to be greeted with open arms.

The vast majority of employees think they don't need to learn anything about marketing. They believe that because:

- they work for an organisation (e.g. church, charity, or government department) they think either it doesn't have to market—or they don't want it to; or
- they work for an employment specialty (e.g. HRM, IT, accounting, etc.) not normally associated with marketing; or
- they do see themselves as a part of marketing, but believe they know everything.

Those who think they are not a part of marketing/customer service have a lot to learn.

This includes the realities that:

- marketing in some form has been around since the beginning of humanity;
- there has never been an organisation which did not market; and

- organisations can never decide whether they will market—they can only decide whether they will do it well.

Many 'non-marketing' employees will resist any attempt to market.

Employers should anticipate that resistance to marketing well may revolve around issues that are much less high-sounding than they seem. These include disturbing the existing power structure and a change in/deterioration of working conditions. But this cannot be avoided.

It's usually a last resort but ...

Many employers begin any first-time marketing efforts as something of a 'last resort', but employees will benefit from these efforts, and they need to know why.

THE BOTTOM LINE

Although marketing represents 'the best game in town' for employees, they may actively resist the hands trying to save them. For their own good this cannot be tolerated.

ACTION EXERCISE 5.1

Marketing ... it's more than you think

For: Employees at all levels   **Format**: Groups
Materials required: Pencils and instructions
Objective: To show that 'marketing well' may mean other than advertising/sales/public relations

Instructions

In this chapter we learned that all employers *have* to market in some way, and that doing this well may mean letting 'marketing' influence what may seem to be 'non-marketing' areas (e.g. other than advertising/sales/public relations). In this exercise we shall see situations in which that might be true.

Form into groups ... then:
In the first 15 minutes read the case below assigned to your group, then discuss the questions following it.

91

'Your' Restaurant Co.

'Your' Restaurant Co. is a family-oriented chain of restaurants. In order to raise business during their least popular nights (Sunday through Thursday) they have started a policy of offering one 'kiddy' meal free with each accompanying adult. These have been a tremendous success, but now are causing some problems as more and more customers complain about slow service, and their kids run riot while waiting for their meals.

Their personnel department has decided that the shifts in these restaurants will never change before 6.00 p.m. After 6 p.m. the number of staff on duty will be triple that for earlier shifts, when there is only one host/hostess and waitress/waiter per restaurant.

1 What is probably causing the problems? (*Hint*: Discuss when young children have to be fed, how they deal with waiting, etc.)

2 What may happen if these problems are not solved? (*Hint*: If you were one of these parent-customers, what would you do?)

3 What area(s) of 'Your' Restaurant Co. will have to 'change their tune' in order to straighten this out?

4 What would you call the area which would now seem to be directing policy after this change is made?

5 Do you think that the ones who have to give in will be happy about this, and why?

The 'Artful Dodger' Museum

'Artful Dodger' is a non-profit art museum in a small conservative town. It survives by charging visitors an admission fee. The art committee chooses from any of several touring art programs for display in the museum. These range from wildly modern (with heavy social overtones) to conservative displays of the 'Old Masters'.

Every time the museum has displayed the works of 'Old Masters' (Van Gogh, El Greco, etc.), it has been packed. New Age displays have not been popular at all.

The art committee (many of whom are recent artist arrivals to the town) has decided, 'These hicks need to learn some culture'. So for the next year, they have booked in tours displaying the wildest of modern art.

1 What do you think will happen? (*Hint*: Will people go to the new displays?)

2 If the 'Modern Art' approach doesn't work, what will happen? (*Hint*: Will the museum 'go bust', change its tune, etc?)

3 If the museum does 'change its tune' who will have to give in?

4 What would you call the area now 'calling the shots'?

5 Do you think the area(s) giving in will be happy about this, and why?

Then be prepared to share your answers in the time remaining.

Conclusion

If organisations are to survive, they *must* make sure that everything they do will satisfy the customer. This means that marketing may be given authority to make decisions that others made before. This may not make everybody happy, but is necessary for survival.

Straightening out marketing

6

How self-destruction works through marketers

THE IVY-COVERED 'CON'—HOW AND WHY THE 'BIG LIE' IS TOLD

Marketers do themselves and those they serve a major *dis-service* by seeming to offer more than they can deliver. They don't tell people the truth about what they do both because they don't want to and they don't know what it is. Here's why this is important—and how to start fixing it.

The customer service syndrome

In the last chapter it was said most 'non-marketing' employees don't think they need to learn about marketing or customer service either because they don't want to, or because they don't see themselves as a part of it. Those who don't see themselves as a part of any marketing/customer service effort represent what is called the 'customer service syndrome'.

This is an ailment afflicting most organisations staffed by 'non-marketing' employees who see *any* customer-related activity as something totally separate from their work. As they may put it:

> *Marketing/customer service is something done 'over there'*
> *(in the Marketing/Customer Service Department).*

Their managers usually echo this belief. So nobody usually gets involved with any customer service programs/issues except those *already* in the Marketing/Customer Service Department.

However, those who are excluded from such a focus are quite frequently the *real* cause of most trouble. They (the people in operations, accounting, warehousing, etc.) are the ones who miss the deadlines, drop the ball and generally refuse to go 'the extra mile'. But no one ever catches up with them, for 'they are not a part of marketing/customer service'.

Strangely enough, the origin of this attitude is in what has already been called the 'big lie' about marketing. This lie is promoted both by marketing practitioners and by academics and goes roughly as follows:

Marketing is a mysterious science which can now (or someday will be able to) make people 'buy' things they do not need or want as much as the alternative(s).

What the 'big lie' represents is something an academic would call a paradigm. A paradigm is the logic that holds a field together—or suggests how it works. The reason this one is called 'classical' is because it represents what most people *think* they know about marketing—if they know anything at all. Where it comes from is pretty easy to see.

Where the classical marketing paradigm comes from

Logic suggests it.

The basis of this thought among the population at large is easy enough to understand. Practising marketers (particularly in the areas of advertising and marketing research) have in some arenas reached the status of professionals, like doctors, lawyers, etc.—all specialists people go to with a problem they wish solved.

If they didn't think the professionals could solve it, they wouldn't bother paying them money to try. For example, one goes to a doctor only if one is sick. And before going, one figures that the doctor is going to charge like a wounded bull! The patient assumes before going that the doctor can somehow make her or him well. Otherwise there would be no reason to go.

Similarly, people go to marketing professionals when they can't flog off enough of something on others! Marketers don't work for their health either. So, before beginning, those who pay them also assume that marketers can somehow make people 'buy' something. Without this belief the process wouldn't even be started.

This holds true for all employers, even non-profits and government departments. The only difference with them is that what is 'sold' may be items like charitable donations, the continuation of some department as worthwhile, and so on. They may have trouble 'flogging these off' too. They all look to professional marketers to do it for them. And this puts the practitioners in a bind.

Practising marketers have to convince those who pay them.

Although wise marketers don't like to make any direct promises, if they can't 'make' people buy things, then what earthly good are they?—especially since they face a demand for what amounts to saying they can, on a regular basis.

For instance, when considering some marketing course of action a nervous client (about to spend big bucks) frequently asks marketers:

> *Can you* guarantee *that what you are suggesting* will *work to reach the goals intended?*

or:

> *If we undertake this marketing course of action,* how much *will sales (or the equivalent) increase?*

The above are mirror images of each other. By signing up to any forecast, the marketer knows he or she is making a promise that may be impossible to keep. However, if such promises are not at least implied, the intended client will be unlikely to part with money for either the suggested actions or what will become the marketer's maintenance and good times fund!

Some marketers think they *really* are this powerful—and, even if they aren't, have obvious reasons to fight challenges to this paradigm which they see as the basis of their income. You might expect something better from somebody not so immediately in the 'firing line' (like university academics)—but rarely will you get it.

Not even the business school academics who feed marketing practitioners knowledge are likely to challenge the 'big lie'. In fact, they are the source of it!

Marketing academics tell practitioners their field can do it.

In assessing who is to blame for the big lie, the 'fickle finger' must point at the marketing departments of some of the best business schools in the world. The reason university academics are most at fault is that they have *always* been the ones responsible for the 'wisdom' used by practitioners of any field. Take engineering, for example. It is engineering academics who are expected to generate the new theories about structure and design used by engineers in the field.

In the same way, medical professors are supposed to be the ones breaking new trails in finding knowledge useful to doctors. This must be true for *all* academics teaching professional subjects. If practitioners were capable of developing similar wisdom on their own, why would society waste money on academics?

The universities most responsible for the 'wrong turn' taken by marketing 'science' are probably American (hence the 'ivy-covered' part of this chapter's sub-title). For not only do the Americans tend to be the world leaders in academic marketing, but also, as a group, they are more resistant to challenges of the status quo than most. Still, what follows about the 'big lie' could be said of most classical marketers.

That these academics *do* buy into it is harder to prove than for practitioners, as they are much more shy about stating what it is they can do. And they give even fewer guarantees than most. They never come right out and say that their discipline can guarantee to make people buy things. But their thinking is mirrored by the leading textbooks which they produce and use. Although a written guarantee is never given, hidden between the lines of every page is a promise that suggests:

> *Do this and this and this, etc. [whatever is covered in the text]—*
> *and the suckers are going to buy!*

Without this implied promise—or some better alternative—the academics have even less to trade for their living than the practitioners. Still, if this implied promise were completely wrong, they should be the ones most likely to see and tell the truth. Unfortunately, they are not likely to turn this corner, as both personal and professional issues blind them to the truth.

Marketing academics lust after the 'respectability' associated with the 'big lie'.

On any university campus it would be fair to say that the School of Business is *not* considered the most respectable part of it—by any but themselves. Though business schools are well funded and bursting at the seams with good students, other faculties (like arts and the sciences) still look down their noses at them. And within most Schools of Business it would also be accurate to say that marketing departments are not at the top of even the business school pecking order.

Marketers are still seen as cheap hucksters teaching 'How to outsell the born salesperson' and 'Irritating advertising' courses. Other departments like law, management and accounting have attained status they haven't. So it is that marketing academics often suffer from a massive inferiority complex that makes them cling to anything offering academic 'respectability'.

Unfortunately, what 'respectability' means to any academic striving for it is a preoccupation with being 'scientific', so that it can be shown to one's peers (across the campus) that 'we are just as good as they'. This obsession with science is at the core of the problem.

The 'scientific method' suggests marketers should (at least someday) be able to make things happen.

Almost from its beginning the marketing academic literature has been full of an argument over whether marketing is an 'art' or a 'science'. There have been articles with titles like, 'When will marketing become a science?', 'Is marketing a science?', and so on. The battle in the literature now seems to have been decided in favour of marketing being a 'science'. This is clearly in line with what marketing academics want to believe about themselves. It all seems so 'respectable'.

What marketing academics view as representing 'science' is interesting. Most frequently any ideas of 'scientific' thinking were borrowed from the so-called 'pure' social sciences—psychology, sociology and cultural anthropology. These social science groups in turn got them from people in 'hard' scientific fields such as physics and biology and their applied 'cousins', engineering and medicine.

This logic underlying the standards by which all research is judged is based upon an approach called the 'scientific method'. The basis of this method is something called 'order-and-pattern'.

'Order-and-pattern' is a belief that things don't just happen by chance. Rather, everything happens because of cause-and-effect relationships which can be studied and understood.

For instance, we burn hydrogen in the presence of oxygen and get water. A scientist seeing this would assume that there *must* be some order-and-pattern causing this to happen. The alternative is a belief in witchcraft, random chance or the will of God, giving humans no hope of ever controlling their world.

Because of this, academic researchers have adopted the scientific method's emphasis on order-and-pattern as their approach to research. What this method assumes is that unravelling this basic order-and-pattern can lead to the advancement of human life in four distinct phases. These are as follows.

Stage 1: Observation

In this stage scientists sit around and watch whatever they are interested in—for instance, chemistry. They burn hydrogen in the presence of oxygen and get water. They do this again and get water.

They do it about a thousand times more and (if they are really quick!) they begin to understand that a *pattern* must be present. If we burn hydrogen in the

101

presence of oxygen, we get water! This kind of thing would be good for at least six major journal articles! At any rate, once the pattern is understood it is now possible to go on to stage 2.

Stage 2: Prediction

Once a pattern is known we can use knowledge about it to predict the future. In this case the scientist who has observed this pattern will now know, 'If we burn hydrogen in the presence of oxygen we are able to predict we will get water'.

This may not seem like much, but if nobody else knows this pattern you could make a lot of money in bars with it! You could do this by betting if you burn hydrogen you can predict what will happen. (Go on—I'll bet you 10 bucks you can't!)

Understand that at this point the scientists wouldn't have a clue about the electrons and protons doing naughty things to each other that produce water. They would just know it works. However, it is hoped that if they study it long enough they will get to the point of stage 3.

Stage 3: Explanation

At this stage scientists not only *know what* is happening, they also *can explain why*. The reason this is good is it enables the scientist to take into consideration unforeseen events. This still does not allow the chemist to *make* things happen until some *tools* which control the items that underlie the process are found. Once this is done, movement to stage 4 is possible.

Stage 4: Control

Control is the ultimate goal (and assumed possibility) of all scientific work. In the case of the hydrogen example it would mean the scientists could achieve the ability to make hydrogen (or any other basic chemical for that matter) do what they wanted it to. For other fields that use this method it suggests similar control is possible as well.

Obviously, control is important to any area of science. But there are few fields which would find the control implied by the scientific method more useful than those associated with business.

This is particularly the case for marketing, in which the control suggested by science implies the ability to do that which the whole discipline wishes so desperately to be able to do—control the customers to *make* them buy or do things. As long as marketing academics cling to this possibility, there is no hope of ever reversing or changing the classical paradigm of marketing. But so what?

What's wrong with believing marketing can 'make' people do or buy things?

If the classical paradigm of marketing is somehow wrong, it causes so much trouble (with few compensating advantages) it is hard to know where to begin.

It ignores human nature.

As shall be shown, the classical paradigm largely ignores the issues of Chapter 2—the nature of human nature. And this allows a potential for control over people (whether as employees or as customers) impossible in 'the real world', where selfishness is rampant. This means any system of thought based upon such an incorrect assessment of humanity starts out 'being built on sand'.

It is wordy and sounds complicated.

It has been said that the 'respectability' of a science is in inverse proportion to the number of words written about it. In other words, go to any library and look up 'nuclear physics'. One is unlikely to find more than one or two books. For, once written, that's pretty much all that can be said.

On the other hand, go to the same library and do a title search on marketing or any of the pure or applied 'social sciences' like psychology and education, and it is likely their volumes will comprise entire floors. This doesn't make it easy for anybody to use, but some have more problems than others.

It makes it hard for 'non-marketers' to understand and internalise required marketing actions.

It is no wonder that most 'non-marketers' don't see the need for marketing-related training. For instance, suppose one is a receptionist asked to answer the phone before it has rung three times. If marketing can (through some mysterious process) 'make' people buy things, how does answering the phone promptly work into it? The obvious answer is: it doesn't. If the 'non-marketer' has ethical concerns the difficulties get worse.

Any ability to 'make' people do things creates ethical problems.

The easiest of these to see happens for 'professionals' like doctors or people in health care. For years they have had professional codes of ethics forbidding marketing of any kind. Many of these have been exposed as (and removed because of) the turf-protecting exercise they often were. But they weren't all wrong.

Suppose for instance that one is a doctor doing frontal lobotomies, but the patient doesn't need a frontal lobotomy. Along comes a tool called marketing which suggests it can make the patient *want* a frontal lobotomy. Do you see any ethical problems here? So it is that many people who could use the discipline refuse to even consider it. And still others exclude themselves from being a part of marketing for the same basic reason.

On a slightly less serious scale, marketing has always faced serious social criticism for encouraging rampant consumption of needless products and services. Marketers' assertion that they can 'make people buy things' hardly helps with this problem.

Suggesting marketing can 'make' things happen limits its influence to promotional areas.

Marketing's influence on an employer is usually limited to the areas of *advertising*, *public relations* and *salesmanship* by any assertion of marketing's 'powers'. The way it works is that these are the areas most people associate with marketing, if they associate it with anything at all. And these same people also take the position that, if marketing is so 'hot', then marketing should be able to 'sell' whatever the organisation makes using *these tools only*—regardless of how the customer feels about it.

In other words, most of the rank-and-file decide that, if marketing can do what most assume it can, and marketers seem to *say* it can, why should marketing ever need to get involved with anything except its own promotional areas?

Suppose customer service is terrible. No problem—marketing can just advertise us out of it. Maybe quality control is bad and the product isn't as good as the competitor's. Not to worry—marketing can come up with a salesmanship gimmick to get rid of it anyway. Perhaps sales outlets are located in places so strange that even the local birds carry maps and compasses! No worries—marketing can come up with a clever public relations campaign to take care of it. When these thoughts about marketing's powers are translated into action, disaster ensues.

Thinking marketing can make things happen produces actions that are arrogant, destructive, and misleading.

Those who run organisations have just as much to gain from believing in marketing's power as marketers, for it makes their lives so much easier. They can blindly 'bull' their way along with absolutely outrageous behaviour—and not see their just rewards coming.

An example was a phone company that suddenly faced fresh competition from a competitor. Even though the competing phone company was offering an identical service 20% cheaper, the older company didn't budge from its pricing structure. It ran lots of clever commercials and sent out millions of full-colour brochures while watching their share of long distance toll calls decline by 25% in about 3 months! They didn't understand why their ad campaign didn't work—I mean, weren't the commercials prize winners?

Professional marketers know their tools can't really overcome problems like the above. But how do they explain it?

The classical paradigm suggests a guarantee with no explanation for its lack.

As suggested earlier, marketing professionals are asked on a regular basis—either directly or indirectly—to give guarantees. Any honest one knows that—in the real world—they can't. So under the classical paradigm they have no alternative to one of the following:

- outright lies;
- mealy-mouthed 'fine print' buried deeply in a proposal; or
- directly limiting what amounts to their benefits from practising marketing.

They would like something that was none of the above. Unfortunately, getting to it would require admitting the most important reason for rejecting the classical paradigm.

The classical paradigm has never been shown to work.

A glance through marketing literature reveals that neither academics nor practitioners have achieved the control suggested by the classical paradigm—ever. One would normally assume that such failure would cause marketing academics to at least question the entire process upon which their field is based. Some have seen the problems associated with it but they mostly don't abandon the paradigm, but rather try to 'fix it'.

Not much new seems to be happening.

Though many might see these as 'fighting words', an honest review of the marketing literature reveals that little real progress has been made in the last 40 years. With the exception of information technology and some changes in thinking regarding physical distribution (once called 'transportation') not much new has happened since McCarthy's 'four Ps'.

This is not to say that marketing academics haven't been busily pounding away at their word processors. They have. It's just that much—if not most—of what has been produced is a 'warming over' of that which went before. Trade channel issues (around since Noah) become 'supply chain' concerns ... and then 'relationship marketing'. Promotional topics which started with Adam and the original 'point of purchase' apple on the tree have become 'integrated marketing communication'.

Much of what is happening in the marketing literature seems not very useful.

The academic response to a scientific failure to get the classical paradigm to work has caused the literature to become increasingly wordy, and separated from practitioner interests. It is a rare practitioner who reads marketing journals very much—and an even rarer one who admits to finding something useful.

What is happening in related social science fields is being largely ignored.

A group called the 'post-modernists' (to be discussed shortly) have 'hi-jacked' many of the other applied social science disciplines. With a few exceptions, this school of thought—which many would consider 'cutting edge'—is being ignored by marketing.

The classical paradigm is not very user-friendly to anything other than western philosophy.

Westerners are not the only ones who have a need for marketing. But any other culture who wants to use the discipline must park many of its own philosophies at the door. Just try to say how feng shui, an Asian paradigm used in business, fits into classical marketing! Or try to easily fit marketing into the problems facing a government department in a communist country. Good luck!

The classical paradigm is dishonest and impossible!

As shall be shown in the next chapter, demonstrating the impossibility of marketing ever being able to 'make' anybody buy anything is astonishingly simple. Why it has taken so long for others to realise this—and replace it with something better—is hard to tell. What has happened instead is that people have tried to work within the existing paradigm, with less than fruitful results.

Trying to 'patch things up' is *not* the answer.

Some marketing academics *have* seen some of the problems listed above, and tried to find a way out of them. For that reason they will be called the 'apologists' for marketing's failure as what they are doing is apologising for some part of it.

The 'moralists'

These people are an interesting bunch. What they try to deal with are the ethical problems caused by the power marketing (supposedly) has to 'make' people do things. They never question this power, but do try to soften it by saying:

> [Harrumph!] Well, marketing may have the power to make people do undesirable things, but of course it would be wrong for marketers to so it. So obviously they won't. [Harrumph]

What's laughable about this bunch is *how* they try to get off any hooks implied by the classical paradigm. They do this by saying that the only thing which keeps nasty things from happening are the *ethics* of the marketers involved—even though few people believe they have any!

The 'number crunchers'

These people (the direct mail people and marketing 'engineers' are in this group) acknowledge that they don't have control over any one individual. But they do have powers of prediction that enable them to foretell how many customers in a group will respond to any marketing action. This is actually just a lower level of control (e.g. stage 3 in the scientific method) that suggests everybody else should be able to get to that level too—so control *will someday* be possible. These 'number crunchers' have no answer for the most important question, ' ... but what happens to your predictions if some competitor does exactly the same thing to the same group of consumers?'

The 'research scientists'

This would be the largest group by far. They admit they don't have control yet, but would be able to get it only if they could secure enough money to conduct further research. They and the police are the only ones who can make an argument for increasing their budgets through what amounts to admitting total failure!

The 'new agers'

This bunch are usually called 'post-modernists'. They are a rag-tag group of academics (considered 'screwballs' by many of their colleagues) who are emerging in all of the social sciences including marketing. Although—being what they are—they probably would resent any attempt to group their thoughts under one banner, it is fair to say they are people who have sensed the failure of the classical social science/marketing paradigm to achieve what amounts to 'one size fits all' rules of action/behaviour.

The way they get to their conclusions is through some concepts of either philosophy or psychology that are very difficult to understand, and are contained in literature that is almost incomprehensible. They have been (at least until now) almost totally without marketing practitioners in their midst.

So with the gay abandon that only academics who don't have to make a living can have, the 'post-modernists' assert that almost none of the cherished concepts within their field have any value. And they don't suggest much to replace them, either. Although this group may seem an unlikely bunch on which to base future practitioner approaches to marketing, we shall return to them later.

What all of these apologists have in common is what amounts to a collective failure to disprove the classical marketing paradigm; determine why it will never work; and then come up with an alternative that will replace it—without losing all of value in the process.

A new beginning is in order.

The only real way to fix all of the problems discussed by this chapter is not to put 'patches' on an old way of thinking (which has never been successful), but rather to start out with a new and fresh foundation. That will be done in the following chapter.

ACTION SUMMARY

It's not my job!

One reason 'non-marketing' employees don't want to hear about customer service or marketing is because they and their managers don't think it is part of *their* job. They think this because marketing practitioners have given them good reason to believe it, due to marketers' *own* attempts to justify their existence.

The cause of the problem

At the core of the problem is what has been called the classical marketing paradigm. This paradigm—or logic which shows how a field works—suggests marketing either can now (or someday will be able to) make people buy things.

Why people believe in 'marketing's magic powers'

There are a number of reasons why people believe marketing can make things happen. These are that logic suggests it, practising marketers need it, marketing academics reinforce it, and the 'scientific method' implies it.

What's wrong with the classical marketing paradigm?

A belief in marketing's powers to make people do or buy things produces many problems. They include ignoring human nature, being wordy or complicated, making it hard for 'non-marketers' to understand and internalise marketing requirements, creating ethical problems, limiting marketing's influence to promotional areas, producing actions that are arrogant/destructive/misleading, slowing development of the discipline, making the discipline non-user-friendly to other than western cultures—and being dishonest and impossible!

'Patching up the paradigm' won't work.

Some marketing academics have sensed the problems associated with the classical paradigm, but their responses don't address all of the problems. These responses have included insisting that marketers should be 'moral', going for a 'lower power' of the scientific method, doing even more research, and dismantling the discipline without suggesting much in the way of replacement alternatives. All of these are less than satisfying.

A new beginning is the only way to start.

Only if marketers (both academic and practitioner) start out with an entirely new platform can the preceding problems be fixed. This will be introduced in the next chapter.

THE BOTTOM LINE

Marketing practitioners and academics have caused enormous problems by suggesting they can now, or someday will be able to, 'make' people buy things. Don't ever believe it—for so doing will severely limit marketing's usefulness within your employer.

ACTION EXERCISE 6.1

Exploring what marketing can('t) do

For: All employees   **Format**: Small groups
Materials required: Pencils and instructions
Objective: To show what people think marketing can do (but can't)

Instructions

In this chapter we learned that many people think they can keep on producing barriers because 'marketing' can somehow 'fix' these. Let's see if this is true.

Form into groups ... then:

In the first 15 minutes try to agree in your groups on some well-advertised 'terrible product' that you hated after you bought it.

1   What was the product?
2   Why did you hate it so much? (*Hint*: Think about features that didn't work, poor quality, perhaps it looked/tasted/sounded awful [depending on the product], etc.)
3   Now that you know what it is *really* like, could any advertising/salesmanship/public relations ever convince you to buy another? ('Fool me once—shame on you. Fool me twice—shame on me.')
4   What does this experience tell you about advertising/sales/public relations' ability to 'fix' barriers?

    Be prepared to share your findings with us.

Conclusion

None of advertising, salesmanship or public relations can overcome barriers that are in the consumer's mind. It is a better idea to avoid these barriers in the first place than to try to 'market them away' once they have been produced.

7

Making the paradigm shift

USED TO BE I COULDN'T SPELL *POST-MODERNIST* … NOW I ARE ONE!

The classical approach to marketing has caused more trouble than it's worth. Showing that it doesn't work is amazingly easy—so is replacing it with something better. Here's how.

Making a start

A good starting point for any new attempt to understand marketing is to form a new definition for it. Lots of people have tried this, but often their ideas have been hampered by the 'you can't see the forest for the trees' dilemma. What this means is that people have tended to define marketing in terms of what it was doing *then*—at one point in time. And this caused the definition to be less useful when times changed.

For instance, up until the middle 1960s most definitions of marketing limited it to selling products (ignoring services) and insisted it had to be done at a 'profit' (thereby excluding not-for-profits and government departments). Hard-fought battles eventually changed this on the part of marketers—even though many 'non-marketers' to whom marketing was (graciously!) offered have been none too keen to use it (see Chapters 5 and 6).

A timeless definition of marketing

One good way to avoid becoming dated is to use a definition flexible enough to embrace all who might ever wish to use the discipline, yet tight enough to set what it does apart. The following does this:

Marketing is the encouragement of behaviour financially beneficial to the encourager.

The most general outcome of all marketing activity is to produce some sort of desired behaviour. The reason for using the word 'encourage' is that it doesn't offer the kinds of promises the word 'make' does. And the words, 'financially beneficial', are inserted to sort out a turf problem.

As anyone with university-level training in the social sciences (e.g. psychology, education, communications science) will confirm, marketing is not the only field struggling with a desire to 'make' people do things. Psychology is all about 'making' people be normal. Education is about 'making' people learn. Communications science is about 'making' people understand, and so on.

Students who have read both the marketing literature and that of any other social science will note a remarkable similarity. It is as though one is listening to music in which the tune is the same, but the words are different. And such students from outside business would also probably agree that these other fields have had no better luck at the ultimate goal of science (control) than has marketing.

The only way to distinguish the goals of marketing from other applied social sciences is to inject the financial issue. Although anyone who likes to split hairs might argue that there are financial side effects of successful outcomes with the other disciplines (e.g. anybody who knows how to teach anything with 100% success is going to get rich!), these are certainly less direct than with marketing. (We shall come back to this issue later.) This monetary 'string' is the key to understanding why marketing cannot now—and never will—be able to 'make' people buy things in the way the classical paradigm suggests.

Understanding why it can't is easiest to see from looking at an extreme case. This is a perfectly acceptable scientific approach. For most scientists agree that a good rule of thumb to use in exploring any theory is to take it to its most extreme point, and test it under the most rigorous of conditions. If it doesn't work there—it doesn't work at all! This can be done easily through the 'Pepsi paradox'.

The Pepsi paradox 'pops' the classical paradigm bubble.

Suppose for a moment that I was an expert in TV commercials and, working late at night in some consumer behaviour laboratory, came up with what every marketing academic goes to bed at night dreaming about—a TV commercial so persuasive it *could make* somebody buy and use some product (like, for instance, Coca-Cola™).

Yes, this advertising approach would be so powerful one could go:

Triple Whammy Zap!—Drink Coca-Cola™!

And people *would*—with 100% power of persuasion! Even diabetics, for whom the stuff might be liquid death, would rush right out and buy a bottle of Coca-Cola™.

If Coca-Cola™ had a commercial this good, would it use it? Are you kidding? Of course it would, and Coca-Cola™ would be making a fortune as people throughout the land consumed its products.

Then, just across the street, at Pepsi Cola™, run by an equally selfish lot, they would see all this money being made and track it back to what seemed to be its beginning (me). Sooner or later a conversation like this would take place:

I hear you gave our competitor a commercial which makes *everyone use their product.*

To this any marketing consultant would reply:

Could be!

After appropriate hemming and hawing the conversation would be continued:

Would you be willing to sell us the same process?

Now, do you think I—or any reputable marketing consultant—would sell a *direct* competitor the same approach *just for money?*

Of course I would! (Call it a weakness!)

So would everybody else. Hey, it's a living! And it follows that time-honoured American tradition of selling ammunition to both sides!

If this took place it would not be long until some innocent customer would be watching television and see the message 'Triple Whammy Zap!—Drink Coca-Cola™!' He or she would immediately reach for the 500 cans and bottles kept in reserve for just such an emergency, when over the television would come an equally persuasive commercial, 'No, Triple Whammy Zap!—Drink Pepsi™!'

If both have what the classical paradigm of marketing suggests, one of only three things can be true:

1 *Possibility:* The customer is going to drown drinking both cans at the same time. Of course this won't happen. The customer's selfishness will keep this from occurring, as he or she will recognise a non-beneficial action.

2 *Possibility:* The customer's mind is going to explode, with grey matter everywhere. Unless something awfully unexpected is developed, this won't

happen either. Again the customer's selfishness (without which he or she would be a robot) will protect the customer.

or:

3 *Possibility:* In this situation marketing cannot be able to *make* people buy something. This seems to be the only real alternative, no matter how sophisticated marketing science may become. And it is important to state that what happened in the case of the Pepsi paradox is not limited to that case. It also applies to all marketing-related activity. Understanding why becomes clearer if one looks at the process behind this sample case, and any that may follow.

The competitive process keeps the classical paradigm from happening.

The general process behind all marketing activity can be explained as follows.

Marketing is about making money.

See the opening definition.

Most people selfishly desire money.

This seems self-evident.

No marketing technique can stay invisible forever.

Just as no military weapons can forever remain hidden, neither can techniques used by commercial organisations to make money stay under the surface for long. Even supposedly invisible techniques (like subliminal advertising—advertisements placed in movies below the conscious ability of the mind to see them) will become known eventually—through these techniques' creators if by no other means.

For it will be to these creators' *selfish* advantage to make sure they do. In other words, if somebody knows how to make money, why would anyone expect they would *not* sell the same idea to other people?

Visible marketing techniques that work can and will be copied by all competitors.

If something is to somebody's selfish advantage, it stands to reason that somebody else will duplicate it. To do otherwise would be foolish.

Once even the most effective marketing techniques are copied by all, they will lose much of their 'power'.

Once any advance is used by everybody, it gives a *relative* advantage to nobody. All the competitors must now look for something 'new' (into infinity).

A sceptic might say, 'but what if [in the Coca-Cola™ example] the consumers didn't actually drink the product, but just accumulated it?' They would now have an enormous storehouse of both Coke and Pepsi. What then?

The answer is that, if they did, the money they were now spending on soft drinks would not be spent somewhere else. The 'somewhere else' competitors would then take up the challenge and *they* would apply the same tool to their ends. Even if this succeeded in building up overall consumption, there does come a time when it can't go on forever. So the same outcome is reached, no matter how one 'ducks' and 'weaves'.

Marketing cannot now—and *never* will be able to—*make* people buy things.

If marketing had *ever* been that powerful, none of what most would admit has been a constant shift towards better and better ways to serve the customer would have been necessary. Once the providers had gone as far as they wanted to go they would have said:

That's it—that's good enough!

They—and everybody else—would then have employed a marketer to advertise customers into thinking the same thing. Obviously this hasn't happened, and selfishness means it never will.

Buried within this truth is something the marketing academicians would rather not hear. It is discussed next.

Marketing can never be a 'science'.

For marketing to be a 'science' in the sense of the word implied by classical marketing, it would have to be able to find some order-and-pattern that was always there—and always 'worked'. Unless somebody comes up with some tool able to overcome human selfishness (heaven forbid!) this can never happen.

For whatever order-and-pattern is found successful with customers is bound to be repeated by competitors. Once this occurs customers will either become bored and change their minds, or say, 'So, what else is new?' as the insatiable nature of their selfishness digs in.

When this happens, the order-and-pattern thought unbeatable will begin to crumble. However, this does not mean that marketing has no contribution to make—nor does it mean it can't use 'scientific' methods to help do it. What this *does* mean is the following.

Marketing works in a manner people haven't recognised before.

What it does, and how, can be observed in the most basic 'sales' situation anyone ever faces—raising children. The reason for using this example is that having children is a relatively universal experience, and infant selfishness makes it a highly *frustrating* one for most parents.

Nowhere is this frustration greater than among social science academics who have acquired so much education they so desperately wish to believe has taught them how to 'make things happen'. But when faced with these small, supposedly 'shapeable' lumps of their own flesh, they find out how powerless all their wisdom really is.

As one world-famous child psychologist put it:

Before I was married I had seven theories of child psychology and no children. Now I am married, have seven children, and no theories!

The obvious reason is that none of these theories worked! I found the same with my own children. This was particularly so the first time I found the need to 'sell' them (as babes) on something—going back to sleep after the 2 a.m. feeding.

Learning from the first 'sales' situation young souls ever face

Ah, the 2 a.m. bottle—the greatest advertisement for abstinence since AIDS! Is there a parent with a soul so dead that, faced with a screaming child at 2 a.m., they haven't wished a year before they had watched TV instead? I know I sure did.

Both my children would go off every morning at 2 a.m. like clockwork. But the harder of the two was my little baby daughter 'Pepper'. (Her real name is Danielle, but if you ever saw her you would know why the nickname stuck—cute, independent to a fault, able to wrap her father around her little finger from an early age—and totally committed to doing things her way.)

With her I would bound up the stairs with a bottle wanting the child to go back to sleep more than anything in the world. As I sprinted up I would always have a grin on my face—for it seemed to me that this was the 'battle of the giants' shaping up here.

Just as in world-wide wrestling ... *In that corner, weighing in at 235 pounds, PhD in marketing and psychology/sales/marketing courses up both arms, we have the challenger, the mad Dr B.* (Mild applause!) *And in that corner, weighing in at*

10 pounds 2 ounces, wrapped in a blanket, non-verbal, but with her face and lower lip stuck out (as if to say, 'Okay, buster, take your best shot!'), *we have the 'champeen', Pepper Buchanan.* (Wild cheering and clapping!)

But what used to really frustrate me was, the kid was going to win! Despite all I *thought* I knew about how to make things happen, she was going to win. There was no way I was going to *make* that kid go back to sleep if she didn't want to, no matter what approaches I tried. (And at 2.00 a.m. anything *does* begin to look reasonable!)

But does this mean you can't *help* a baby go to sleep? Of course not. There are all kinds of things you can try. First you put a fresh nappy on to make sure it is not wetness keeping her awake. Then you stick a bottle in her mouth so that it is not hunger keeping her awake.

Then you wrap her in a blanket so it is not coldness keeping her awake. Then you turn off all the lights and noises so that there are no distractions keeping her awake. Then you rock her softly and maybe, just maybe, she gets bored and says to herself: 'Self! Boy, this is dull. I think I might as well go to sleep'. (And she goes to sleep on her own because she doesn't have anything better to do.) But don't let that make you think you 'made' her go to sleep, because if she had a better option she'd take it! The upshot of all this is that you didn't *make* the baby go to sleep.

You don't *'make'* a baby go to sleep ...

All that you, or anyone else, could do was to take away all those things that kept her awake. Whether he or she goes to sleep at night or not will be up to their own selfish little nature, which it probably inherited from you, and is God's little way of getting even! But no way did you make the child go to sleep.

Neither do you *'make'* people buy things.

In time these rotten selfish little babies who can't be *made* to go to sleep grow up to become rotten selfish little adults who can't be *made* to do anything else (like buy things)—for pretty much the same reason. Therefore, it will always be impossible to achieve the goal of 'scientific marketing'. However, what *can* happen with babies (as insomniacs) suggests what is possible with adults (as consumers). And this produces a new paradigm.

A new paradigm of marketing

Putting all of the preceding together points to the following:

Marketing doesn't make people buy things; all it does is take away the things (called barriers) that keep consumers from buying.

This will be referred to as a 'post-modernist' paradigm, to recognise the work which has gone before. Although (being what they are) the post-modernists discussed in the last chapter may not like being put into any category, they *do* reach the same conclusions as this book—namely, that 'one size fits all' rules capable of *always* making people do things (as suggested by the scientific method) will never be found.

Just because they haven't identified what causes this to happen (selfish human nature)—and also haven't replaced the beliefs they demolish with something better—does not erase their contribution. All this approach does is to build on their earlier work, as science always should. However, that is not the only contribution a post-modernist paradigm has to offer.

What's right about a post-modernist paradigm?

It is based upon a realistic view of human nature.

The element of human selfishness is missed in other approaches. This got everything off to a wrong start. Human nature is a fundamental part of the post-modernist paradigm.

It is simple.

No big words here! Anybody, even someone with only a primary school education, can understand it.

It is easy for 'non-marketers' to make a part of their job.

The example in the last chapter of some receptionist answering the phone clearly shows why a slow response could be a barrier.

It explodes the domain of marketing by making everyone a part of it.

This will be expanded upon in Chapter 9. But when one looks at marketing as removing barriers, it quickly becomes clear that nobody in any organisation (at least those who are necessary!) *cannot*, by failing to do their job, create a barrier.

It makes understanding and explaining marketing concepts a good deal easier.

Many marketing tools (for instance advertising) can seem dark and mysterious arts—at least until they are looked upon as a means to take away barriers.

It makes no claims it can't back up.

There are no promises here. All that is implied by marketing is the removal of things that may be a barrier.

It explains why marketers can't give a guarantee.

This one is linked to the preceding. Marketers can never control two things: (1) what some competitor may do which will overwhelm a marketing strategy; and (2) whether consumers will or won't change their minds about what they *think* is a barrier.

It resolves some issues troubling to professionals/not-for-profits.

To many 'professionals' marketing is still a dirty word. But a post-modernist paradigm takes much of the 'sting' out of it. One doctor, who was in charge of a national breast cancer self-examination program, learned about the post-modernist approach. His response was, 'I can't get the government to give me money for "advertising". But I sure can get money to *remove the barrier of knowledge* which keeps women from breast self-examination.'

It puts ethical responsibility (largely) where it belongs—with the purchaser.

This is related to the above. In the case of the doctor doing 'frontal lobotomies', explaining to medics that marketing can't really 'make' somebody want a frontal lobotomy is quite reassuring—even if it doesn't totally get marketers off all ethical 'hooks'.

For the issue still remains of whether 'undesirable' products (e.g. cigarettes) should be offered at all. But again some of the 'sting' is taken out.

It explains some troubling academic issues.

It has always bothered marketers that they have never effectively 'proven' that advertising 'works'. If it is true that all advertising does is to remove some barrier of knowledge—and knowledge might not be the problem—why advertising might not work is much more understandable.

It is comfortable with all known theories, tools and concepts of classical marketing.

As shall be shown, the sky does not fall! All existing tools can be embraced by post-modernist marketing. And it actually expands the need for marketing research by making all marketing knowledge time- and situation-specific (more about that later). So such research needs to be done *more*, not less than the classical approach.

It is useful to non-western, non-capitalist cultures.

Again as shall be shown, ideas that may seem alien to westerners can be worked into post-modernist marketing with little trouble.

It is cutting edge.

There is no question that the issue of post-modernism must be embraced in an applied social science discipline like marketing—as it is in all the others. And this can be done without losing anything in the bargain.

It suggests a tantalising possibility about other disciplines.

Although post-modernism is coming to marketing from other social science disciplines, they have made little progress with it. Suppose that the way ahead suggested by marketing's post-modernist paradigm is applicable to our social science 'betters' as well. And these more 'respectable' fields have to *learn from* marketing. Oh, the joy of it!

It provides a great platform from which to build a post-modernist marketing management structure.

Once a sound foundation is in place, it is possible to move more quickly to issues which will be of interest to practitioners. A good start for all of this is to build from this paradigm to a definition of marketing management.

Post-modernist marketing management

Putting the paradigm into a form more useful to practitioners goes like this:

Post-modernist marketing management is formal producer minimisation of important barriers to desirable consumer behaviour.

Notice that what is defined here is the *process* by which marketing is applied to real problems. Because this process is so important there are a number of words in it which are worth defining before going any further.

Formal

By 'formal' all that is meant is *planned*. Marketing does in a planned way that which *always* gets done in some way. Since things that are planned usually work better than things that aren't, this adds to any power the marketer might have.

Producer

As used here, the term 'producer' means anyone who depends on others to make a living. If you depend on others for any part of your living, then by this definition you are a producer. And you must be prepared to market.

What this implies is that *every* employee—whether worker, manager or owner—is included, and no organisation—whether business, charity/non-profit, or government department—is exempt.

This also says that, as a producer, it will be your job to make sure that the process happens.

There are a few products, such as illegal drugs, for which the consumer *may* be willing to assume responsibility for the process. For example, a junkie desperate for a 'fix' may do anything to get it. But these situations are few and far between. It is better as a producer for you to control the process, as it is *you* who most benefits from this control.

Consumer

A 'consumer' is anyone on whom producers depend to make a living. At a minimum they are the ones who control the cash, but limiting one's view this tightly can be wrong. A good way to see this is through a typical shopping excursion involving children who need shoes.

As any parent will know, because of their energy children seem to wear their shoes out *from the inside* very quickly. So every 3 months or so most go out shopping for replacements. As parent and child go through the doors of the 'Discount Shoe Place', one might think that the doors should be wider. This is not because the kid-and-parent combo is so large, but because there are so many consumers going through at once.

At the most basic point there is *the kid*. Although he/she probably doesn't yet pay for his/her shoes, parents quickly learn that it's foolish to put clothes on kids if they don't like them. If you do they will solve the 'problem' by losing or destroying them. So, *he or she* has to be happy with them.

Next there is *the paying parent*. He or she pays for the shoes, so must think they are good value, look nice, won't hurt the kid's feet, etc.

Then there is *the other parent*. She or he has an interest in the child as well, and certainly doesn't want the neighbours nudging each other when the kid goes past and saying:

There's the child from the orphanage!

Rounding this out is the *government* which sets standards for footwear, the various consumer groups and magazines, etc. The list seems (and is) endless, but any one of them, if not happy, could destroy the producers who make and sell the shoes.

The process gets even messier for non-profits/charities. They have the *donors* who provide the cash, the *watchdog groups* who monitor them, the *consumers* of charitable generosity, etc., all of whom can stop the charity in its tracks through dissatisfaction.

Government departments work the same way. Someone who ran a government department which altered equipment like cars and tractors for people who were disabled asked a marketing consultant to review his marketing plan.

When reviewing his plan, the consultant commented that he had done a brilliant job of planning to take great care of *one half* of the consumers whom he served. His plan *did* do a good job of detailing how to give good service to the disabled. The consultant also insisted this was only half the job.

When the manager angrily demanded who else could possibly be involved, he was asked, 'Do the disabled pay you for your work?' When he explained that they didn't, that it was funded by a government health department, he began to see what was meant.

Among his consumers were also the *bureaucrats* who administered his funds, the *legislators* who determined his budget, the *voters* who elected the legislators, etc. All of them were people upon whom his organisation depended, and overlooking any could be deadly.

Desirable consumer behaviour

What this term means is the behaviour marketers want from the consumer (or in some cases *don't* want). This latter alternative covers an area called 'de-marketing', which basically is an attempt to use marketing to discourage consumption of some sort. It is said to have happened during the oil crisis when petroleum had to be conserved. Other examples would be attempts to discourage 'unsafe sex', speeding or driving after drinking.

Whatever the case, there are normally some consumer behaviours which are essential to the continued survival of the producers who depend on them. Most often these involve selling the consumers something, but other factors, such as getting the consumers to like the producer, tell others about the producer, and not sue him or her, and so forth, are also potentially present.

For charities/non-profits the list looks remarkably the same. Here what may be the most important goal may not be just getting the donor's money, though this is important. It may also mean serving some poor people in a way they find satisfying, raising moral standards, decreasing pollution, or some other desirable goal.

Government departments are no different; they always want to make sure that their revenue stream (called a 'budget') not only continues, but gets bigger. This inevitably involves keeping bureaucrats, taxpayers and those with whom the department deals not only happy, but thinking positively of them.

Whatever the case, *all* desirable consumer behaviours should be known before beginning, for if these are not in mind from the very start, the process can have little chance of success.

Barriers ... the key to understanding post-modernist marketing

The word 'barriers' is emphasised because they are (ultimately) the focus around which this entire book—and approach—revolves. At its simplest point a barrier can be defined as:

anything that prevents a consumer from doing what producers want.

Because of marketing's total lack of power to make people buy things, barriers must be its basic building blocks. We will explore what these barriers are, and how they can be used to aid organisational survival, in the following chapters.

ACTION SUMMARY

The classical marketing paradigm won't ever work!

Showing why this approach *can't* work begins with a new definition of marketing:

Marketing is the encouragement of behaviour financially beneficial to the encourager.

This definition should never go out of date, doesn't make any promises, and separates marketing from other disciplines (e.g. education, psychology) also interested in *making* people do things. The word 'financially' also explains why marketing can't make people buy things if one understands the competitive process underlying marketing activities.

The competitive process reveals why the classical paradigm can't happen.

The competitive process can be summarised as follows:
- Marketing is about making money.
- Most people like making money.
- All marketing techniques become visible, either because *they* can be seen, or their *creators* find it to their advantage to publicise them.
- Visible techniques which make money *will* be copied, so they no longer provide any advantage.

Therefore, marketing cannot make people buy (or do) things. However, it can help to reach employers' goals in a different way.

Marketing works in a manner people haven't recognised.

A clue to what happens with any activity trying to encourage behaviour can be found in the most basic 'sales' activity people ever encounter—trying to get one's baby to sleep following a 2 a.m. feeding. Some analysis shows that one doesn't *make* such a baby go to sleep; what one does is *to take away the things that keep it awake*. Marketing does the same thing the same way.

Marketing doesn't 'make' people buy (or do) things; all it does is take away the barriers which keep people from buying (or doing) them.

Called the 'post-modernist' paradigm, this approach to marketing solves a number of problems by being realistic about human nature, being easy for 'non-marketers' to internalise, explaining marketing concepts, not making impossible promises, suggesting why no guarantees can be given, lessening ethical problems, being both 'cutting edge' and comfortable with all approaches to business, and providing a basis for post-modernist marketing management.

Post-modernist marketing management

Applying the post-modernist paradigm to practical uses suggests marketing management is 'formal producer minimisation of important barriers to desirable consumer behaviour'. In this definition 'formal' means planned. 'Producers' include anyone dependent on others to make a living, and implies that it is this dependent group who must take responsibility for the process. A 'consumer' is anyone who influences an employee's ability to make a living. 'Desirable consumer behaviour' is whatever producers want consumers to do (or not do). And a 'barrier' is anything that keeps desirable consumer behaviour from occurring.

Barriers are the basis of post-modernist marketing.

Once this is understood, an examination of the whole concept of barriers can help employees to see how everyone (including them) is involved in marketing.

THE BOTTOM LINE

The post-modernist marketing paradigm says it doesn't make people buy (or do) anything—all it does is take away the barriers which keep them from buying or doing what producers want. Keep this in mind the next time something you are trying to make happen doesn't, and ask, 'What am *I doing* to hinder what I desire'?

ACTION EXERCISE 7.1

Why no 'gravy train' is forever

For: All employees   **Format:** Small groups
Materials required: Pencils and instructions
Objective: To gain an understanding of why *nothing* guarantees success forever

Instructions

In this chapter it was said that, because of human selfishness, anything that 'works' to make money always gets copied by competitors, and then it no longer provides much advantage. Today we will see this process in action for ourselves.

Form into groups ... then:

In the first 15 minutes your group is asked to come up with some product or product feature that seemed startlingly 'wonderful' when it came out. (*Hint*: For instance, air conditioning in cars, microwave ovens, home video games.) Try to come up with something that your group thought impressive enough when new, so that everyone thought seriously about going out to buy it.

1 What was the product or feature?
2 Was it pretty much unique to one producer when introduced?
3 How long did it take before other producers were offering it as well?
4 Looking at this process, what do you think always happens when somebody finds a way to make money that 'works'?
5 Given this fact, do you think there is anything about our employer that gives us an advantage in making money—and will this last 'forever'?

Conclusion

There is no 'magic' about marketing, or anything else, which some competitor can't copy, and render 'us' equal with 'them'. Because of this, it is important for us to always be looking for ways to serve our 'customers' better than others. The next chapters will show us some of these ways.

ACTION EXERCISE 7.2

How our pay cheques happen

For: Employees at all levels   **Format:** Small groups
Materials required: Pencils and instructions
Objective: To understand who the organisation's 'consumers' are and what behaviours we wish of them

Instructions

In this chapter we learned that a consumer is someone who controls the money that eventually becomes our salaries. Today we will discuss who they are, and what we wish them to do.

Form into groups ... then:

1 In the first 10 minutes list all the people who *can* influence the money that comes into our organisation. Who are they? (For example, customers, donors, taxpayers, spouses, children, advisory groups, government agencies.) Please be as complete as possible.

2 In the second 10 minutes discuss for each group named what it is that we (selfishly) want from them (e.g. buy from us, give us money, think well of us, not cut our budget, not sue us).

3 Do you believe that our behaviours always encourage the above goals? (Answer yes/no and explain why.)

   Then be prepared to share your answers with us in the time remaining.

Conclusion

Employers rely on a large number of people for their continued existence. There are an equally large number of behaviours which must be encouraged for the organisation to survive and thrive. It is important that we learn what these are.

8

Barriers, the basic building blocks of post-modernist business

ANSWERS TO 10 OF THE 'NINE MOST ASKED QUESTIONS' ABOUT BUSINESS-DESTROYING BARRIERS

A post-modernist approach to marketing can provide a *unique* way for an employer to achieve customer service success—if the employer knows how it works. Here's how to do it.

We don't make 'em buy—we take away barriers.

We have looked at marketing as the idea not of making people *buy* things, but rather of *taking away* barriers (the things that keep them from buying). This idea achieves its greatest usefulness once a number of questions about barriers have been explored. The most common barrier questions (and their answers) are as follows:

Q. What's a barrier?

    A. Anything that keeps consumers from doing what producers want.

Barriers happen everywhere.

It must be understood that absolutely *anything* that producers do can become a barrier for consumers. For commercial enterprises these could be unattractive products, snotty service on the part of an employee, too high a price, annoying advertising messages, etc.

Non-profits/charities/government departments tend to have pretty much the same barriers as commercial ones. For instance, failing to answer a phone within about two rings is just as deadly for a charity, a church or a government department as it is for a business.

Some creative thinking is often required for a non-business employer to see what form barriers could take, but in their most basic appearance barriers are pretty much the same for all. And, for all types of employers, the list is endless. However, producers don't always have to do something about barriers.

Not all barriers are created equal

Some barriers must be dealt with, others can be left until later.

Q. It does look like almost anything *could* constitute a barrier. But your definition calls for the minimisation of *important* barriers. Which barriers are *important*?

> **A.** Any barrier is an important barrier if a competitor increases 'sales' by avoiding it.

In this case the word 'sales' means any time a competitor gets their hands on money which would otherwise have come to your employer. For instance, in a car company this could mean money received when a Ford is sold instead of a Toyota.

For charities/non-profits something could happen to cause one church to grow at the expense of another, or one charity to have a successful fundraising campaign that would make another campaign fail. For government departments, something could happen to cause one department's budget to be increased, and the money to be taken out of some other(s).

An example of this was a country whose airforce faced a major scandal about some funds which were (in the eyes of taxpayers) 'wasted' through spending a huge sum on renovating the base commander's house. The airforce got its budget cut—while the army did quite well next fiscal year.

What has to be understood here is that there are no absolutes. *The only thing that is really important is what one employer does compared with its competitors.* If there are no competitors, or everyone else is equally bad, something which consumers don't like may not be an *important* customer service barrier.

For instance, one United States airline gave such rotten service that at one time it was known as 'Agony Airlines'. Often its flights were overbooked, the staff didn't answer their phones, its terminals were usually unspeakable, and its staff had all attended the East German Border Guard School of Hospitality—prior to Gorbachev! The reason that none of these were *important* barriers is that, for many of their destinations, *there were no competitors* or, if there were, often these were just as bad.

Understanding this can help employees realise that service standards that may have been acceptable in the past may not be acceptable now if competition is much sharper. Often the idea of what is 'good enough' tends to be rooted in the past.

Q. Are some barriers more important than others?

> **A.** Absolutely. Sometimes one barrier (or the lack thereof) is worth a great many others.

A good example of this is people who smoke. They generally are well aware of all the barriers—cancer, heart and lung disease, horrible smell and horrendous cost—but they keep right on smoking. The satisfaction smoking gives by feeding their addiction outweighs the barriers for them. However, the relative value of the barrier may not stay the same.

Times change—so do barriers.

Q. Does the importance of barriers change over time?

> **A.** Certainly, as people change their minds about what they like (and dislike).

A good case of this is the television program called *I Love Lucy* that is still shown in various places as a rerun. Fifty years ago this was the most popular television show in the world. Watching it today tends to be a shocking experience, for there are all kinds of themes (husband dominance, wife submission, threatened wife abuse, etc.) that could never be other than barriers to a modern audience.

Charities find similar changes. Twenty years ago any charity with an aim of aiding homosexuals would have had a hard time, but now attitudes have changed, and there are many with that focus. Similarly, some churches who used to 'pack 'em in' now have a difficult time even surviving. And others—who might have had a difficult time attracting anybody a century ago—are now growing rapidly.

This is also the way for government departments. Sometimes they seem to go on forever. But if society changes its mind about the value of what a department is doing, it will not survive.

Just ask the secret police of former dictatorships about this one! The days of those they dealt with used to be numbered. Now the days of those who used to do the 'dealing' are. But, just because society—through changing attitudes—may eliminate barriers, don't think your employer (by itself) will be able to.

Why not go 'the whole hog'?

Q. Why just *minimise* barriers? Why don't we go the whole way and *eliminate* them?

A. We can't.

There are a number of reasons why this seemingly reasonable goal can never be reached. One of them is that *some barriers belong to the customer alone* and it is very difficult to change them. A local organisation which sells alcohol to the public is a good example. It takes the position that, if somebody is a teetotaller, and/or just doesn't like to drink, it is much easier just to *accept* that barrier for *that particular* customer, and not try to change it.

Similarly, there are probably some people who, for their own reasons, may never support research into AIDS. And it seems likely that some government departments, such as those with the power to tax, may never create a great deal of affection for themselves.

Generally, unless people have barriers based upon obviously incorrect information, it will be very difficult to change their opinions. It is usually much easier just to give up and work around them.

Advertising agencies will sometimes challenge this position by stating, 'We must re-educate the public'. But generally this tends to be a great waste of time/money, and can take forever. Just look at how much money has been spent trying to stop people driving while drunk!

A second reason barriers can't be eliminated is that *removal of a barrier for one often creates barriers for others*. People's tastes differ, and so it will always be difficult to make everyone happy.

For example, New Zealand is a right-hand-drive country. This creates all kinds of problems for visitors from countries who are used to the other way around. One way New Zealand could remove a barrier for Americans and most European tourists would be to move the steering wheel over to the left. But this would create tremendous difficulty for New Zealanders, Australians, the British and the Japanese—all of whom are used to right-hand driving.

There is no one who understands this problem better than government departments. Almost any change in any of their regulations or activities is bound to set off a political flap that makes World War II look like a Sunday School picnic.

The best any employer can ever do is to decide to focus upon some group of consumers as what is called their 'target market', rather than trying to make everybody happy with the same thing. An example would be a retirement community which decides to cater to Dutch people with their food, activities, and architecture. They know people who aren't Dutch may not like this, but they also know you can't satisfy everyone.

Even if it were possible to take out a barrier for one consumer without creating another, this still wouldn't eliminate all barriers. The reason for this is *it is impossible ever to make any one individual totally happy*. As stated at the beginning, human selfishness is insatiable. No matter how good a deal a person is given, they can always think of a way it *could* be better.

Businesses always know this. Even if they have nursed some customers for years by giving them free advice, carrying them on their books at no interest for ages, and bending over backwards to be helpful, this guarantees nothing. The minute some competitor gives these customers a 'free toaster', some of them will be down the road.

People who work in charities quickly learn this principle—or go mad in the process. Some of them can get quite cold-blooded about life as they harden up to how 'it really is'. Ask any minister or priest how difficult it is to keep a church full of people happy for any length of time; their job sometimes makes running a war zone look easy. And one *can* go too far.

There *are* limits.

Readers may be pleased to learn there is a limit to how far one can go in minimising barriers.

Q. Can you ever go too far in minimising barriers?

> **A.** Absolutely! Minimising barriers can (eventually) get completely out of hand.

There are two ways this can happen. One is by increasing cost to the point where a new price barrier emerges (e.g. cost constraints). The other happens if taking out too many barriers destroys what the organisation is trying to do in the first place (mission complaints).

Cost constraints

It must be admitted that there are some occasions when barriers are the result of inefficiency or outright ignorance, so removing them can be cost free. For instance, an organisation may find that its phones are not answered during lunch times, and this is costing it customers. Rearranging lunch times so that there is total coverage may not cost anybody anything. Or a business/charity/non-profit/government department may discover that its old accounting system (using green eye shades and quill pens!) is costing it dearly. Replacing it with a more modern computer may, in the long run, save money.

However, there does come a point where minimising barriers *will* begin to cost money. At this point it is a good idea to remember the following:

There is no such thing as a free lunch.

What this means is that, whenever anything is added to what an organisation does, the cost of doing it must come from somewhere. The 'free lunch' will always have to be 'paid for' eventually—one way or another.

It was once suggested to a group of postal employees that they could remove a lot of barriers by being open 24 hours a day, 7 days a week, quadrupling the staff level per shift so no one ever had to stand in a line, installing a free food buffet with caviar and pheasant-under-glass, offering free wine for all, and having a string quartet play soft music on the side. The only problem was that if this were done it would cost $25 just to send a letter across town (to say nothing about airmail!). It was likely that nobody would be prepared to pay this price.

As suggested by the preceding, removing barriers for firms will eventually mean that either profit will go down (with all that this implies) or prices will go up. This cannot go on forever.

For non-profits or charities, what will often happen is that the money spent to take away one barrier may mean that there is less to spend somewhere else. This can create a barrier of its own.

That this is a constant problem is made plain by the watchdog agencies who either formally or informally monitor how much donor money is spent on other than the object of the charity; they, or somebody else, will make a terrible fuss if they think someone has stepped over the edge.

For example, a rest home for the aged caused a terrible flap by running some innocent advertising ('We've got a nice place. If you need a home, come and see us', etc.). The result was indignant letters to the editor, people removing their parents from the home, and at least one case of somebody threatening to burn the home to the ground. Why?—because they were seen to be 'wasting' money on advertising instead of spending it on patient care.

Mission complaints

The other way to go too far is if taking away barriers changes or destroys what the organisation is trying to achieve. An example of this would be churches who could really build attendance by preaching that sin was okay and adultery fine. But this wouldn't do much for the morality that churches see as their goal.

From putting all the preceding together it can be seen that cost, the impossibility of eliminating barriers and the barrier-based approach to marketing seem to contradict each other. If marketing consists of minimising barriers, but not all barriers can be taken away, then how does any one competitor 'win'?

The 'secret' of post-modernist marketing success

Q. If you can't remove *all* barriers, then what *is* the secret of marketing success?

A. Having fewer barriers than the competitors.

The secret of marketing success is so simple it took me 20 years to see it. It has been stated before—in an old movie called *Lost Horizon*, in which it was said:

> *In the valley of the blind, the one-eyed man is king.*

The reason is that the 'one-eyed man' would be able to do things others couldn't. Stated in barrier-based marketing terms, what this means is:

> *The 'winning' competitor in any market arena will be that one with the fewest barriers compared to its competitors.*

In other words, the 'winner' in any competitive area will be the competitor who has (relatively) the fewest barriers. For businesses this means that who 'wins' will be the one who presents the *consumer* with the fewest barriers by making (relative to the others) 'four Ps' decisions that are most in line with what customers want.

A good example of this is Microsoft. Bill Gates has made a fortune because Microsoft's software—relative to other alternatives—is as close as anybody currently comes to what computer users want. Another would be McDonald's. The golden arches represent gold to franchise holders because everything offered from under them is carefully planned to be closer to consumer needs than competitors offer.

For charities/non-profits what this may mean is that, relative to all other charities to which contributions may be made, they are the most attractive and the easiest to donate to. As an example, a charity had excellent success with a 'red nose day', on which it raised money by selling plastic red noses (cut-out plastic balls with rubber bands to hold them on) for $2.

This was brilliant marketing as it was one of the few charities which actually gave donors something back for their money. What it gave was fun for both adults and children, who seemed to enjoy the noses equally. Also, the visibility of the red noses ensured that others knew the wearer had *given*, and made those misers who hadn't stick out from the crowd. There were even chicken badges for those 'too chicken' to wear a nose. And it was all for a good cause. It was a very successful campaign.

133

Similarly, successful government departments may be the ones on which taxpayers are *least* reluctant to see money spent, for what they do seems *most* compatible with what the taxpayer wants. As an example, local fire departments have a terrible time raising money to pay firefighters. But they can raise enormous amounts to purchase a new engine. It seems some people just like them. The saying that 'men are just boys grown up' seems appropriate here.

Again, what all this means is that the most successful marketers will be the ones presenting the fewest barriers to their consumers. However, buried within this truth is an issue well worth raising.

You're never 'the best'!

Q.   Is the 'winning' marketer the best?

A.   No, they're always the *least worst*.

There are a number of good reasons for keeping this in mind. One is that it is usually the statement closest to the truth. Think of the various firms with whom you do business. Are the ones you deal with really the best that you can imagine them to be in your 'dream-world of dream-worlds'? Or are they just the best of a rather hopeless lot? It would be surprising if the latter were not the case.

The other reason for keeping in mind that 'the winner' is always the 'least worst' is (over and above corporate pride) thinking that an employer is the 'best' is the most dangerous thing its employees can do. For normally it means that they will not change.

As an example, only 15 years ago anyone who said the Japanese car industry or retail giants like Sears or Kmart might someday come close to facing receivership would have been thought crazy, but both of them have recently stared that possibility in the eye.

The reason their very existence became threatened is that they probably allowed themselves the luxury of thinking they were 'the best'. When this occurs the employees believe that there is *never* any reason to change anything they are doing—why tamper with success?

As stated earlier, what is (and is not) a barrier changes over time. If organisations do not allow for change reflective of that experienced by their consumers, they are asking for trouble. For existing organisations the source of any failure does not seem to be that they are doing what they did in the past much worse. Rather, failure seems to happen because customer preferences (barriers) change. And some new competitor twigs on to that better than the old, thereby stealing the previous 'winner's' business.

This was certainly the case for the original Ford Motor Company. When Henry Ford's 'You can have any colour as long as it's black' philosophy first drove down costs, it worked very well. Unfortunately, Ford appears to have thought it was 'the best', and refused to change that single-colour policy when the public grew tired of it. Along came upstart Chevrolet with a choice of colours, and took the market away from Ford.

Many churches have experienced similar problems. For a while main-line US Protestant and Catholic churches refused to budge in any of their positions with regard to what represented appropriate worship. Eventually newer churches with more relevant teaching, modern music, and guitar-playing pastors made serious inroads.

It's not hard to find government departments who take the same line. Employees who believe their employment is guaranteed 'forever' will fight tooth and nail any attempt to change. It may take the public longer to hurt them, but if the department presents enough barriers, it will. For example, the postal service in some countries is so miserable that private parcel and courier organisations have taken most of their business away from them.

In all cases, maintaining a humble 'we are the least worst' stance is a good way to maintain the flexibility required for continued survival. The question then becomes, 'The least worst among whom?'

Competitors are the key.

Q.   What's a competitor?

A.   Any organisation an employer wishes didn't exist!
People attending single-profession functions (e.g. pharmacist conventions, florist associations) don't like to think about it, but for many of them, 'more for me is less for you'—and vice versa. Because of this, the shared camaraderie present at such occasions may be a bit strained!

The reason is that any means of making money generally exists in an environment very much like one where there are three undertakers in a small town. Is there anything any of them can do individually or collectively, to increase the total amount of business available to them all by having a 'one cent sale'? (E.g. 'Somebody died? Bring a friend. We'll "throw them in too" for only a penny!')

Generally, no matter what kind of business is involved, there are only so many 'stiffs' to go around. And more 'stiffs' for you is fewer 'stiffs' for me (and vice versa).

Within broad limits this is always true. However, seeing this is often made difficult because people normally think in terms of one type of competitor when usually there are four. These are 'the four Fs' of post-modernist competition.

Firm competitors are ones everybody recognises.

These are organisations that serve the same needs in the same way as some employer. For businesses, they are opposing companies (e.g. Ford versus GM). For charities they are others who collect money from the same people or who serve similar causes (e.g. Save the Children versus Christian Children's Fund). Government departments didn't used to have them, but many do now (e.g. the post office now faces competition from private courier companies).

Form competitors are harder to see.

These are organisations that serve the same needs as some employer, but in a different way. For example, firms like Universal Studios who produce movies are a *form* competitor in the entertainment field to firms like NBC who produce television programs.

Charities/non-profits may find their biggest form competitors are ways other than giving money to make a contribution to worthy social causes. For instance, if someone feels that working afternoons at the Humane Society is a reasonable substitute for giving money to a charity, then the two are form competitors. Or sometimes a non-profit may face a situation like their commercial brethren.

Many churches are now finding it quite a struggle to give spiritual leadership. Not only do they have to cope with other Christian churches (firm competitors), but also non-Christian denominations and fortune tellers (form competitors).

Government departments are classic cases in which form competitors may be the most important ones encountered. A case in point would be employees of an electricity utility who may believe they have no competitors, but the form competitors of natural gas, solid fuel, solar energy and so on are all waiting for them. Similarly, postal service employees may or may not face an opposing post office, but the emergence of e-mail should be of major concern to them, as should faxes.

Fiscal competitors are 'piggies at the same trough'!

These are organisations who compete for the same part of the consumer's budget as some employer. Firms who sell luxury items such as giant-screen televisions may find a key financial competitor may be someone else (such as the travel industry) who competes for the same 'luxuries' budget in some consumer's mind. In another case, funeral homes know the costs of their wares are often in direct competition with other ways any heirs might spend an inheritance (e.g. trips to Hawaii), and must seem to represent superior value to those left living.

This is particularly true for charities/non-profits who discover that people often have some figure (e.g. 10% of their income) in mind as the maximum sum to be spent through charitable giving. This may be split up among charities or non-profit endeavours which have absolutely nothing in common except that they are all fed by the same hand.

This notion of being 'little piggies all lined up at the same trough' holds particularly true for competing government departments. Inevitably there is only so much taxpayer money to be spent. Money spent on social welfare is money that education won't get (and vice versa). Thus the departments are direct competitors even though their people may never even see (let alone think of) each other.

There is a fourth category of competitor for which this line of reasoning does not apply. However, most firms still wish this kind of competitor didn't exist.

Feeling competitors are invisible ... but there anyway.

Feeling competitors don't fit into any of the preceding categories, but instead are organisations totally separate from some employer but against whose standards that employer will be bench-marked. They are particularly important in situations in which the consumer feels inadequate to judge quality, and so may depend on superficialities to separate competitors.

A classic case of this happens regularly with university students (particularly MBAs) and their language/grammar/punctuation skills. Such students usually get quite annoyed when assignments are marked down because of errors in these areas. They take the position that only the content—not the presentation—of their work should be considered.

They miss the point. The intent of their education is to prepare them to write business reports, proposals, summaries (etc.) for people who won't necessarily know whether their content is any good or not. If they did, students' employers wouldn't need the employee to write these submissions for them!

So, not having any other guide, such employers will frequently use something they *do* understand (like language/grammar/punctuation) to make any judgments about quality. As one employer who often has to sift through hundreds of resumes to fill his jobs once put it:

The first thing I do is throw away any c.v. which is sloppy or has any grammatical errors. If they can't get such simple items right, how can the rest of their work be any good?

137

The world probably shouldn't be this way, but it is. And anyone who ignores these issues sets themselves up for an ambush.

Another illustration can be found in how people evaluate professionals like lawyers, doctors and engineers. Most people can't tell whether (for instance) the lawyer they use is any good or not. If they knew this much they might not need the lawyer! However, they certainly can tell lawyers with crumby offices, ones who don't return phone calls, and ones who dress sloppily. These lawyers may be perfectly competent, but these 'feeling' issues can make or break them.

This fact was certainly not lost on one nursing home operator who replaced all the vans used to transport patients with stretch Cadillac limousines. (They weren't very expensive as he bought them 'used' from mortuaries with whom he usually had a working relationship anyway!)

As he put it:

Most people don't know how to judge nursing care, but they know a Cadillac when they see it. They seem to assume that (like hotels) the presence of a Cadillac must indicate superior quality care.

Charities/non-profits often assume (with some justification) that looking poor increases the donations. This may be true, unless the donors also feel it indicates shabby or unprofessional management.

Government departments have to walk a similarly precarious line. They can't be seen to be wasting taxpayer money. But they also can't seem to be 'unprofessional'. Good luck on figuring out where to separate one from the other!

How to have fewer barriers

Seen in this way, there is *no* organisation which has no competitors, and therefore has no need to market. Every employer always faces a competitive arena in which survival goes to 'the least worst'. Given that this is the case, the next problem becomes how best to do this.

Q. How can any organisation have fewer barriers than its competitors?

A. By:
- taking out their own barriers; and/or
- making one for a competitor.

You can take out your own barriers ...

Often organisations are doing some incredibly foolish things that, if eliminated, would result in better business. This is what is meant by *taking out their own barriers.* A good analogy is going to a doctor, twisting one's neck, and saying, 'Doc, it hurts when I do that'.

The response will of course be:

Don't do that. That will be $50, thank you very much.

One company selling very expensive items was doing something like this. They refused to take a certain credit card for payment because it took a bigger 'bite' from their proceeds. Unfortunately, the card they wouldn't accept could be converted into free air points for a major airline, and the firm's customers (who were high flyers) wanted the points.

When the reluctant firm finally figured out they were losing much more money on the business they pushed away (by not taking the card) than it would cost them to get it, they decided to (grudgingly) accept the credit card. Sales soared.

One charity found something similar. It got marvellous results by allowing contributions to be made over the phone and charged to donor phone bills. Why this hadn't been done before (even though contributors requested it) nobody knew.

Government departments usually have so many barriers it is hard to know where to begin. One university discovered (to its horror) that, of its six biggest competitors, it was the only one who didn't have pre-enrolment packs available at least 3 months before registration (when they were most requested).

When it changed from sending out letters saying, 'Wait until the month prior to registration to get your materials' to sending out enrolment packs the minute they were requested, its enrolments soared. But this 'taking out your own' approach is not the only way to achieve fewer barriers.

Or you can make barriers for others ...

The other way to have fewer barriers than others is to *make one for a competitor.* This does not mean blowing up its trucks or burning it to the ground! What it does mean is being willing (or able) to do something the competition doesn't, and which the consumer wants. Viewed in this way, doing something for a customer becomes a barrier for competitors if they don't match it. The competitor is at just as great a disadvantage as if the other had always done something for the consumer and it hadn't.

This was the secret behind the dramatic turn-around of Chrysler Corporation in the 1990s. They began offering glamorous, exciting cars like the Plymouth Prowler and the Viper. Not only did these special vehicles sell well, but when people came into showrooms to see them, the sales of their entire line soared.

One church took the unusual step of opening a coffee bar behind its meeting rooms with desserts, sandwiches and beverages available for sale. They also made a practice of getting the name and address of any stranger who attended and gave them a pack explaining the benefits of belonging to the church, containing a self-addressed stamped envelope asking if the pastor could make a personal visit, with a coupon good for a free beverage at the coffee bar following the service. This let them meet the newcomer in a comfortable surrounding.

This church saw its membership grow fourfold in a few short years. Others, who at best gave you a weak cup of tea, saw their membership decline.

Coming up with good examples of government departments doing something innovative is difficult, but not impossible. One university offered an 'executive' MBA (Master of Business Administration) on weekends in all the major cities in the country. This grew to the point where it graduated over half of all the MBAs in the land, even though almost every city where it was offered had a competing university with its own MBA program. The problem for the competitors was that they had full-time programs which met Monday to Friday over a 2-year program. Working executives just couldn't afford to spend this much time on them.

In all cases, although the successes were treated with some awe, there was no magic present. All that these 'success stories' did was find a way to be a little 'less worse' than their competitors.

It doesn't take very much.

It is important to understand that *it doesn't take very much* to do this. One shopper put it very well when she said:

> People don't have to do very much to make a major impression on you as a customer—for so often nobody does much of anything.

A case in point is Joe CarNut's choice of service stations. Joe loves cars, drives big ones long distances every week, spends a fortune on petrol, and is very fussy about keeping his vehicles spotless. The way one service station got Joe's business is by having a car wash attached to its operation with a couple of unique features.

Most service stations in the area had a car wash attached, and for all of them the way they worked was the same. One went into the station, requested a car wash, paid for it, and got a little piece of paper with a number code written on it. The motorist would then drive around to the back, put coins into a vacuum cleaner to clean out the inside, and then drive to the car wash where he/she faced a small key pad with numbers. What the driver was supposed to do was punch in the code supplied by the station, wait for a green light to go on, and then drive in. This created an interesting problem.

What does Joe CarNut (and everybody else) now do with the little bit of paper with the numbers for the key pad on it?

Some might be tempted to say, 'Get a life!' But for Joe—and others like him—this represented a real dilemma. For the car was now clean—and if the bit of paper were dropped on the floor, it wouldn't be spotless anymore. But if one were to drop it out the window, that's *littering*.

One service station saw this quandary and devised a tiny trash bin below the number pad—into which the bit of paper could be dropped. Hey presto! They got all of Joe's business (and that of other fanatics like him). Lest you think this foolish, if you were Joe—and all service stations were alike in all other aspects (e.g. prices, location) but this one—what would you do?

Isn't this often true? Think of the cases in which some producer impressed you. Was what was done *really* that marvellous? Or do you remember it because it was done against a background of competitors who were so terrible? A truthful answer to this question—for *any* employer—suggests that there is always so much hope for the future.

Turning hope into success

Turning this 'hope' into 'success' by having fewer barriers requires *finding* them so you can work on them. How to do this will be shown in the next chapters.

ACTION SUMMARY

Barriers—the basic building blocks of post-modernist business

Barriers are a simple way for employees to understand what is necessary for their own survival.

What employees need to know

In order to use this knowledge, employees need to know that barriers:
- are anything that keep a consumer from doing what producers want;
- become important if they are used by one competitor to secure money away from other competitors;
- may not be equal in importance, so must be looked at both in isolation and in total;
- can change in importance over time; and
- can never be totally eliminated.

Barrier-based success

Both survival and marketing success are a matter of having the fewest barriers, e.g. being *less worse* than competitors, who are those organisations whom some employer wishes didn't exist.

Competitors are the key.

These competitors come in a number of different categories:
1 firm (some competitor who does the same thing in the same way);
2 form (some organisation who serves the same needs in a different way);
3 fiscal (some employer who competes for the same budget);
4 feeling (anyone by whose standards a competitor is judged, even though they don't directly compete).

How to win

Having fewer barriers can only be done through taking out one's own barriers, or creating a barrier for a competitor by being willing or able to do something they can't or won't. This may not take very much.

Looking in all the right places

Having fewer barriers is essential to any employer's success, and knowing where to look for them can help with this process.

THE BOTTOM LINE

Keep in mind that you are never 'the best'—you are always (at best) 'the least worst'. Be constantly on the lookout for ways to take away your own barriers or make one for competitors in a never-ending battle for fewer of them.

ACTION EXERCISE 8.1

How good are we?

For: Employees at all levels   **Format:** Small groups
Materials required: Pencils and instructions
Objective: To show how we might tell if we are as good as our competitors (or better)

Instructions

This chapter said that marketing success was a matter of being 'less worse' than our competitors. What we will do today is to see what that might mean for us.

Form into groups ... then:

First 10 minutes:

Look at the four different kinds of competitors. For our employer, go through these four and (where appropriate) name for each category two organisations in competition with us. Where the categories are not appropriate leave them blank.

Firm: (Organisations who serve needs like us in the same way.)

1

2

Form: (Organisations who serve the same needs as us in a different way than we do.)

1

2

Fiscal: (Organisations who compete for the same share of some budget.)

1

2

Feeling: (Organisations not related to us, but by whose standards we may be judged.)

1

2

Second 10 minutes:

Discuss within your groups the following questions:

1 Which of the above do you think are our most important competitors?

2 Does anyone in the group know anything about them?

3 (If 'yes') Are we as good as them in all aspects? (Be honest here. If we could learn something from any competitor, it is to our advantage to do so.)

(If 'no') In light of what we have learned about barriers, would it not seem to make sense to learn about (and copy) these competitors?

4 What would be a good way to do this? (E.g. get their promotional materials, visit them as 'customers', ask our customers what they think, talk to our sales people.)

Conclusion

In order to survive, every organisation needs to be 'less worse' than its competitors. This is not easy. And, despite what employees may *think* they are doing, customers may not paint so rosy a picture. We must be constantly looking for ways in which we can go 'one better' than our competitors. We will next discuss where to look for barriers so we can do this.

The power of post-modernist marketing

HOW MARKET-ORIENTED ARE YOU REALLY?— HERE'S HOW TO TELL

It becomes much easier to do something about barriers if you know where to look for them. This chapter tells you where to start.

Post-modernist myopia

A classic marketing article once described something called 'marketing myopia'. What this meant was being too 'near-sighted' in defining what an employer's 'business' was. For instance, the railroads thought they were in the 'train' business and didn't see they were in the transport business. So they lost out to airlines and buslines by being too limited. Most do the same thing when deciding where to look for the marketing barriers pushing their consumers away.

Slipped under a post-modernist microscope, most employers look even more like 'Mr Magoo'! For the extent of what they define as 'marketing' and those they see as their 'consumers' is way too narrow. These pre- post-modernist employers have really missed a key point.

The 'omnipotent/impotence' of post-modernist marketing

'Omnipotent/impotence' seems a contradiction—but is nonetheless true. Namely, if marketers would only give up and admit that their discipline is powerless to 'make things happen' (i.e. *impotent* as a science in the sense of the classical marketing paradigm) and adopt a post-modernist approach, the function (or job) of marketing would become supremely important (*omnipotent*) within any organisation. How this works is as follows.

Being 'least worst' sets the scene.

As discussed in the last chapter, marketing success is defined as becoming that competitor having the fewest barriers. In the 'dog eat dog' real world, competitor responses to this success will greatly enlarge what is meant by 'marketing'—in a manner very much like a poker game.

Post-modernist marketing is like a poker game.

Suppose a situation has little or no apparent marketing activity—at the start. Eventually some competitor decides it wants something 'more', and produces a simple black and white brochure to get it. If nobody else has anything like it, this may work (remember Joe CarNut in Chapter 8). This is like 'raising' in a poker game.

If it does work, it may take a while for competitors to see what is happening. When they do, they must meet this raise (e.g. also offer a brochure) in order to survive. And they must 'raise' again by (for instance) making it colour in order to stay in the game.

If the colour approach works, then the first competitor must not only offer a colour brochure as well, but they must also do something more (like advertising). If this is successful, the second competitor will have to not only advertise, but also try having a trained salesperson ... etc. ... etc. ... etc.

Competitors run through the 'marketing' barriers pretty quickly.

In a rather short while everybody will be doing almost everything classically thought of as 'marketing'. All competitors will be advertising like mad, have steely-eyed salespeople with a quick wit and glib tongue, and be employing enough 'spin doctors' (public relations) to make cyclone experts envious. But there will be a problem.

Everybody is 'marketing' like mad ... and getting nowhere.

The reason for the lack of progress is that the 'marketing' efforts begin to cancel each other out. But nobody can stop. For if they did, they would have more

145

barriers than their competitors. Against this 'If you've got a tiger by the tail—don't let go!' backdrop, a search begins for more barriers to vanquish. This has a predictable outcome.

Lookin' for barriers in all (the other) places

If the area most people see as 'marketing' (namely, promotion) is pretty much dredged dry, the crosshairs of post-modernist marketing management begin to shift elsewhere. When they do, what is considered 'marketing' changes, as does where to look for barriers.

For instance, somebody begins to notice that the policy of the finance people allowing 'no credit to anybody anywhere any time' (which really keeps the bad debts down!) may be a bit too restrictive. A decision is made to see if more business comes in if we start offering credit. And (click!) *finance* is now a part of marketing.

Then, constant complaints about errors in billings—not to mention taking months to produce them—begin to rear their unlovely heads. So the order goes out to accounting, 'Produce bills ... without errors ... our customers can understand ... on time'. And (click!) *accounting* is now a part of marketing.

Or somebody begins to notice that the personnel in the warehouse (all of whom were dismissed from the US Marines for excessive cruelty) are a tad non-user-friendly—and this has cost us at least one customer. So a conscious effort is made to hire nicer ones. And (click!) *HR* becomes a part of marketing.

The net effect of all this is to produce the biggest turf grab since the Americans got Manhattan for a few beads! For where all this goes is predictable.

What's not a part of marketing?—nothing!

Given enough time and competition, something about this process becomes very obvious. No *necessary* employee—and no activity—is *not* a part of marketing. The reason for emphasising the words 'necessary' and 'not' is to make a very important point.

As stated in the earlier chapters, most people don't want to acknowledge that they are a part of marketing. What they don't realise is that, if some employee is so deeply buried in the bowels of an employer that they *can't*—either directly or indirectly—produce a barrier (and therefore can be excluded from marketing), there must be only one outcome. These 'non-marketing' people must either be sacked or retrained!

For if they didn't exist nobody would notice, but as long as they are present they must be paid, and this creates new price barriers when it feeds into costs. Seen in this way most employees are able to understand the 'omnipotent/impotence' issue in a very personal manner. Truly, if one adopts a post-modernist approach, everybody *must* be a part of marketing. And the matter doesn't stop there.

Your barriers don't stop at your boundaries.

Sometimes employers find that the areas causing problems are not even within their own organisation, but rather in outside outfits associated with it. In this situation what is causing the problem may be somebody else's employee, but customers don't make this distinction. All they see is something kept them from getting what they wanted when they dealt with a firm, and they are not interested in the finer points of it.

A firm who sold whole-house carpeting was a good case in point. It seems its own personnel were first-class, but it had to contract the carpet installation to outside firms whose employees saw no good reason to get things done quickly. So the retailer sold the carpet, its own people delivered it, but it often didn't get installed in time to meet some customer deadline. All the customer would think (and tell everyone who will listen) is, 'That lousy retailer. He promised me installation by a certain time and didn't deliver. Don't ever deal with them'. This became a major problem.

A port authority faced something similar. It discovered that its personnel were doing a wonderful job of moving cargo through their facility. But the people from the government-controlled customs area (who had to clear most incoming freight) were totally oblivious to anything resembling speed. And the port was getting a reputation for being a bottleneck.

In all such cases what is happening isn't 'fair', but that will make no difference to anybody. It's the producer's problem, not the consumers'. All the organisation taking lumps can do is to try to link in the outside provider's workers to their shared problems. In the above situations both the retailer and the port authority paid for its outside contractors to go through the customer culture training upon which this book is based.

Accepting all of the above really explodes the areas in which a post-modernist specialist can search for barriers. But organisations don't normally recognise that 'everything is marketing' all at once. They do it in a stair-step process, the major landmarks of which can be used to judge *your own employer's* marketing development, while at the same time showing how wide a barrier-seeking net can be thrown.

How to tell how marketing oriented you are

Truly, everyone has to start somewhere. Historically, most marketing authors have suggested the beginning for most is what is called the 'production' stage during which there is no discernible marketing effort happening. As has been stated before, it is impossible not to have some form of marketing—no matter how primitive—present. So this phase has probably been mislabelled. A post-modernist viewpoint suggests a more descriptive title would be 'the accidental marketer'.

Stage 1: The accidental marketer

What is meant here is that, at the beginning, many employers get their start through a process which has more luck than science in it. By some fortunate set of circumstances the organisation comes up with a solution to some problem that people want. And the provider starts making money hand-over-fist by selling this solution (either a product or service). In this happy state the major focus is on making more of whatever it sells, along with reducing costs (so more is made on each item). The production and accounting people reign supreme. There is no area even faintly identifiable as 'marketing' to be seen.

This doesn't mean that the marketing tasks represented by deciding on the shape of the 'four Ps' aren't happening. They are. However, the decision process behind them is very informal, and sometimes done with little real thought. This doesn't last forever, as foul-ups between production and those paying for its output begin to happen.

If enough of these occur the organisation will move on to the next phase.

Stage 2: The sales era

This starts innocently enough. Usually, somebody will emerge from the production area whose job it is to coordinate what is being made with those who want to purchase it. Initially their job is just to 'push paper' back and forth between the outside world and the production area—without much thought. As long as people are 'beating down the doors' with money in their hands, this is probably all that is needed.

Unfortunately, competitors eventually see all this money being made and begin to move in—just at the moment when all who want whatever is being sold begin to think they have enough. So whatever means 'sales' for the organisation slumps. (What constitutes 'sales' may not always be in dollars. For instance, sometimes sales are called 'census' for rest homes or hospitals, 'equivalent full-time students'—EFTs—for universities, 'circulation' for libraries, 'case load' for social workers, and so on. But these figures are *always* present—and noticeable through having some numerical connection to employer finances.)

At this point the 'paper pushers' begin their evolution into real, live salespeople by recognising that sometimes they can help the production/consumption process along by telling what are now 'customers' more about what they sell. Slowly the salespeople begin to move away from feeling they are a part of production into becoming something separate—which now may even be called a 'sales force'. And if they grow in number, something called a 'sales manager' may be hired to manage them.

The important thing to understand about this stage is that the people in sales have nobody else related to the process (e.g. advertising) reporting to them, and they have absolutely no influence on what they sell. In other words, they are told, 'Go thou, and *sell* something'. But they are not allowed to even *think* about influencing any area but sales.

If nobody else has salespeople this may work for a while. But the 'poker game' of competition discussed earlier will begin to heat up as others respond. Sales may again slump, creating panic in management ranks. Depending on the type of employer, this may lead to one of two occurrences. Let's start with the one requiring less noticeable marketing effort.

Stage 3: The 'committee' phase

This one happens a lot with employers who sell more than one product/service or offer their wares in more than one location. (Schools are a prime example.) If one of these pre-conditions is not present employers usually go directly to stage 4.

What happens in stage 3 is that someone in an organisation big enough to have choices notices that some product/service or some location is doing better than others. And an assumption is made that something about this situation is 'magic'.

So a committee is formed to study what is happening. And a plan is hatched to clone this 'success strategy' down through the rest of the organisation. What is seldom recognised is that the successful offering/location may have very little 'magic' to offer—because its success is caused by some (usually temporary and accidental) lack of real competition. Nobody sees this, and instead it is decided that this offering/strategy 'glows in the dark'. So it is duplicated throughout the employer.

At best this usually does little harm. And at least the people on the 'marketing committee' formed to study the 'success strategy' may get a free trip out of it! Something useful may even be found. But this stage usually doesn't last more than a year. Key decision makers still see their sales charts heading downward. This causes them to 'do something'.

Stage 4: The 'first-time marketing manager' *moments*

What is generally done by employers in real trouble is to hire their 'first-time' marketing manager. Unfortunately for the people hired into this job, they usually last a maximum of about a year to 18 months before they are fired (with great satisfaction) by the rest of the firm! (These people are not always called 'marketing managers'. Some may be called by some other name like 'business managers'.) Whatever their title when these people are (almost always) let go, their employer generally blames them—and thinks their firing was person-specific. Most often this is not true. The reason first-time managers get into so much trouble is situation-specific.

Why 'first-time marketing managers' get into trouble

Why this happens is due to a number of causes, the biggest of which is the problem associated with the 'classical' marketing paradigm. These people are hired on the basis that 'marketing is magic', and with just the right salesmanship approach, just the right advertising gimmick, or just the most clever public relations campaign, they will be able to *make* sales go up.

Because of this belief they are signed on with little idea of what they are supposed to do, and even less of how they are to do it. However, the one standard part of their job description is the charge given them, 'Go thou, and *market* something'. What this means is they are to stick to the promotion area (e.g. sales, advertising and public relations only). And 'keep your hands off the rest of the organisation!'

One thing that distinguishes this phase from the 'sales' era is that those areas related to marketing (like advertising and catalogue production) may be dragged kicking and screaming from wherever they have been. (For instance, primitive advertising departments often grow up from 'graphic artists' in 'print shops'.) Such a change sets the teeth of everybody in the employer on edge. For it means that the power structure has been changed—and some criticism implied.

Even if this change doesn't happen, there *has* been an addition to the management team. And this always *can* represent a possible threat to others. This apprehension is not made better by the fact that, up until now, all the other managers have been sitting around 'polishing the crown' of those above them, hoping somebody will die, retire or move on (creating a possibility of promotion). Suddenly there is this new kid on the block called 'marketing' who just might know something they don't.

This is sometimes made worse by the fact that first-time marketing managers often come into an organisation thinking, 'I am God's gift to this outfit—I'll show these hicks a thing or three!' What they are forgetting is the reality of Chapter 5—namely that the 'four Ps' decisions associated with marketing always get made somehow, with or without *formal* marketing. And this attitude is not only arrogant, but untrue. Whether or not such arrogance is expressed, knives come out and are honed—just in case.

However, for a while no serious alarm bells go off, for everybody knows the 'marketing manager' has no *real* power. This is generally confirmed by her/him having a lower salary, worse office, or some other indicator of status less than other managers—and no power over anything but promotion. The consensus becomes, 'Let her/him play with their brochures. Who knows, some good may come of it'. All and sundry go back to normal.

For a short period of time things may go well as the 'marketing manager' goes quietly about their job sharpening up the only (promotional) areas to which they are allowed access. And if no competitor has something similar, this may work. However, the clock is ticking for everyone. One of two things may happen next, both with the same result for the first-time marketer.

Why 'first-time marketing managers' get fired

A possible alternative is that the 'first-time marketer' never leaves the promotion area. What this usually will mean is that—after competitors catch up—nothing noticeable happens with sales. And a decision is made that, 'This person is ineffective—why do we need them? Off with her/his head!'

Unfortunately, the other possibility—that of the marketing manager really trying to *do something*—is even worse. Again working with promotion (only) begins to yield no visible results. But in this scenario the marketing manager finally acknowledges the limitations of a promotion-only focus by staggering back—bruised and bleeding—and declares, 'I can't do this no more'.

Like cats circling their prey, the 'non-marketing' managers will respond to this possible opportunity to slit their fellow manager's throat by asking, '... and why is that?' At this point the marketing manager may, in an ill-timed expression of honesty, blurt out the fatal words, ''Cause what we are selling is rubbish!'

This usually turns out to be a most unfortunate turn of phrase! What the manager really means is that something outside his/her control is not how customers want it—the product should be changed, the price is too high, the places of sale too inaccessible, etc.

All of this may be true. But it represents criticism of all the people currently responsible for these areas. What the organisation produces and how it does it doesn't just happen—*somebody* made it that way. And here is this upstart marketer not only daring to say 'the emperor has no clothes', but implying that he/she should have the authority to change it! At this point the days of the marketing manager are numbered. And how they will perish is pretty predictable.

How 'first-time marketing managers' will be eliminated

Those unhappy about a marketing manager can't attack openly, so they wait and play to the manager's most likely weakness, a product of the manager's hiring.

Most often if a major employer doesn't have a marketing manager, it probably exists within an industry or profession that is not exactly 'cutting edge' in this regard, either. So it is unlikely that there are many candidates who will have *both* industry and marketing experience.

This requires making one of two choices. Either the employer must hire somebody from within the industry (or employer) and try to make them into a marketer, or hire somebody who is a marketer, and make them industry/profession aware.

The first choice often is made if the employer is not too desperate. In this case some pleasant person without much to do is appointed 'marketing manager' and, predictably enough, little really happens. This results in the 'Why do we need them?' scenario. End of game.

On the other hand, if some marketer without industry/profession-specific knowledge is hired, they leave an opening a mile wide for others to attack. Namely, 'They aren't "professional"'.

In most cases they probably aren't. Without at least a year's background in their new employer's culture the first-time marketer will sooner or later commit a professional faux pas—and their peers will be there waiting for them.

A classic case of this happened when a rest home chain hired its first marketing manager from real estate. This made sense for, in a way, rest homes are a form of residence.

After a short period of time this manager decided to hold a 'sales contest' (based on occupancy levels). This *sort of* made sense. And he decided to announce the results at a quarterly 'sales meeting' attended by the homes' managers at which the 'winners' (all of whom were either registered nurses or people with a Master's degree in social work) would be applauded. This *could have* made sense.

Unfortunately, this manager chose to bring into this setting something borrowed from his real estate experience. At his first quarterly dinner not only were the results announced, but also the 'winners' were served steak—while the 'losers' ate beans. And the manager hired a singing telegram service to send somebody dressed up as a 'killer bee' to come in and serenade the attendees (most of whom were intense feminists!) with an absolutely filthy ditty about what 'no-hopers' the losing contestants were. His days (actually minutes) were numbered from that point.

The moment of truth

Whether real (like this) or imagined, the non-marketing personnel who feel threatened will collect these industry-insensitive showings and make sure the CEO hears about them. Eventually, when they think they have enough, they will march into the CEO's office and announce:

Either they [the marketing manager] go—or we go!

Faced with such an in-house revolt it will be a rare (and brave) CEO who doesn't give the marketing manager their walking papers. After a while the organisation will realise that it still isn't 'flogging off' enough of whatever it makes to survive. And it will either die (some *do* choose this route) or go—kicking and screaming—into the next phase.

Stage 5: The full-scale marketing department

Once again a marketing manager will be appointed, and (for sure) all areas related to a classical sense of marketing (e.g. advertising/sales/public relations) will be grouped under their command. What makes this period different from the prior one is both a sense of resignation that this is required (from the rest of the organisation) and a recognition by top management that this person *must be a manager among equals.*

In other words, not only will this marketing manager have salary and 'perks' similar to managers in the other functional areas (e.g. production, accounting, finance, HR), but they will have authority *equal* to them.

So marketing will have an input into any decision being made within the firm. How big this input may be—and whether it is listened to—may very much depend on the whims of the CEO. But they will have *some* input.

This is about as far as most employers go. However, those facing a particularly tough market or those with unusually wise management may go to another level.

Stage 6: Marketing dominance

In this stage an entire organisation recognises the reality of a post-modernist viewpoint—namely that there is *nothing* within any employer that *is not* (directly or indirectly) a part of marketing. Note that this does not mean that the marketing department is necessarily all powerful. But marketing *considerations* are. It may or may not be led by the marketing department.

Where it generally starts is with a usually wise and market-centred CEO who both drives and protects the process from those in the organisation who, given their 'druthers', would take it right back to an earlier stage of development. Without such a CEO internal politics will make the situation deteriorate pretty quickly.

Regardless of who is calling the shots, what this phase means is that, before making any decisions—even those in 'non-marketing' areas like finance or accounting—the first question asked must be:

How will this affect our customers?

153

Answering this correctly may require quite a bit more head scratching for some areas than for others. The 'production' area can be pretty straightforward. As an example, before purchasing equipment which can make red 'widgets' (only), it must be considered whether the market really wants red 'widgets' or would prefer something else. Other areas may be more obscure.

For instance, before structuring its financial affairs a firm must balance off its cost of capital (feeds into total costs and hence selling price) against risk (feeds into what sales must be made 'when'—particularly important for products/services which are seasonal). The key to all of these is tracking through any employer's system how any decision will eventually come out the other side to those who support them.

It is easy to see why 'marketing dominance', though complicated, will give the best results by opening up the largest areas of an organisation for the kind of barrier scrutiny that is the subject of this chapter. This opens up an interesting question.

Where are *you*?

An exercise at the end of this chapter explores this question more completely. But it must be asked:

If not at the safest point (marketing dominance), why not?

Indeed! However, extending the domain of marketing *within* an employer through working up the ladder of marketing dominance is not the only way to increase the number of barriers which can be considered. The other way is to minimise the barriers one presents to what shall be called 'rarely considered consumers'.

Rarely considered 'consumers'—another area for barrier scrutiny

Other areas for improvement (usually overlooked by classical marketing) can come into better focus through re-examining the post-modernist marketing management definition. Remember that in Chapter 7 post-modernist marketing management was defined as follows:

Post-modernist marketing management is formal producer minimisation of important barriers to desirable consumer behaviour.

And it was said that a 'consumer' is anyone on whom producers depend to make a living. Most people look at this definition and limit their vision to 'consumers' (called 'customers') who have a direct impact on income flow. More myopia!

People who spend money with some organisation are not the only consumers who can affect an employer's ability to survive. What about banks, employees and so on? Do they affect producers' survival? Of course they do! A classical approach to marketing will sometimes look at some of these as a part of what are called the 'marketing environments' impacting on decision making. But this misses the point, for it doesn't show how these areas could be turned into a market advantage.

And they can. A post-modernist analysis can do this through extending barrier scrutiny to these rarely considered consumers, thereby exploding the possible barriers to be minimised. Finding out how requires addressing two questions:

1 What do these 'consumers' provide that an employer needs so desperately?
2 How could they be sufficiently annoyed (through barriers) that they wouldn't provide it?

The following will briefly explore these issues for a number of such 'rarely considered consumers'. It will then provide an example of how other organisations have used this information to give themselves an 'edge'.

How 'rarely considered consumers' can be a source of market advantage

Employees' families

Let's start with the workforce (sort of), but not confine our focus to those on the payroll. We have already dealt with those workers in Chapters 3 to 5. Employees' families make a big contribution too. They do it by supporting and encouraging the worker, not complaining about work-related demands, going along with job requirements like shifts, moving from one area to another, not suggesting the worker quit, and so on.

Ways this can be lost are by ignoring the family, forcing the worker to perform under what their family thinks are unusually harsh conditions, ignoring the importance of 'family days' like birthdays and holidays, requiring the family to shift where the family doesn't want to go, failing to acknowledge family needs, and so forth.

One hospital noticed that it had a terrible time getting enough nursing staff. The problem wasn't that nurses weren't out there—they were. But their working 'shelf life' was very limited due to their starting young families. This hospital responded to the problem (barrier) of young children by providing an in-house creche for employees. End of nursing shortage.

Suppliers

Although these people are paid for what they provide, *to whom they give it* at times of shortage or emergency and *under what conditions* they provide it can be a major problem. Ways to annoy suppliers can include excessive 'crunching' of prices, late payment and 'panic' orders with unreasonably short lead times.

A book distributor accidentally neglected to pay the account he owed to a publisher (he thought his accountant had paid it, and the accountant thought he had). This caused the publisher to hand his account over to a debt collection agency. When the distributor figured this out he not only paid his account in full, but asked what the debt collection agency would have charged the publisher for having been assigned the account—and paid that too.

Since he didn't legally have to do that, the credit manager for the publisher was sufficiently impressed he decided to continue to ship to the distributor without advance payment—although this was normally required for any accounts which had *ever* been deficient. This sped things up heaps, and allowed the book distributor to prosper.

Banks

Financial institutions provide the capital which is the life blood for many employers. Understandably, they get nervous about releasing this money if anything suggests they might not get it back.

One nightclub entrepreneur needed banks to lend him start-up capital on a regular basis. For nightclubs generally worked best if set up in one area for about 9 months—then closed down—and set up in a different area with another theme for 9 more months. The nightclub owner discovered that if, in his prospectus, he called his business a 'nightclub' he never got the cash. But if he called it a 'jazz club' he did. From that time onward his prospectus always said he was setting up a 'jazz club' and he was able to access finance when nobody else could.

Cultural/ethnic/religious special interest groups

There are few markets in the world in which there are not minorities with organised special interests. These people generally have the media or political clout to make a major problem if unhappy, and/or in some other cases can represent a major market. When these minorities erupt the person against whom they are protesting usually richly deserves what they get, for the minorities have generally been offended beyond anybody's patience.

A good example of this was one market in which there were two skiing resorts about 10 miles apart. The resorts fell into areas populated by two different tribes of indigenous peoples. One resort ignored these natives, treated them with scorn, and made all its decisions independently of them. The other resort went to great efforts to understand them, made a contribution to their fund-raising efforts, attended their tribal events (to which it always got an invitation), and always consulted with them before making any decisions. The manager of the second resort reported that he never had any problem with getting a resource consent, while the first resort couldn't put a spade into the ground without setting off a major protest.

Environmental special interest groups

These people are similar to the above. If unhappy they can either directly or indirectly shut most employers down. What will make them do this is usually somebody operating in flagrant disregard of what these special interests want. This is very dumb.

An insurance company fixed its clients' damaged vehicles through a franchised association of auto body shops. Instead of fighting the 'clean air' advocates, the company required its authorised agents to install air filtration systems in their spray booths to stop putting contaminants into the air. This got it an award from an environmental group, a 'green' reputation, and its agents were never attacked by the 'greenies' (unlike its competitors).

The list of 'rarely considered consumers' is endless.

Clearly the above just scratches the surface of a group which can include employees, unions, taxation authorities, government agencies, insurers, etc., etc., etc. How each one works will vary with the situation, but they do provide a largely untapped source of potential barriers. They also can add to the wisdom of Chapter 1. Just as one doesn't *lose* a customer, but *drives* them away:

> *You never lose a resource (e.g. employee, endorsement from special interests, outside approval) … you drive it away!*

How you drive these (and more traditional) consumers away is through barriers of your own making. How to find them will be discussed in the following chapters.

ACTION SUMMARY

One can't find barriers if you don't look in the right places.

It is easy to be too 'near-sighted' in considering where to look for business-destroying barriers. A post-modernist approach can avoid this problem.

The power of post-modernist marketing

If marketers would ever give up and admit they are powerless (impotent) as a science, marketing becomes all powerful (omnipotent) as a function. In a post-modernist sense marketing is like a poker game in which one side 'raises' through some successful action—requiring that action to be matched—and then bettered by some competitor—and so on. This eventually leads to an unavoidable conclusion.

There is *no* employer activity which *is not* a part of marketing.

Employers usually reach this conclusion in a number of stages which include 'accidental' marketing, the sales era, the committee phase, 'first-time marketing manager' moments (after which the first-time manager is almost always fired), the 'marketing department' period, and marketing dominance. 'Dominance' is the safest place to be, for it places the largest number of barriers under scrutiny. This is not the only way to extend the power of marketing.

'Rarely considered' consumers represent another opportunity.

These are people who are generally far from any purchase, but directly or indirectly affect the employer's ability to survive. They can be used to create an advantage through considering what it is they provide which is needed by producers, and what barriers could make them reluctant to give it. These people can include such individuals as employee families, suppliers, banks, special interest groups, and an almost endless list of others.

A post-modernist approach expands the areas in which barriers can be studied.

It does this by expanding the domain of marketing within an employer, as well as considering consumers normally overlooked by other approaches. How to find barriers will be addressed in the next chapters.

THE BOTTOM LINE
Barriers won't be found if your idea of what constitutes marketing and consumers is too limited. Use a post-modernist approach to keep this from happening and you are bound to do better than competitors shackled by outdated approaches.

ACTION EXERCISE 9.1

How market-oriented are we—really?

For: Employees at all levels **Format:** Small groups
Materials required: Pencils and instructions
Objective: To consider if we are 'market-oriented' *enough*

Instructions

This chapter said that marketing's influence could be measured in a number of steps. Today we will consider how market-oriented our employer is—and if that is 'good enough'.

Form into groups ... then:

First 15 minutes:

Look at the following levels of market orientation and the characteristics which set them apart. For our own employer, go through these and discuss which one best describes our situation.

Stage 1: The accidental marketer

Employers at this level have no formal marketing department. And the majority of emphasis is either on producing more of something or finding a way to reduce costs.

Stage 2: The sales era

People in this category have some sort of sales force, but no centralised advertising department. And the sales force has absolutely no influence on what is being sold.

Stage 3: The 'committee' phase

In this situation an employer either offers several products/services for sale and/or offers them in several locations. If one of these is doing noticeably better than the others, a committee is formed to find out why—and tries to clone it outward.

Stage 4: 'First-time marketing manager' moments

In this (usually) short-lived stage a marketing manager is hired but given no authority over decisions other than promotion (advertising/sales/public relations). This marketing manager doesn't have salary, perks or power equal to managers in other areas. They are resented by other functional areas of the employer.

Stage 5: The marketing department period

In this situation a marketing manager is hired, but given salary, perks and power roughly equal to other managers. Marketing has a say in everything which is happening, but this is not greater than that of other managers.

159

Stage 6: Marketing dominance

This is the highest level. At this stage marketing considerations (e.g. how will this affect our consumers?)—but not necessarily the marketing department—are all powerful. This customer emphasis is true for every area including 'non-marketers' like accounting and finance.

Second 15 minutes:

Discuss within your groups the following questions:

1 Do you think this is 'good enough'?
2 If not, why not?
3 If you don't think this is good enough, what would have to change to get to a more meaningful level (e.g. attitudes, management structure)?

Conclusion

The safest employers to work for will be those which do the best job of serving their customers. Extending marketing to do this may not be easy or comfortable. But in the long run, it will be best for all.

ACTION EXERCISE 9.2

Serving all the consumers

For: Employees at all levels   **Format:** Small groups
Materials required: Pencils and instructions
Objective: To show how we might better serve 'rarely considered consumers'

Instructions

This chapter said that a 'consumer' is anyone who affects a producer's ability to make a living. It was also said that this extended market consideration to groups far removed from any purchase. Today we will consider what 'rarely considered consumers' may be important to us … and how they might better be served.

Form into groups … then:

First 5 minutes:

Look at the following groups of 'rarely considered consumers' and see if you can find any which seem to be giving our employer particular difficulty. Discuss and choose the one with whom you think we are having the most trouble and go on to the next part of the question. The groups from which you can choose are the following:

- banks;
- media (e.g. newspapers, TV);

- insurance companies;
- religious/ethnic/cultural special interest groups;
- environmental groups;
- regulatory agencies (e.g. government regulators);
- suppliers;
- employees;
- employee families;
- taxation authorities;
- any others you may wish to add.

Next 15 minutes:

1   What is it this group supplies which is so vital? (In other words, what do we get from it when 'things are going well', or sometimes, 'What happens with it if things aren't going so well'?)
2   What will happen if we don't get what we want from this group?
3   What are we doing to annoy it?
4   Would it be a good idea to learn more about these people?
5   How could we do this?

Conclusion

Whether it be a customer, employee, government approval, resource constraint or anything else associated with consumers, we never lose it—we drive it away. It is vital for us to learn how this is happening—and stop it.

Clearing out self-destructive barriers

10

Barriers, bothers and business

THIRTEEN WAYS TO HEAR 'WHISPERS' OF
BURIED BARRIERS THAT SCREAM 'YOU ARE
SELF-DESTRUCTING!'

Once one knows *where* to look for barriers it becomes necessary to learn *how* to find them. A post-modernist approach offers more ways to do this than classical marketing. Here's what they are.

There's more than one way to find barriers.

A post-modernist approach offers two techniques for finding barriers—the classical only provides one. A post-modernist marketer can look for potential barriers, and work backwards to solve them. Or such a post-modernist can use the tools of classical marketing (albeit in a different way) to either find or avoid them altogether. This chapter and the next deal with the first of these strategies; the following ones outline the post-modernist/classical approach.

If the key to marketing success is having fewer barriers, it becomes important to have a way of seeing what *might* be a barrier. Before beginning this process it is worth repeating something said earlier. Not all barriers are equal in significance.

165

There are *barriers* ... and there are *bothers.*

What this means is that not all barriers need to be dealt with. It is possible to do quite well with a large number of known barriers lying around, and there may be no really good reason for getting rid of some of them. Therefore, a distinction shall be made between a barrier and a bother.

A *barrier* is a problem important enough that something *must* be done because it is costing an employer money. A *bother* is something the customer doesn't like, but will put up with because they can get no better elsewhere. So it is really not what the post-modernist approach defines as an 'important' barrier—and it may be possible to ignore it.

Of course a bother may be a 'baby barrier' waiting to grow up, so organisations which find one *should* keep an eye on it. But it may not make much sense to do anything about it—for now. Why not can be seen from what happened to air service in one city. Only two airlines served this market. And one of them offered only prop-jet service. The other offered both turbo-props and more modern jets that were faster, more spacious and had better meal service.

It happened that the one with the big jets eventually needed them elsewhere. When an announcement was made that their big jets would be replaced by prop-jets and commuters (described by locals as '60 000 rivets flying in close formation'), there was a terrible hue and cry.

This was clearly at least a *bother.* But, assuming nothing terrible happened with regard to market share or that people did not get so unhappy because of it they started driving, taking the train or not travelling at all, this would not be a barrier. At least it wouldn't be *unless* the other outfit decided to offer something better.

One finds a lot of these situations. Employers should never get complacent about them—but neither should they always feel forced to act when they sense consumer dissatisfaction. If they do, they may find themselves reducing profits, adding to price or in some other manner creating a barrier—with no pay-off to them.

Helping employees to understand this is not a bad idea. Otherwise it is hard to explain why they should be interested in giving outstanding customer service when their employer is willing to tolerate what seem gigantic barriers of their own. The employer seems to be talking out of both sides of its mouth. This is never helpful.

With this background it is now possible to start looking for what may be a barrier. Just exactly what is a barrier for any employer may be as diverse as the many kinds of employers which exist. So, for any specific organisation, it is not possible to say *exactly* what is—and is not—a barrier. But this doesn't mean one can't develop some useful rules of thumb.

Finding the 'footprints' barriers leave behind

Barriers always leave behind what amount to 'footprints'. These tend to be common to businesses, charities/non-profits, and government departments. These 'footprints' will be called 'whispers of buried barriers', for that is how they appear. Rarely do they run past with a flag on them. And (particularly to employees) they may not seem a 'big deal' at the time.

Rather, they tend to be 'whispered' in subtle ways which are all too easy to ignore. But if people are trained to listen to these 'whispers', they can do a great deal to stamp out problems as they occur—or those who listen to them may recognise an opportunity in the making. These whispers are as follows.

Whisper: *Too many rules*

What this means is that consumers are being forced into a mould convenient to the producer, but not necessarily what the consumers want. A classic case of this was provided by a bank and its own insurance company.

A new customer took out a mortgage with this bank and requested his payments include credit life insurance which would pay off the mortgage should he die. The bank officer said he would like to do this, but couldn't. When asked why not he explained that the customer was 47 years old and was taking out a 20-year mortgage.

However, the insurance company would insure only up to 65 years of age—and the mortgage would run past this cut-off for the borrower involved. So the customer suggested he be given coverage until he was 65 and he would take his chances from there. The response was that this couldn't be done either. It seems the bank required the term of the mortgage and the term of the insurance to be the same.

What that really meant was that the bank's rules ensured they couldn't write a policy on anybody over 45 with a mortgage of 20 years or more (even though that was where some really big and lush mortgages take place). This cost them heaps of business. Rules for the convenience of the provider always do.

The next whisper is a little bit more visible, for an employer's own employees are noticeably a part of it.

Whisper: *The giving of too many explanations*

This whisper is often introduced by the phrase, 'Well, you have to understand that ...', followed by some explanation of why consumers can't have it the way they want. Has it ever occurred to you how ridiculous this opening is?

Why should any consumer *have* to understand anything? It is the *consumer giving* the producer money, *and not vice versa*. Something that isn't working the way consumers want is the producer's problem, not the consumer's.

Such was the case with one hotel and its room service menu. Room service was provided by the same kitchen as the one supplying the restaurant. However, the room service menu was extremely limited in terms of its choices. One guest walked past the restaurant, read the menu and noticed something she wanted to eat.

She called up room service and asked if she could have the item on the restaurant menu, but was refused. She was told she could only order off the room service menu. She then asked if the item could be sent up if she was charged extra for it. The answer was a firm 'no' followed by this explanation:

Look, lady, we get this kind of request all the time. What you have to understand is we can't make any exceptions because we are run off our feet down here.

The guest thought to herself, 'That could be self-correcting', and slammed down the phone. She was so angry that not only did she go out to eat, but vowed never to use the hotel again.

Bear in mind this book is *not* advocating a *refusal* to give explanations. Sometimes they may be quite necessary. It is just that the giving of an explanation always signals the presence of a consumer unhappy with something. Why else would it be necessary to give it? And this can point towards a barrier. The presence of such a barrier can be signalled even more loudly by employees' discomfort at producing it.

Whisper: *Employees feel uncomfortable doing something to consumers.*

This is a bit stronger than the last one. In this case it is often the employees on the firing line who sense that something they are required to do is not a good idea.

Employers may refuse to listen because they assume the employee is just too lazy or thin-skinned to do what is necessary. This may or may not be the case. A key issue is whether the employees are making their jobs *easy* or their employer *equal* or *ethical*.

Sometimes barriers are present because they genuinely have to be, or there is no good reason for getting rid of them (see 'bothers'). In this case the employees may just be trying to make their job easier so they don't have to deal with the consequences of the situation. But this isn't always the case.

Failure to listen to employees trying to make their employer either equal or ethical can be deadly. 'Equal' means trying to make an organisation's offerings about the same as a competitor's. 'Ethical' means trying not to do something that isn't right.

A prime case of 'equal' was provided by a phone company. It had a chain of retail branches selling phone equipment (phones, faxes, answering machines and so on). Due to a top-level command, this firm refused to carry the Panasonic™ brand even though it was the best-selling brand name in many key categories.

One manager who disputed this policy was told in no uncertain terms:

Look, get with the program! We don't like listening to snivelling complaints from the likes of you. There are plenty of people around who would like your job.

Actually, right now there are *even more* people who would like the job, as this phone company recently shut down all of its retail phone shops. It seemed to feel there just wasn't enough business!

The other time employers *must* listen to employee concerns is if they involve *ethical* issues. Because good ethics are both morally satisfying and (usually) good business as well, ignoring such concerns can be disastrous.

This was certainly the case for a pharmaceutical company. It demanded its sales representatives sell one of its products—hard, because the product was beginning to show some serious side effects, which the company was trying to ignore. A few salespeople left over this. Those who didn't might as well have, for eventually the story broke wide open and the lawsuits continued for years.

As shall be discussed later, what is (and is not) ethical is usually for the employee to determine. And this may vary with the individual. That is not the case for the next whisper.

Whisper: *Too many apologies*

The main difference between this and the preceding is here even the employer knows it is doing something wrong, or it wouldn't need to apologise. This is not to say that there are never situations needing apologies.

But apologies should be like fine china, reserved for *special* occasions, because somebody was human and messed up. Any time they become matter-of-course, and not the exception, apologies can indicate a serious problem.

This was the case for one salesperson for a pet-food company. A consultant followed him around for a day as he did his normal calls. He was quite proficient, and not a bad salesman. But one thing the consultant couldn't help but notice was how frequently he apologised for a home-office problem.

On every other product he *always* seemed 'temporarily' out of stock. At every call he had to apologise because something the customer needed wouldn't be available—in some cases for weeks. The problem was so typical the firm had little stickers printed up which could be attached to the counters where the product *should* be. These basically said, 'We're sorry but this product is temporarily out of stock. New stocks will be available soon'.

It wasn't that these stickers weren't a good idea—they were. What seems incredible was that a company could have a problem so bad that they made up *stickers* to fix it, and did not see themselves treading on thin ice. If any other pet-food company ever got *its* production sorted out, the one employing this salesman would be 'dead meat'.

At a lower level of complexity was a marketing consultant who had run out of business cards. He just didn't get around to having more printed up, and when asked for one by potential business-on-the-hoof he always said, 'I'm sorry, I've run out of them. I must get some more printed'. One day he saw this list of 'whispers' and recognised himself in this one. He still wonders how much business he drove away by not giving possible customers a way to get in touch.

Whisper: Some customer jokes about something.

Often people are too shy to come right out and complain, or they don't want to threaten their relationship with a supplier (see 'rarely considered consumers'). So they put what amounts to criticism in a joke. This is less obvious and sometimes results in both sides having a good laugh. If it is ignored, the person having the last laugh may be a competitor.

Something like this happened to a transport company. When its driver drove up to a key client with important supplies he was greeted by the logistics manager with, 'Not too bad—*you're only three days late* this time.'

Government departments are hardly any better. One manager of a tax authority was once greeted by a friend who went up to him and said:

> *Good morning. For a secretary press 'one', for a bureaucrat press 'two',*
> *for somebody who knows something, press on regardless.*

In both situations much more than joking was involved. In the first case, the customer was trying to say, 'You do not keep to the schedule I need', and in the second, 'Your electronic answering machines are *annoying*'.

Any one of these could be a barrier. What the producer should say is, 'Thank you' and then do something about it. But they seldom respond to any complaints that way.

Whisper: A customer states/acts as if they are unhappy about something.

Complaints always come across as a criticism of what someone is doing. And for that reason they generate pain, which often produces anger from the recipient. The feelings of 'This isn't fair … this customer doesn't understand what problems I am facing … how dare they complain, etc.' immediately come to the surface. As stated in the beginning of this book, this is absolutely true. It's not the customer's job to care. That's what they pay producers (like you) for.

Still, anyone who serves others may find it easy to sympathise with a world-famous chef who is so enraged by complaining customers that he has an unusual response to items sent back to the kitchen. The first thing he does is spit on them! (Think about that before you send your steak back to be re-cooked!)

Though entirely human, these automatic responses should be choked down because, when a customer complains, they are in fact doing those to whom they complain a favour. Research has shown that if one customer goes to the trouble to complain, there are many more who feel the same way, but haven't done so. The customer who complains is warning of a barrier which, if fixed, should benefit those who are cautioned.

Recognising this has greatly aided in the production of this very book. Every time students have had some problem with earlier versions, it has resulted in changes or additions which later students have said made it better.

Even churches need to be sensitive to hidden customer complaints. Sometimes their members will come right out and say what they think is wrong. Or it may be hidden. As one pastor put it:

> *I know I am in trouble when they shake my hand after the service and say,*
> *'We are praying for you'.*

Although this is whispered softly, others get a whole lot louder.

Whisper: *Somebody thinks you don't offer something the customer wants.*

What is meant here is that a customer has money which, for some reason, producers seem to be refusing to take. The reason for the use of the words 'thinks' in this whisper is to restate a truth covered at the beginning. Namely, perception is much more important than reality. If the customer thinks you don't offer something—in their mind you don't.

An example of this was a supermarket which learned through a survey that its Asian and Indian customers thought it didn't have much in the way of an ethnic food section. In fact it did, but it was not publicised and it was located in a part of the store which was hard to find. So, no matter what the 'truth' was, both the Asian and Indian communities stayed away from this store in droves.

At any rate, whether real or perceived, this whisper occurs in four different forms.

The producer is out of the desired merchandise.

The dumbest form this takes was shown by a guy who ran a Thai food buffet in a food court. Every single day he was out of food by about 20 minutes past noon. Bunches of people went up to his counter, saw only a few scraps, and went on their way.

No doubt he thought he was saving money by not having unsold food which might have to be discarded. What he didn't realise was how much more he could have made from the customers who were driven away. It would only take once, and they wouldn't come back.

The customer asks for merchandise you don't sell.

For businesses, this one is usually most noticeable when the customer comes in and says, 'I was interested in _____. Do you have any?' If the answer must be 'no', this occasion should be treated like a complaint, because asking about merchandise not available is a 'complaint' about what's (not) available for sale.

An example of this was a car company who offered the same basic vehicle in a 'sport' version with dramatic styling on the front end (but no climate-control air conditioning or leather interior) and a 'luxury' version with both climate air and leather (but not the 'sporty' front end). In walked a customer who wanted the styling of the 'sport' version with the luxury of climate-air and leather. The salesperson couldn't sell it to him directly, but knew that the factory could easily make it by simply accepting certain production codes. The factory refused the salesperson's request, and the customer bought somebody else's car.

Whenever any customer is denied a request, an apology for not having it, and a declaration of intent to get it, is the best answer. One lunch place demonstrated this idea with a sign over their sandwiches saying:

> *If the sandwich you want is not here please ask.*
> *We will make it for you and make sure it is here next time.*

Just how 'wise' this restaurateur is may be reflected by the fact that she operates in a mall at the 'wrong' end of town in which there are almost no successful businesses but hers.

At least one church found a way to capitalise on a similar situation. When it realised it wasn't getting much in the way of bequests, it set up a 'memorial fund' to which people could make contributions in somebody's name if they wished. All it required was a brochure explaining how to do it and what would be done with what was given.

It has been the recipient of thousands of dollars in cash. It seems that there were always donors out there who wanted to give something. It was just that they *couldn't* 'buy' because the non-profit wasn't 'selling'. Sometimes this isn't actually the case, but it might as well be.

The customer thinks competitors offer something you don't.

Once again, perception is more important than reality. Often a sharp competitor salesperson can get people thinking that others don't offer what they do—and those losing business are too dumb to realise it.

A customer looking for a new car had decided on make and model, and went to a local showroom eager to make a purchase. But she bounced off of a poor salesperson who didn't show off the features of the product and basically said, 'Here it is, let me know when you are ready to sign'.

The customer left without buying, but on her way home stopped to pick up a part for her husband's car. As she walked back to the parts department she slowed at a display of its new model. A good salesperson saw her interest and asked, 'Can I show you our new model? I'm so awfully proud of it'. He went on from there to demonstrate the CD player, the climate-air, the power adjustments on the seats, etc., etc. She left having bought the car—and she didn't even know she wanted one!

Interestingly enough, this customer later found out that her original choice had more features, cost less and was bigger. But, because nobody had told her, she couldn't buy it.

In many cases the most maddening thing about a missed opportunity is frustration over *how long it has gone unnoticed*. This is certainly true for the last form that unmet customer whispers take.

The customer tries to 'cobble up' what they want.

If a producer doesn't make what customers really want, the customers may try to make it on their own. This usually indicates they want it really badly. An example of this was a post office whose employees had watched customers struggle up to the counters with home-made parcels tied together with tape and string for about 50 years. When the post office offered its own 'handi-boxes' (preassembled cartons), they sold like hot cakes. How much money must the post office have lost in the years before this?

> **Whisper:** *A competitor has something desirable you don't.*

What makes this one different from the case where people *thought* a producer didn't offer something is—in this case it's true. They don't have it.

Most employers act as though they live in a perfect world where competitors don't exist. This is almost never true. When looking at barriers it may be worth 'bending' a famous saying to fit what is usually the situation:

The competition isn't everything—it's the only *thing.*

As small children, people are taught to never look over our shoulders at what others are doing. Rather, they are told to go along and do their own thing as though the others didn't exist. In business this is not smart, because whenever a competitor is willing or able to do something some producer can't, that employer and its employees are living on borrowed time. The consumers *will* find out about it and, when they do, will vote with their feet.

One discounter really understands this. It has a policy that if a customer can find any product sold within its store cheaper elsewhere, then the discounter will meet the competitor's price.

The wisdom to be gained from this is to be totally knowledgeable about what your competitors are doing. How else can you know they have something you don't—and make sure you fix the situation?

In all of the preceding cases the 'whisper' is fairly easy to see, but this will not always be the case. Sometimes the organisation won't have a clue as to what the problem is. However, there will be something left behind to tell it that it has a problem—somewhere.

Whisper: *Somebody else solves a problem you should have.*

Sometimes there is an indicator that may suggest this is happening. This occurs if *somebody does work you should have*. If your employer is a business this could mean learning that a contract your organisation should have received went somewhere else.

For a charity or government department it may mean some other unit does a job which should have been yours. When this happens trouble may be brewing. Budgets usually stretch to cover work done. When somebody else starts doing 'your' work, it is normally only a matter of time until they also start getting 'your' money.

An example of this for non-profits/government departments would happen if a flood occurred, and the Red Cross did work that Civil Defence should have (or vice versa). Sooner or later the idle agency will find itself in trouble as its budget gets cut.

When any of these events take place, employees should not just shrug their shoulders and forget it. It is to everyone's advantage if they keep in mind that they never just 'lose business'—what has happened is that some barrier (of theirs) *drove it elsewhere*. If they can find out why, perhaps they can fix it.

If you would like to provide 'added value' from these *whispers*, understand that they—and most of this book—don't apply to commercial relationships *only*. They work with *all* relationships, including husband/wife, parent/child and so on. An illustration of that working with this 'whisper' was a 'workaholic' who resented the fact that his wife asked him to stay home from work one night a month to take her to the symphony. He was overjoyed when a neighbour volunteered to do this for him. His joy lasted about a year ... until his wife ran off with the neighbour. What we have here is a massive customer service failure. She decided that her husband's customer service level had fallen to an undesirable point, so she switched her 'business' to an alternative supplier!

What this requires is noticing when 'business' is lost, and then taking the trouble to ask, 'Why?' Customers may or may not tell you, but one thing is certain: if you don't at least try to find out what happened, there is a good chance that it will happen again. There are at least three ways one can notice business has gone elsewhere.

An old customer stops buying.

In one situation a customer of a major supermarket chain was given what she thought was extremely rude service by one of their employees. She tried to tell the manager—who couldn't have cared less. He seemed to figure, 'What's one customer?'

What he didn't realise is something called the 'life value' of a customer. What this means is that surveys show most customers have a 'shelf life' of about 10 years. In other words, take what someone spends per year times 10 and that is roughly the amount of volume lost.

In this case the shopper had a big family and spent at least $200 per week with the supermarket. This amounts to over $10 000 per year. Applying this formula means the manager 'blew off' over $100 000.

It isn't as though they didn't know it. The customer tried to tell the manager, who recognised the customer and probably noticed she didn't seem to be coming in anymore. Beyond that, because this customer shopped using a store preference card (which could be used to track purchases), the headquarters could have seen she wasn't buying. But they just didn't seem to care.

A 'sales pitch' is unsuccessful.

This 'sales pitch' could apply to either a business or charity/non-profit. When this occurs one shouldn't just give up and go on to the next, but try to find out what barriers kept the sale from happening. A good way to do this is to go back to the customer who hasn't bought and say something along the lines of:

I hope you are happy with your purchase decision, but I am really proud of my products/services. Could you tell me any one thing which tipped the balance away from what I was selling?

Then 'shut up' and listen. You may learn what the problem is.

The grapevine says somebody else is getting the business.

Here you really have to swallow your pride and go, hat in hand, to somebody and admit: (1) I know I didn't get the chance even to talk to you, (2) you went elsewhere, and (3) why?

An agent for professional speakers tried this one. She knew that other agencies were getting business that she wasn't for one of her performers. She asked 'why' and learned that, unlike her competitors, she was trying to 'close' the business herself. But her competitors let the speaker go and talk to their clients directly, and this seemed to work better. She changed her tactics and got a great deal more business. The reason she did is related (in a backward way) to how the next barrier works.

Whisper: *Somebody is 'talked out' of what they really want.*

Letting the speaker in this situation talk with the agent's client enabled him to tailor what was done to what the client thought he needed. Sometimes 'super salespeople'—in a fine demonstration of what is wrong with classical marketing—go in the opposite direction. They may not have what the customer wants (see above), so they try to fast-talk the customer into what they do have … which may not be very satisfying.

One salesperson for an office supply firm made this mistake. He had sent a client a desk which turned out to be scratched when delivered. What the purchasing agent handling the deal really wanted was a replacement, but he talked her into taking a discount instead. This later caught up with her when the executive in her firm who got the desk complained—and the purchasing agent got in trouble. This eventually cost the 'super salesperson' the account. So although he 'won the battle' he lost the war. Although this case was a big 'one shot' failure, sometimes barriers show up in a pattern of smaller irritations that add up to something greater.

Whisper: *Something provides an unnecessary cost.*

Remember, 'there is no such thing as a free lunch'. In the end it will always be paid for—somehow. Employees usually don't see this. They act as if they are working with a bottomless pit of resources. Eventually the chips they 'let fall where they may' add up.

A striking example are all the industries which have gone offshore for their production. Often this has been forced by a long history of either unreasonable salary demands on the part of staff, or a management refusal to replace outdated equipment—sometimes both—which so raised the costs of products/services that they became impossible to sell, and something had to be done. But costs aren't the only things which mount up over time.

Whisper: *Some staff member abuses common courtesy.*

This one is directly related to the 'feeling' competitors of Chapter 8. Remember that most customers don't have the knowledge to tell whether what a producer is providing is any good or not. So they rely on things they do understand, like 'common courtesy'.

One of the most frequent barriers people express is, 'Their staff is snotty'. Examination of this reveals that what it really means is that the offensive staff don't stick to even the most basic rules of human conduct. They don't say simple things like 'please' and 'thank you'—nor do they say, 'goodbye' on the phone, and so on.

Customers tend to count these up over time. Faced with a history of this kind of conduct, they have every right to question whether the rest of the outfit can be any good, if the provider can't even get this simple issue right. They may be, but the customer may not wait around to figure it out.

In order to avoid this problem one major financial services provider (whose clients *must start out* with a *minimum* portfolio of 10 million dollars) had a secretary/receptionist who was making over $100 000 per year!! When asked about this the CEO replied:

> *I realise this could be excessive. But the customers just love her. She is so polite and interested in them and their problems. I swear that when she goes on vacation our sales slump.*

He was probably absolutely correct in what he was doing, and other employers would do well to follow this example. As one person once put it:

> *Pay peanuts—get monkeys!*

The last barrier to be discussed is actually an extension of this common courtesy issue.

Whisper: *Too many broken promises*

One of the more basic rules of human conduct is to be sure to do what one says they will do. Organisations violate this every day—by missing deadlines, failing to send out brochures when they say they will, not showing up on the day promised, etc. A famous comedian summarised how serious this is with the following comment:

Ninety per cent of life is just showing up!

One plumbing firm made this truth into a market advantage by stating what seems a simple promise in their advertising:

If we're not there on time, it's 2 hours free!

In other words, if they made an appointment and failed to keep it, they would give the first 2 hours of their labour free. This must have been a big problem in their market, for their sales really skyrocketed. Having completed this chapter's pledge by presenting the 13 barriers promised at its beginning, it is worth stating two more all-important points.

The 'whispers' work for *all* consumers.

One is that these whispers apply to more than commercial customers. Generally, with a bit of bending, they will also be effective in pointing out problems an employer is having with the 'rarely considered consumers' of Chapter 9 (not to mention personal relationships!). And wait, there's more!

These aren't the only 'whispers'.

There is no way that the preceding list of whispers includes everything that goes wrong. However, these are some of the most frequent indicators. And it does tend to be true that if they are happening too much, there are serious problems elsewhere. That brings up an interesting point.

How much is too much?

This is a little like trying to answer the question posed by a famous laxative commercial for prunes: 'Is one enough, is two too many?'

There are no absolutes here. But, in general, if anyone hears the same 'whisper' twice in one week, somebody should start listening. And that brings up the next logical question:

We found a barrier. What do we do with it?

So now what?

That question demands an answer which will be provided in Chapter 13 after we have looked at other ways to find barriers.

ACTION SUMMARY

There's more than one way to find barriers.

Post-modernist marketers have more options than their classical peers. They can either look for potential barriers—and work backwards to solve them—or use the tools of classical marketing to find or avoid them.

Barriers and bothers

Not all potential barriers must be addressed. A barrier must be dealt with if it is costing some employer more revenue than the cost of removing it. A bother is something customers don't like, but will put up with because they can get no better elsewhere. Bothers may sometimes be left alone.

Whispers of buried barriers

Barriers can take different forms for different employers. But the traces ('whispers') they leave behind tend to be the same.

The 'whispers' that indicate a possible barrier are many. They include:

- There are too many rules.
- There are too many explanations.
- Staff feel uncomfortable about doing something to consumers.
- There are too many apologies.
- A customer jokes about something.
- A customer states/acts as if they are unhappy.
- Somebody *thinks* you don't offer something they want.
- A competitor has something desirable you don't.
- Somebody else solves a problem you should have.
- Somebody is 'talked out' of what they really want.
- An unnecessary cost is present.
- Some staff member abuses common courtesy.
- There are too many broken promises.

And that's not all, folks!

This is not an all-inclusive list—and these points apply to both commercial customers and (with a little bending) the 'rarely considered consumers' of Chapter 9. However, when any of these is found, there are usually many more.

How much is too much?

Any time employees hear about any one barrier more than twice in any week, it indicates trouble worth fixing. How to do it will be discussed in the next chapter.

THE BOTTOM LINE
Barriers will destroy your business if you let them. Build a sensitivity to the 'whispers' they leave behind so that you can detect them—and do something about them.

ACTION EXERCISE 10.1

Hearing 'whispers' of our own buried barriers

For: Employees at all levels   **Format:** 4–8-person groups
Materials required: Pencils and instructions
Objective: To seek barriers within our own organisation

Instructions
In this chapter we saw the traces barriers leave behind in various organisations. These can affect any employer's ability to survive. After forming into groups we are going to see what they might look like for us.

Form into groups ... then:
Keeping in mind this is not an attempt to attack anybody, in the first 10 minutes you are asked to look at the various 'whispers' that barriers leave behind. Within your group you are asked to choose from these 'whispers' one which you think represents a possible barrier we could have, and describe what form it takes for us. (In other words, when, where, and how do we do something that leaves behind this 'whisper'?)

Choose from the following situations:

1 There are too many rules.
2 There are too many explanations.
3 Staff are uncomfortable about doing something to our consumers.
4 There are too many apologies.
5 Customers joke about something.
6 Customers state/act as if they are unhappy about something.
7 Somebody thinks we don't offer something they want.
8 A competitor has something desirable we don't.
9 Somebody else has solved a problem we should have.
10 Some customer has been talked out of what they really want.
11 We provide an unnecessary cost.
12 Some staff members are abusing common courtesy.
13 We break too many promises.

In the next 10 minutes:
Being careful to be sensitive to the feelings of others, discuss what we would have to do in order to keep this from happening again.

Then be prepared to share your answers with us.

Conclusion

Barriers can be present in any organisation at any time. We must be constantly watchful to both avoid them and catch them when they occur. The 'whispers' which indicate a barrier should always be on our minds. When one is found it is important for every employee to alert others and make sure it does not continue. This is not being critical or disloyal. It is being helpful to ensure the survival of all of us.

11
Post-modernism merged with mainstream marketing

WISDOM GREATER THAN THE SUM OF ITS PARTS

Most post-modernists figure that, since the 'one size fits all' rules of classical marketing don't always work, then *everything* within that approach is useless. And mainstream marketers similarly believe the post-modernists are 'screwballs' with nothing to offer. This is wrong and a needless waste. Here's a better way to go—one that puts the best of both worlds together—to produce insights available to neither one alone.

The post-modernist paradigm is the foundation.

We have already seen how the post-modernist paradigm can be used to build a different (barrier-based) approach to marketing. And the 'secret' of success for that approach is to isolate barriers so they can be dealt with. The tools of classical marketing can greatly help this process, but understanding how requires a proper foundation. Let's start with how barriers begin.

Where barriers come from

A good way to do this is to go back to the beginning (of time). Remember caveman 'A' and caveman 'B' of Chapter 5? When they (and the rest of society) decided to take the first step towards marketing, what they basically did was to agree to *specialise* by solving one problem only.

It's all about solving problems.

They probably didn't see it that way, but when caveman 'A' decided to do all of the farming and caveman 'B' all of the hunting, they weren't just making products. What they were doing is *agreeing* to solve *just one* problem. For caveman 'A' it was raising food and for caveman B getting animal skins for clothing.

Do it well—or die!

It was critical to do this well. If caveman 'A' had a little difficulty with storage and produced food that was mouldy, or caveman 'B' had gotten sloppy with his spear work and made clothes that were draughty, nobody would have traded with them ... if there were *better alternatives*. In other words, if caveman 'C' offered food without mould (or clothes without holes) both 'A' and 'B' would be short lived, for they would be producing barriers *by not solving some part of their problem as well as their competition.*

Every provider who followed after them would continue this 'survival of the fittest' (least worst) theme. As a result, it is easier to see what a barrier represents. A barrier indicates some producer is solving some consumer's problem in a better way than competitors.

Another good way to see this is Joe CarNut of Chapter 8 and his car wash. The job of cleaning his car included getting rid of the bit of paper left over after he had punched his computer code into the little keypad. One chain of stations solved this problem for him by providing a little trash can under the keypad, and the others didn't. So the one who solved his problem *most completely* got his business—while competitors watched him drive by.

This is the way it always works. Whenever anybody 'wins' by having fewer barriers, it is because they are doing a more complete job of solving some problem. So the job of every marketer—which started thousands of years ago— is to solve other people's problems by making better decisions than have others about what to do with their resources. If they do this correctly, they will have fewer barriers—and win. This idea of *making better decisions* can provide a thread with which to understand what is happening, and how best to do it.

Marketing is all about making better decisions for consumers than for competitors.

This idea of solving a problem is represented by Figure 11.1. What it shows is how every competitor begins—with total barriers.

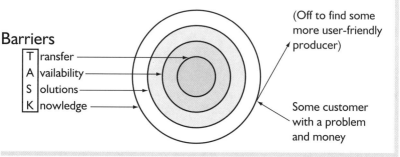

Barriers

T ransfer
A vailability
S olutions
K nowledge

(Off to find some more user-friendly producer)

Some customer with a problem and money

Fig. 11.1 An organisation without marketing resources

This figure shows a producer who has not yet begun to do anything with regard to marketing (either formal or informal, as no resources have been committed to it. Such a marketer will present barriers at four levels that look a little like an onion, and spell the acronym, TASK, underscoring the notion that a barrier represents an unsolved problem. Just exactly what order these barriers may take probably varies from situation to situation. But assembling them in this manner is a good way to understand what they do.

'Knowledge' starts the process.

Starting at the outside of the 'onion' is the barrier of knowledge. A consumer who doesn't know about a producer (e.g. who they are, what they do, where they are) will bounce right off this barrier—or others—and go to another more 'user friendly' producer.

An example of this was a group of university students who said that, at midnight or later, they often got hungry and wanted to order a pizza to be delivered. Being students at midnight, they might not be able to find the phone book and therefore would not know whom to call. So these students would be bouncing off the *knowledge* barrier of 'What's the phone number of that pizza joint?' We will next follow these students further through this 'onion' analysis, so that each layer can be understood.

'Solutions' either do or do not solve consumer problems.

Assuming the students did figure out how to get through, they would bounce off the barrier of 'solutions' if (for instance) the pizza parlour only offered pizzas with anchovies, and one of the students either hated them or was violently allergic. The area of 'solutions' refers to whether or not the product/service offered solves the consumers' problem.

Availability' puts a product/service where it can be bought.

However, if the students got through the barrier of knowledge *and* the parlour made pizzas they liked, the hungry ones would bounce off the barrier of 'availability' if that pizza provider closed an hour before they called, didn't deliver to their area—or the students thought it looked grotty. This is always the case with 'availability' as it usually has at least three dimensions: physical location (e.g. where is it?), time (when is it open?), and facilities (what's it like?).

'Transfer' moves value from consumer to producer.

Last, but not least, if our heroic students persevered and got through to the parlour, found pizzas they liked, and the parlour agreed to deliver them, they would still bounce off the final barrier of 'transfer' if the provider either charged unreasonable amounts (e.g. a five thousand dollar delivery fee!), or had reasonable prices, but when the delivery person arrived wouldn't take credit cards, and the students had no cash.

Note that 'transfer' means more than just price and may not always involve money (e.g. really desperate students could have tried swapping their watch for a pizza!). But it implies moving something of value between consumer and producer.

The same general situation holds true for non-business providers like charities and government departments. They all solve some sort of problem in return for money. And they have to let people know their solution is available through some sort of knowledge-penetrating promotion (often called 'public service' advertising). This problem solving requires they offer a solution through either products or services. They have to figure out their solution's availability by determining where it will be offered (called 'parishes' by some churches and 'regions' by governments). And some sort of transfer of value (called 'donations' for charities and either 'taxes' or 'fees' by governments) must be arranged.

185

Putting all of this together shows what post-modernist marketing does for all producers.

Post-modernist marketing means opening up barriers.

How this works is shown more completely by Figure 11.2. Within it these barriers have been opened, much in the manner of the earlier pizza discussions.

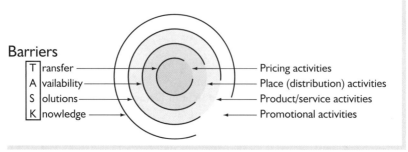

Barriers

T	ransfer
A	vailability
S	olutions
K	nowledge

Pricing activities
Place (distribution) activities
Product/service activities
Promotional activities

Figure 11.2 The 'four Ps' from a barrier perspective

Post-modernist marketing meets McCarthy

What Figure 11.2 shows is how a post-modernist approach can use the classical marketing 'four Ps'. Again using the pizza example, the tools of *promotion* can open up the barrier of 'knowledge' (e.g. the students reported remembering a catchy promotional tune for the telephone number from television, so they dialled it).

The whole area of *product* summarises what amounts to 'solution' barriers. (For those who don't make products, *services* represent the same thing.) In the case of the pizza parlour it was important that their menu make their solutions seem satisfying.

What has classically been called *place* or 'distribution' opens up the barrier of 'availability'. In the pizza example, for the barrier to be open the parlour would have to still be operating after midnight, look reasonably clean, and deliver to the students' location.

Finally, what has mostly been called *price* is expanded upon by using the word 'transfer'. This includes not only price, but how value is moved from one to another (e.g. barter, credit cards).

Putting the preceding together with the idea of somehow solving the customer's problem better than others results in Figure 11.3.

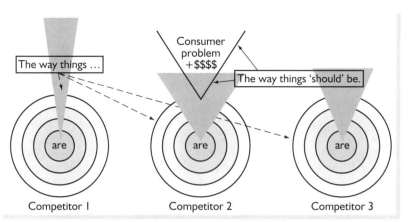

Figure 11.3 The post-modernist marketplace

The post-modernist marketplace

Figure 11.3 reveals the type of environment in which most marketers really operate. Each competitor arranges his or her barriers in the way they think best (see competitor 1, 2, and 3 in the figure). And there is a consumer with a problem ready to 'try them on' through what most call 'shopping'.

The consumer problem is pictured as a wedge going outward (to infinity) in order to symbolise something said earlier—human selfishness is insatiable, and there will never be a way to give the consumer everything she/he wants. And attached to the consumer problem is *money*, in order to make an important point.

Money is a by-product.

Most marketers think money is their sole objective, and get so fixed on this target that they miss what they are actually doing. In fact, the most important issue is for the marketer to solve the consumer's problem *more completely than other competitors*. If that is done the money will follow.

Let's go shopping!

The way consumers 'shop' is to (consciously or unconsciously) compare for themselves 'the way things *should* be'—namely, the shape of their particular problem—to 'the way things are' (the set of barriers offered by each competitor in their attempt to solve the customer's problem). Whichever competitor seems to match up best *in total* (e.g. is 'the least worst') shall have the fewest barriers, be chosen as the 'winner' and will get the money.

187

A good way to visualise this process can be gained from the nursery school tale of *Goldilocks and the Three Bears*. In an attempt to get porridge that was to Goldilocks's taste she tried one batch—too hot, and a second batch—too cold. But the third batch was 'just right'. All shoppers do pretty much the same thing.

Post-modernist marketing is all about decision making.

Seen in this way post-modernist marketing is all about arriving at decisions that will make 'the way things are' for some competitor closest to 'the way things should be' for their consumers. There are two different viewpoints for so doing.

Macro- and micro-marketing

All of marketing can be broken down into two separate camps—one called 'macro' and one called 'micro'—which often don't agree with each other. What makes these two different is the answer to one question surrounding the objective of marketing effort:

The way things should *be according to whom—and in order to do* what?

Depending upon how this question is answered, very different outcomes will be produced.

Macro-marketing has a social perspective.

Those interested in macro-marketing find some sort of social objective most important. Whatever is done in the marketplace, they want society to be well served. People with a 'macro' (and often dim) view of marketing question its impact on the environment, those who are poor, etc. This may be quite different from the other side.

Micro-marketing is interested in the goals of an organisation.

Within broad limits determined by the marketer's own ethics (or lack thereof), a 'micro' viewpoint is mostly concerned with achieving the goals of some organisation. There are times when these can come into conflict with macro-marketers.

Macro/micro conflicts do happen.

When there is a difference of opinion between marketers about social versus organisational goals, this is called a macro/micro conflict. An example of this would be US supermarkets who found that their shops in ghetto areas were the subject of much more shop-lifting (not to mention the occasional fire bombing!) than those in wealthier areas. So, in order to make more money (the micro viewpoint), they decided not to locate in poorer neighbourhoods.

This made macro-marketers very unhappy. For it meant poor people couldn't get to the lower prices supermarkets generally had—and this was de facto racism (the poorer neighbourhoods were generally black).

Who's right? In this particular instance—and in most cases—that very much depends on one's personal point of view. This is left to you, the reader.

However, given the subject matter of this book, most of it will take a micro perspective. This does not mean a macro viewpoint is totally unimportant, and some macro concerns will be incorporated into what follows. However, the reader will more easily understand the rest of this volume if it is limited (mostly) to one or the other.

Classical micro-marketing is about *always* making 'good' decisions.

Starting with a micro point of view, it can be seen that a marketer's job is all about making 'good' decisions—namely, those that work out well from the standpoint of the marketer's employer. Thus it is that classical marketers have generally defined micro-marketing as follows:

> *Micro-marketing is a discipline used to advance the goals of an organisation in a logical and complete manner.*

Unfortunately, this can't be done.

But *always* making 'good' decisions is impossible!

'Always making good decisions' would mean that marketers were able to 'make' people buy things in the manner thoroughly disproved in Chapter 7. For there are two things no marketer can ever control. One is what a competitor may do (e.g. it tends to really upset an advertising campaign if some competitor cuts prices by 75%!), and the other is the ever-present ability of consumers to change their minds about what a barrier is for them. So the objective of *always* making 'good decisions' is not open to a post-modernist. This requires a new definition of micro-marketing.

Post-modernist micro-marketing is different from classical micro-marketing.

Introducing the uncertainty attached to a post-modernist viewpoint changes things quite a bit. The only post-modernist micro-marketing definition that will 'wash' must go as follows:

Micro-marketing is a discipline used to advance the goals of the marketer *by advancing the goals of an organisation in* as logical and complete a manner as possible ... at the time.

There are a number of major differences between the classical and post-modernist definitions that are worth highlighting. For they show many of the advantages of a post-modernist approach.

... the goals of the marketer ...

What this recognises is that those doing the marketing are not robots. They will *not* take actions favourable to their organisation if they feel those are detrimental to their own personal goals and career.

An example of this was shown when a group of executives were asked the following question. Suppose you were marketing manager for a firm and you were considering making a major investment for that firm. And also imagine that you were 100% certain that if that investment were made, the returns to the firm would be fivefold ... but nothing would happen for at least 3 years. Assume also you believe that, if nothing happened after 3 years, your managers would lose sufficient patience as to fire you. Would you do it?

Not one executive said they would! Would you? Probably not, and neither would most.

... in as logical and complete a manner as possible ...

What this part recognises is an essential part of the appeal of post-modernist marketing. It makes no promises it can't back up. It just does what is *possible*. The post-modernist definition also recognises one last issue ...

... at the time ...

This segment stresses a reality of post-modernism—that things change over time. Not only do people change their minds over what represents a barrier (see the *I Love Lucy* example of Chapter 8), but marketing knowledge expands as new additions come on line. An example of this is all the work in informational technology. Twenty years ago this whole area probably wouldn't have been considered essential. Today it would.

Putting all of this together produces an observation essential to merging post-modernism with classical marketing.

All post-modernists can do is avoid making 'bad' decisions.

Understand that 'bad decisions' are not ones that work out badly. For always avoiding making decisions that work out badly is a mirror image to always making ones that work out well. In order for either of these to happen marketing must (ultimately) make somebody do something. Otherwise whoever had a sure-fire way of making a 'good' decision would find it copied by competitors—and away we go. No, making a 'bad' post-modernist decision is quite different.

There are only two ways for a post-modernist to go wrong.

From a post-modernist perspective, there are only two ways to make a 'bad' decision. These are contained within the following definition:

A bad *decision is one which,* when reviewed, *is found to have one or both of two errors in it:*

- *a failure to consider information the decision maker could* reasonably *have been expected to consider; and/or*
- *a breakdown in* logic—*either in how information was gathered or what was done in light of it.*

This approach is totally in line with the post-modernist position outlined so far. And it should produce decisions as good as can be expected, given the true nature of what marketers are able to do. It also contains a number of differences that are worth discussing further:

... when reviewed ...

This item recognises the career dimensions of marketing; it is not frozen at one point in its development, nor locked in one cultural setting. For the reviewer might come from many backgrounds, or any point in time.

... could reasonably have been expected to consider ...

What is 'reasonable' will be locked in the mind of the reviewer and depends on his/her background. This will be discussed shortly.

191

... a breakdown in logic ...

As shall be shown, the word 'logic' shall be the tool which reunites classical marketing with a post-modernist perspective. What it really means is that there are no gaps in the thinking process leading to any conclusion or action. This key is essential to understanding what shall follow. Putting all this together demonstrates a number of benefits suggested earlier.

What's right about post-modernist micro-marketing?

It is the same approach used by the most 'respectable' professionals in the world.

If what amounts to malpractice is suspected of a doctor, the two questions used to examine them are:

1 What tests did you run (i.e. what information did you gather and how) before deciding on what to do?
2 What procedures did you undertake (i.e. what did you do after the information was obtained) following those tests?

This certainly looks very much the same as the only two ways to make 'bad' decisions. The first has to do with considering information the doctor could reasonably have been expected to consider. The second looks at the logic of what was done.

It is all that can really be done.

Most of this book has been about proving why no certainties exist. Sometimes—particularly if a 'disaster' happens—this may either be comforting or save a career. For making a decision that works out badly may *not* destroy a marketer's future (it would be a good idea not to do this too often!). But making a 'bad' post-modernist micro-marketing decision will. For it means the marketer concerned has been irresponsible.

It doesn't 'throw out the baby with the bath water'.

Just because the promises of classical marketing can't be true, this doesn't mean it has nothing to offer. There is much that can be found within classical marketing that can be useful.

It is simple to understand.

Again, there is no mystery. 'Nailing' bad decisions down to two easily understood errors can make remembering what they are easier (and therefore make them less likely to happen).

It recognises human nature.

By not promising more than it can offer, being based upon why it can't (e.g. human nature/competition/changing minds), and incorporating the career needs of the marketer, it gives a far fuller picture of what will happen than other approaches do.

It is not culturally exclusive.

Because 'bad' decisions will be 'in the eyes of the reviewer', this approach can take into consideration the cultural background of that reviewer. So concepts alien to a classical approach can be built into the system.

For instance, if a marketer were working within a Christian organisation, some reviewer might ask, 'Did you pray before making this decision?' Or, if the marketer were in Hong Kong, someone might ask, 'Did you consult a feng shui master before building this bank headquarters?'

Classical marketing would probably not even consider these questions. But depending upon the situation, and the reviewer, a 'no' response to either could be deadly.

It is time sensitive.

This one is somewhat rooted in the preceding issue. As long as a reviewer appraises the knowledge available only to the marketer *at the time of making the decision*, the results of the review may be a great deal more just.

A good case of this *not* happening is the Edsel. Though (with the full benefit of hindsight) people like to say this was a tremendous marketing gaffe, judged from a post-modernist viewpoint, it probably wasn't.

What happened is that, during the early fifties, Ford marketing research suggested a gap in the market for a large, medium-priced car and Ford made the Edsel to fill it. Unfortunately, in the 3 years it took to bring the car to the market, the market headed off towards compact cars. And the Edsel came on the scene just in time to meet a market that was no longer there. This was nobody's fault, except for whoever decided to go ahead with the project (if that person knew that—by then—the market had changed).

Last, but not least, a post-modernist micro-marketing perspective has one key benefit, which was the reason for writing this chapter.

Post-modernist micro-marketing can incorporate all of classical marketing.

How this works is suggested by the words 'information' and 'logic' in the definition of a 'bad' decision. As discussed in earlier chapters, classical marketing is all about gathering information related to 'order-and-pattern'. Order-and-pattern screams out 'logic'. So it isn't hard to see how all the millions of hours put into finding it may be useful to any marketer.

The next chapter will show how this can be done.

ACTION SUMMARY

Post-modernists don't have to reject classical marketing.

In fact, so doing is not only unnecessary, but also undesirable. Classical marketing has a great deal to offer the post-modernist, if we understand how to use it.

Merging post-modernism with mainstream marketing

Barriers are the basis of the post-modernist approach. They happen when some competitor solves a problem less completely than others. For all organisations, barriers can exist at four different levels within what looks like an onion. These levels are knowledge, solutions, availability, and transfer.

Post-modernist marketing means opening these barriers up through activities classically called the 'four Ps'. Actions within promotion open up 'knowledge', products/services open 'solutions', place/distribution opens up 'availability', and 'transfer' covers price.

The post-modernist marketplace

A post-modernist sees a market as having a consumer with a problem (and money attached) choosing from a number of competitors who have arranged their barriers in the way they think best. The consumer's problem defines what for him or her is 'the way things should be'. The competitor barriers display 'the way things are' for them. That competitor for which 'the way things are' is closest to 'the way things should be' in the mind of the consumer shall 'win'. The job of the marketer is to try to make this happen by making 'right' decisions.

Macro/micro issues

All of marketing can be studied with either a 'macro' or 'micro' perspective which relates to 'the way things should be' according to *whom* and in order to do *what*. A macro viewpoint is interested in social issues, and a micro one is concerned with achieving organisational goals. These two may be in conflict. The focus of this book is mostly micro-marketing.

Classical micro-marketing

Classical micro-marketing is all about making 'good' decisions (e.g. that will *always* work out well) due to producing a pattern of barriers closer to the 'way things should be' than the competition does. This is impossible, for no marketer can control competitors or the changing minds of consumers.

Post-modernist micro-marketing

All a post-modernist can do is to avoid making 'bad' decisions, which are not ones 'which work out badly'. This is equally impossible as always making 'good' decisions.

For a post-modernist, a 'bad' decision is one which, when reviewed, is found to fail to consider information the decision-maker could *reasonably* have been expected to consider, and/or have a breakdown in *logic*. This approach has a number of advantages going for it, including recognising human nature, being the same one that professionals (like doctors) use, being all that can be done, being culturally inclusive, being time sensitive, and representing an easy way to link back into classical marketing.

Classical marketing can serve the post-modernist.

The millions of hours classical marketers have put into discovering order-and-pattern can be useful to providing the post-modernist decision maker with much of the information they should consider, the logic underlying how it should be gathered, and what should be done in light of what is known. It is not perfect, but it is better than nothing.

THE BOTTOM LINE

There are only two ways to make a 'bad' marketing decision:

1 fail to consider information you could *reasonably* have been expected to consider; or
2 have a breakdown in logic—either in how information was gathered or what was done in light of it.
   Make sure you do neither.

ACTION EXERCISE 11.1

Learning from past failures

For: Employees at all levels   **Format:** Individuals or 4–8-person groups
Materials required: Pencils and instructions
Objective: To review what can be learned from the past

Instructions

In this chapter we learned that there are only two ways to make a 'bad' decision. They are to:

1 fail to consider information one could reasonably have been expected to consider; and/or

2 have a breakdown in logic—either in how information was gathered, or what was done in light of it.

Consider the following either in groups or as an individual.

In the first 10 minutes:

Keeping in mind this is not an attempt to attack anybody, in the first 10 minutes you are asked to think about any market action (e.g. advertising campaign, new product, new location, change in price) that has been less successful for us than we hoped.

Discuss what this was and anything you know about it.

In the next 10 minutes:

Being careful to be sensitive to the feelings of others, discuss:

- Was any information overlooked, which then led to the disappointing results?
- What was it?
- Was it available to decision makers at the time?
- Was there anything you think could have avoided the disappointment? `
- Did the information available suggest that the actions seemed to make sense?
- Why/why not?
- What can be learned from this experience?

Then be prepared to share your answers with us.

Conclusion

Marketing is not magic. Sometimes things don't work out as well as we wish. However, if all decision makers gathered all the information they should have at the time—and what they did made sense—there is nothing more that can be done. And no shame is present for those who did their best.

But we must all avoid taking any future actions that might include any of the above errors. If you ever see any actions being taken that you don't think make sense, tell somebody. It is your job, too.

12
Marketing made easy

FOUR SETS OF 'FOOTPRINTS' THAT FIND BUSINESS AND BARRIERS

The millions of hours which have gone into classical marketing have *not* been wasted. All that is needed is a way to use that knowledge in a post-modernist manner. Here is a way to do it that (into the bargain) will make marketing tools much easier to understand.

Only two ways to go wrong ...

Recall from Chapter 11 that a bad decision, when reviewed, is one found to have one of two errors:

1 failing to gather *information* one could reasonably have been expected to gather; and/or
2 a breakdown in *logic*—either in how information was gathered, or what was done in light of it.

This brings up an interesting question.

What information is a 'reviewer' most likely to use?

What information is likely to be used to consider whether the marketing decision was 'the way it should be' will depend on the background of the reviewer. But given that the decision to be reviewed is a marketing decision, and 99 per cent of marketers (at least until now!) have a classical background, it is easy to make a good guess. Most of whatever is used to measure a 'bad' decision will probably come from classical marketing concepts, as well as from some other situation-specific elements. This is not bad news, for at the core of classical marketing is something equally essential to a post-modernist.

The core of classical marketing

At the centre of most classical marketing (particularly that learned from marketing academics) is the concept of order-and-pattern discussed in the beginning chapters. The end result of research into the order-and-pattern of marketing has been to develop 'rules of thumb' (now called 'empirical generalisations') about what information to gather, how to gather it, and what to do in light of it.

If this sounds to you very much like what post-modernists do, you are absolutely correct. There is only one real difference.

The difference between classical and post-modernist marketers

Both types of marketers are looking for some way other than random chance to make their decisions about 'the way things should be' for consumers. However, the classical marketers tend to suggest that whatever they find (particularly in the very academic ranges of theory) is timeless. The post-modernist approach of this book knows it can't be, because human nature is always asking, 'So what have you done for me lately?' And competitors are always coming up with new answers.

Still, what the classical marketers have done *does* have value. The way for post-modernists to bridge into this value—while not sacrificing their firmer grip on reality—is to understand that there probably *is* some order-and-pattern in human affairs. But it doesn't last forever.

Marketing is a *historical* discipline.

What this means is that people who study marketing barriers from *any* perspective are mostly historians (whether or not they admit it). In other words, what they find could be summed up as, 'Uh, we think that at one point in time this was (or did) lead to a barrier of some sort—maybe'. The only thing that ever changes is how this history is expressed.

What causes a problem is that all marketing decisions are concerned with how to make decisions covering *future* issues. But the only information marketers ever have to base these decisions on happens in the *present*, which becomes the *past* as soon as it has taken place. However, there is a thread that keeps classical marketing insights from being worthless.

The thread that holds marketing 'science' together

There is only one thing that gives any marketing patterns any claims to being anything resembling a science. It is the consistency of human behaviour. Put another way, what holds everything together is:

People tend to do tomorrow whatever they have done today.
But this does not go on forever.

This is the source of most marketing patterns/logic. For short periods of time, treating information from any source about market desires as fixed does no harm. And it is pretty much all there is. Beyond that, it is definitely better than nothing. However, it must be kept in mind that it won't last forever.

How long is *too* long?

Exactly when any marketing information or theory is past its 'use-by' date depends on the situation and the person likely to review any decision. However, it is essential to consider this time factor. And this factor surely does no harm to the need for constantly updated research.

This vastly increases the possibilities for researchers, along the lines of the arguments made for the post-modernist paradigm in Chapter 7. For as times change, there is a never-ending demand for new research to record the patterns of what is happening/has happened lately.

Where do 'mainstream marketing' patterns come from?

The 'history' depicted by mainstream marketing patterns may take one of many forms. This chapter will look at four of these. They will be the macro and micro marketing environments, demographics, and marketing research. It will then suggest how to combine this information into a successful overall strategy.

However, it must be understood that this is only one chapter covering topics, each of which has been the subject of entire books. And there are many more topics to choose from, as well.

This chapter is far from all-inclusive— but there's an easy way to learn more.

This chapter will brush only briefly upon a few key issues by discussing what is *different* about a post-modernist use of them. Once readers have 'gotten the hang' of this, those who want to learn more would do well to look at any major 'marketing principles' textbook, and extend the post-modernist approach they have learned. Which one is not important, for they all tend to look pretty much alike! But it is important to note what they all have in common. Next is some general guidance on how they can be used by a post-modernist marketer.

How to use mainstream marketing texts to gain post-modernist insights

After some sort of general introduction, most principles of marketing texts have a section on what amount to ways of seeing patterns that *could* lead to a barrier (e.g. macro/micro environments, demographics, market research, and consumer behaviour). These are normally followed by a chapter on a 'little black box' called segmentation/differentiation/positioning through which informational patterns about a market enter (on one side) and lead to marketing programs (on the other).

The next sections generally progress into some equivalent of the 'four Ps' and look at either items within these classifications which *could* be a barrier, or suggestions for what seems to be 'best practice' for *handling* these barriers if they are present. End it all with a chapter or two on international and ethical issues, and you've got a complete text, most of which can be used in a post-modernist manner more easily than the mystery surrounding mainstream marketing.

What will next be examined is how a post-modernist looks at some of the most useful of these classical marketing tools. This will be followed by examples to show any principles, and ways to apply this knowledge to your own situation. An easy way to understand the thinking behind every classical marketing tool is to see all marketing information as being 'footprints in the snow of time'.

'Footprints in the snow of time' lead to barriers.

What this analogy means is clearer if a simple scenario (not involving business) is presented. Start out by imagining that you are living in an area which gets lots of snow, and you decide one night to have rabbit stew for dinner tomorrow.

You get out a cookbook and the recipe chosen begins, ' ... first get a rabbit'. So the next morning you go out to your backyard and notice there are animal footprints in the snow covering it. These show that a rabbit crossed a corner of your yard heading in a certain direction last night.

So using the same assumption as marketing—that what happened in the past will be repeated in the future—you see where the rabbit tracks came from and seem to be going, and the next evening you hide behind a bush on that path hoping that (maybe) that furry fellow will come past again. If you are right, it's rabbit stew for dinner!

Market-related information is a great deal like this. It looks for 'footprints in the snow of time' which show where consumers have 'been' in the past. And one hopes that from this information one will be able to predict 'the way things should be' in the future, then use that input to form a program. Let's now look at the first part of how to do this.

The marketing environments

One place where this historical approach is particularly noticeable is in considering what have been called 'the marketing environments'. These are the conditions expected to be present when marketing decisions are put into action. They come in two 'flavours': the micro-environment and the macro-environment.

The micro-environment has been studied before in a different way.

Remember the 'rarely considered consumers' of Chapter 9? They included such elements as employees (covered more completely in Chapters 3 to 5), employee families, suppliers, the media, and anybody else who 'might stick an oar' into anything that happens to an organisation.

The classical approach to these is not the same as that in Chapter 9, which attempted to find ways to create advantage by marketing to them. The classical approach pretty much tends only to look for trends in what has happened with them in the past in order to see what they may do in the future. And realises that this could impact on any decisions being made.

Example

A case where history didn't 'hold up' was an automobile company that usually made certain it had at least three sources of supply for any components it purchased. One place it made an exception was a firm who sold it the small light bulbs that lit the instrument panel (the most expensive model had 23 of these). The reason for allowing this exception was that this bulb supplier had never had a labour strike in 60 years of operation.

Unfortunately, one year the light bulb manufacturer had a bitter strike that shut the factory down for a year and a half. Without another source of supply this left the automaker desperate. Its choices were to buy them from others (not enough capacity available to fill all needs), shut down the assembly plant (horrendously expensive) or send out the cars with only a few bulbs and replace them in the field. They did this, but it *really* cost them (the instruction manual for one model on how to insert the bulb went, 'First remove the windshield and headlining ... '!).

Questions to ask yourself

Look at the list of 'rarely considered consumers' in action exercise 12.1. Spend a few minutes considering what about each of them is important to you (e.g. what do you give you that you need?). Then try to determine all you know about their past and present history. Is anything changing which will impact on their likelihood of giving you what you need? How? Should this be reflected in any future plans?

The macro-environment is concerned about PESTs!

The macro-environment represents issues happening outside an employer that may have a severe impact on 'the way things should be'. One way to remember these is that some marketers think of them as PESTs. This is an acronym for:

- **P**olitical factors;
- **E**conomic/environmental factors;
- **S**ocial factors;
- **T**echnology factors.

Political factors

A major concern for all firms is what will happen to the rules and regulations which can either advance or slow up their ability to survive. Although these may be beyond any one employer's control, taking them into consideration is essential.

Example

Many automakers vigorously opposed any attempt to toughen government standards regarding exhaust pollution. However, another firm quietly watched what was happening to these and other standards, and built a product to meet what they were likely to be in the future. Then, when the standards came into practice, it would have the only product capable of being sold. Game, set and match!

Economic/environmental factors

These two don't really have a great deal in common, but have been put together in order to fit within the PEST framework. The economic environment has to do with what is happening in all the factors relating to the economy—interest rates, business confidence, exchange rates, employment and so on. Environmental trends sometimes are noticeable in government regulations. What they signal are changes in what have, in the past, been considered of little value—clean air, water, forests and so on. With both of these factors, definite historical trends can be seen and used to identify potential barriers.

Economics example

One Australasian university noticed that the exchange rate for its country's currency versus the US dollar had become worse for several years, and wasn't really expected to improve. This made its English language education very cheap (compared to US universities) for students in mainland China. So a plan was hatched to attract these students via a 'package deal' expressed in US dollars.

Environmental example

Concern about the environmental impact of plastic soft-drink bottles became such an issue in one country that it looked like they would be banned altogether. In order to beat this barrier a plastics manufacturer set in place a massive recycling plan to pick up these bottles and try to find uses for them. Even though they have yet to figure out what to do with these (the firm has warehouses full of them!), this 'recycling' allowed them to continue to be sold.

Social factors

These have to do with what is happening in the lives of people within a market area. Are they marrying/not marrying, are there new cultures coming into the area, are traditional values eroding?

Example

One church noticed that its base of regular members was deteriorating, but also sensed that there were a large number of people seeking spiritual leadership. So on a Saturday night, they decided to offer a 'For Sinners Only' service. The church was packed and this led to ongoing events for people who felt 'unchurched'. Some of these resulted in individuals and/or entire families finding their way to the Christian faith.

Technology factors

What this category has to do with is the relationship between people and machines. It can include new methods of production, or it might be involved with 'Silicon Valley' concerns like the Internet. Employers either stay current with these or die.

Example

One authority on small (10 employees or less) businesses believes that one of their major barriers is credibility. Many people just aren't inclined to trust some small outfit about which they know very little. This expert believes that a way to fight this barrier is by securing a website and making sure this appears in all their promotion. The idea is that people will assume, 'Wow, if they have a website they *must* be with it'.

Questions to ask yourself

The best way to keep from 'unpleasant surprises' caused by any of these PESTs is to be consciously aware of them, and how they might impact on your enterprise. Being able to answer 'yes' to the following questions would be a good start:

- Do you regularly read any national business newspaper?
- Do you subscribe to and read the journals attached to your profession?
- Could you list the two most important issues facing your employer within each of the PEST categories?
- Have you made any changes in your operation within the last 2 years which reflect shifts in any of the PEST categories?
- Do you know of any changes like these that your competitors have made?
    Although all of the preceding can mostly be communicated with words, sometimes the 'footprints' are left behind in the form of statistics.

Demographics—the 'footprints in the snow' studied through statistics

Demographics are a good way to follow what is happening to the people who will ultimately become customers—and predict the problems they will want producers to solve for them. These are usually left behind in the form of statistics (mostly gathered by governments) and concern various factors that can be measured in numerical terms. These include such items as age, sex, marital status, gender, income and so forth. One of the hottest items being discussed within this area is a real 'footprint in the snow' which can be seen by studying such statistics.

The 'pig in the python'

For many 'footprints' the best way to see where people and their problems are heading is to view them at several points in time, and learn from this sequence what seems to be happening. This is certainly true for what has been called 'the pig in the python', which has to do with age patterns. These patterns can be seen by examining Figure 12.1.

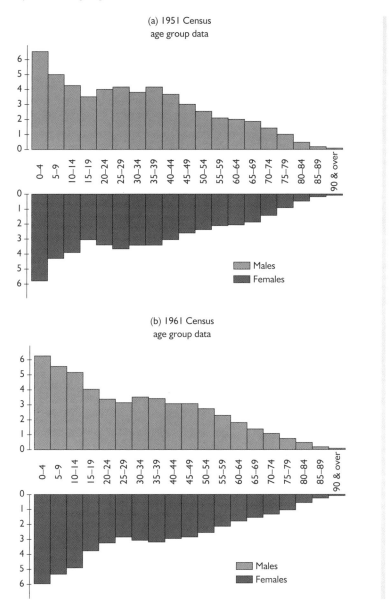

(a) 1951 Census
age group data

(b) 1961 Census
age group data

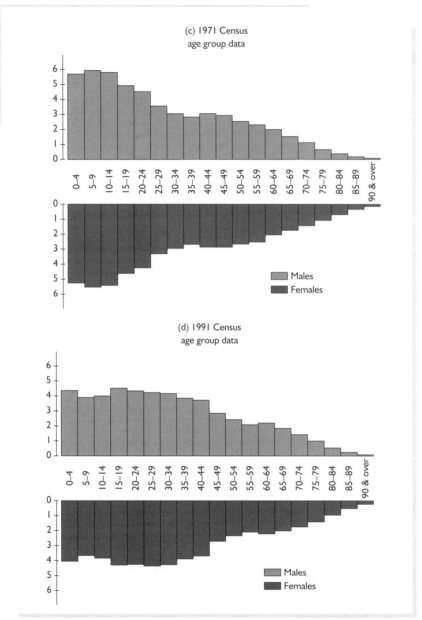

Figure 12.1 Illustrating the 'pig in the python'

What these show is age distribution by group over time. The males in the population are shown across the top, and the females along the bottom. A graph has been used because it makes these 'footprints' visible. And this graph has been laid on its side to get the notion of the 'pig in the python' across. (Don't worry too much about the exact numbers shown, for the specifics of these tend to vary from country to country. But the pattern of the python is pretty much the same in most western [and some Asian] nations.)

It started about 1945.

What these graphs show is a pattern which got started around the end of World War II when most service people returned home, and the *second thing* they did was to buy a new car! The results of this activity are shown in Figure 12.1(a). For the largest bar on the chart represents children 0–4 years old—what has come to be known as the 'post-war baby boom'.

Fig. 12.1(b) shows that this boom continued all the way into 1961. Up until the mid-1960s age demographics were a great example of the predictability of classical marketing. Right up until then people *did* keep right on doing tomorrow what they did yesterday (at least with regard to having children). And this made population patterns most predictable.

For several centuries population had moved in 20-year cycles, as children were born, became of childbearing age, and had children of their own. Given that the baby boom started in 1945, it could have been expected that the next surge in population could be expected in the mid-sixties and reported in the '71 (Fig. 12.1(c)) census. It didn't happen.

In the mid-sixties things really changed.

It appears that a *technological* change, the first effective oral contraceptive (since the word 'no'), was developed, and many people decided not to have babies. Though the 1991 census showed a modest increase in birth, it certainly wasn't the expected carbon copy of the 'boom' of 1945.

All this has created the 'pig in the python'—a 'ticking time bomb' for many producers.

Besides showing all these changes in childbearing, Figure 12.1 reveals something even more interesting: the 'pig in the python' which is the subject of this discussion. Where this got its name was from the appearance created by the population charts displayed. If one views them one after the other, they certainly do look like a boa constrictor that has swallowed a pig! There is a definite bulge that seems to be working its way through the numbers.

From Fig. 12(d) it can be seen that, in 1991, the age of the leading edge of this bulge was around 40 to 45 years. These were the people born in the post-war baby boom. And behind this bulge (starting about age 20 to 25) there is a definite drop-off for quite a while.

What this means is that there is a huge block of similarly aged people moving through most countries' population numbers, with very little following it. Barring some major medical or other life-threatening disaster, these people will start reaching retirement age in about 10 years, and they represent one of the largest single groups of what will be consumers.

People in the 'pig' will have different problems.

Because they are older, and physical abilities normally erode with age, these people will probably be sicker, weaker, have worse eyesight, and make a major change in 'the way things should be' for many employers. Few are doing much about this. They should, for these 'footprints' are quite visible. And the needs/problems attached to them are most predictable.

Example

One cosmetics manufacturer offers a very expensive ($85 for a small tube) cream of wrinkle-preventing cream. A department store salesperson selling it noted that it was very powerful, and could be dangerous if misused. So it was very important to follow the directions for use. One consumer bought this cream and got out the instructions that were printed on a piece of paper slightly larger than a matchbook. The all-important instructions were in (at best) a two point font!—and couldn't be read even with a magnifying-glass! One would imagine that somebody should have realised that those most likely to want wrinkle-prevention cream *just might* have weaker eyesight—and their 'fine print' instructions would be a barrier.

Questions to ask yourself

The only way not to be foolish about changes in the demographics of your consumers is to ask yourself (and answer) some of the following questions:

- Is there anything about the problems my employer solves which could be related to age, gender mix, country of origin, income or any other demographic factor?
- Do I know what is happening with regard to these factors?

- What will any noticeable changes mean for 'the way things should be' about the problems we solve? (List them.)
- Are we making any of those changes?
- Is there anything we are doing that recognises the changes brought about by the 'pig in the python'?
- What?
- Will these be better than those of competitors?

If your answer to any but the first two of these questions was 'no', you are probably living on what could be borrowed time. For the barriers related to the above factors are relatively noticeable by all. This is not always the case for all marketing tools.

Market research—looking for 'footprints' in a more active manner

Most of the preceding tools require learning how to read what is happening from a number of publicly available measures, and using this to find barriers. Little more than staying aware of 'current events' seems to be required.

However, sometimes more is needed, so some employers set up formal market research departments to actively seek out barriers, or hire this expertise for themselves. Such activities frequently take two forms: setting up a marketing information system (MIS), and/or formal market research.

The marketing information system— an 'early warning radar' for barriers

Some readers may be surprised to see 'MIS' defined as a *marketing* system, for this is often taught as being a *management* information system. From a postmodernist viewpoint, this is clearly mislabelling. For as discussed in Chapter 9 there is nothing that is not (ultimately) a part of marketing. However, call it whatever makes sense to you.

Whatever label the MIS may be given, what it represents is kind of an 'early warning' radar left on constantly to monitor information about what is happening 'out there'. This often has two dimensions: marketing intelligence and marketing 'science'.

Marketing intelligence

This has mostly to do with keeping an eye on competitors—their products/ services, plans, and so on. And, because competitors are not particularly keen on sharing this information, how it is received may be through one of three ways:

1 *Overt* intelligence is gained from freely available sources. It is amazing how much can be learned just by attending professional meetings, reading newspapers, and doing the kind of things recommended for monitoring the environments.

2 *Covert* intelligence is 'cloak and dagger' stuff. It ranges from buying competitor products (to examine what they are doing) all the way to practices as extreme as planting spies in competitor firms.

3 *Unsolicited* intelligence is information about competitors that 'walks in the door'. It does it because somebody (somewhere) 'talked to Moe ... who was related to Zoe ... who told Joe ... who works for the other outfit'.

Example

Many believe that a good case of marketing intelligence backfiring was the Ford Mustang. Although the company line was that this product was a tremendous success for market research, some insiders say otherwise. They contend that what really happened was that Ford, not wanting another Edsel, made up prototypes of the Mustang and showed them to both dealers and the public before offering the car for sale. Apparently, these people stated that they *hated* the car. But Ford executives decided to plunge ahead anyway. Rumour has it that competitors GM and Chrysler somehow gained access to the Ford research showing a negative reaction, and made a decision not to produce a sporty car of their own. The success of the Mustang caught Ford's competitors flat-footed. These competitors didn't have a similar product for several years!

Questions to ask yourself

Issues concerning intelligence have to be looked after both in terms of what is gathered about competitors and what they may be able to learn about you. Considering the following may help:

- Look again at the questions about the environment. Do you follow them with regard to competitor activity as well?
- How much do you know about the 'four Ps' for your competitors?
- How recent is this information?
- Do you protect yourself against 'covert intelligence'?
- How? (E.g. do you have paper shredders, do background checks on employees, have your offices swept for 'bugs'?)
- Do you have a system in place to feed back information about competitors which your staff may have learned?
- Have you used anything from it in the last 2 years?
- Are your own employees made aware of items which should not be discussed with outsiders?
- How recently has this been reviewed?

Marketing science

The above are not the only things which should be tracked. Another is what may be happening in 'marketing science'. Any advances in these areas may be reported in a number of ways:

- *Books* come out from time to time which may serve the needs of marketers by telling them something about order-and-pattern for their area. These may range from popular-press releases like this one to academic texts. They can be helpful.
- *Marketing journals* may also report results of research that can be used. A case of this was an experiment into whether money attached to the top of a mailed questionnaire actually increased the response rate of people who sent it back. Knowing this would be critical to determining 'the way things should be' for any mailed questionnaire.
- *Professional meetings* are another way to gain recent information. At one meeting of academics the results of a Master's thesis into the negotiating behaviour of South Americans was published. This could have been invaluable to somebody trying to export to a South American country.

Example

A company was considering the possibility of attaching a coupon to its product, offering 50% off the next purchase. Crucial to whether or not to do this was to get some idea of how many would be returned (e.g. if everybody sent them back, the marketer was in big financial trouble!). The marketer concerned discovered that a book had been written about coupons, and decided to use its insights to make his decision. They turned out to be correct.

Questions to ask yourself

As with almost all of the preceding sources of 'footprints' a key issue for avoiding a 'bad' decision is to be sure that at least *something* has been done to secure any information available. The easiest thing to evaluate is a zero! In other words, if a disaster happened and absolutely *nothing* had been done to check for available information, it would obviously be at best embarrassing, and at worst deadly. However, if reasonable efforts have been made, what is done represents a judgment call that may be acceptable.

So positive answers to the following questions should be best:

- Have you read any new business books in the last 6 months?
- As a result of this reading have you made any changes in what you do?
- Do you subscribe to professional marketing journals?
- Have any of their articles had an impact on your employer in the last 2 years?

211

- Do you attend any professional marketing meetings in your area?
- Do you even have a good way to know when they are happening?

Positive answers to the preceding groups of questions will have a profound effect on the 'survivability' of any employer. However, sometimes they are just not enough, and formal market research will be required.

Market research made easy

Formal market research is more problem-centred than the preceding items. Most of them are things which may represent a barrier, but they are not always items people have gone out and looked for. They tend instead to have been caught in a net of processes set up to constantly monitor the outside world. Formal market research is different.

Formal market research is set up to either avoid or solve a problem by finding barriers related to it. 'Avoiding' a problem would be best illustrated by a decision to launch some new product or service an employer has never offered before. In this case it might be essential to determine everything (e.g. knowledge, solutions, availability, transfer) about 'the way things should be'. 'Solving' a problem might mean discovering the barrier behind some fall in sales—after the fact.

Whichever the case, all forms of post-modernist market research start out the same way and follow the same steps. Each step in this process provides an answer to one of several basic questions. The first begins the whole process.

Step 1: How all research worth doing begins

From a post-modernist viewpoint, all research worth doing begins with an 'itchy feeling on the back of some decision maker's neck' that goes this way:

> *I believe there are now/could in the future be barriers keeping us from making money—and those barriers can be resolved at a reasonable cost. (Yes/No)*

The reason 'worth doing' was mentioned is that some market research is done without the objective of solving some *specific* problem (e.g. 'Why do people buy bread?'). This tends to be a very costly way to learn anything, as it is really just a 'fishing expedition' that may or may not discover something useful.

Why the idea of 'barriers keeping us from making money' is included in this definition should (by now) be obvious. And words assuming that these 'barriers can be resolved' must be present, or there is no reason to begin. (E.g. what good is it to find barriers that can't be taken away?) Last but not least, the 'yes' or 'no' ending does warn that the assumption starting the process may not be true. (E.g. barriers may not be found, or they may be too costly to resolve.) This is part and parcel of post-modernist marketing, and it's only fair that people should know. Seeing how the whole process is driven by this desire to remove revenue-robbing barriers leads to the next step.

Step 2: *Where* is the money being lost?

What this means is there are only four ways any employer can lose money, and it is useful to pin down which of these are the focus of research. These four ways are:

1 sale of an existing product/service to existing customers (e.g. we are Ford; why are people leaving us to buy GM products?)

2 sale of an existing product/service to new customers (we are Ford; why aren't GM buyers purchasing from us?)

3 sale of a new product/service to existing customers (we are Ford, but have a new four-wheel drive product. Why aren't people who normally buy Ford sedans interested?)

4 sale of a new product/service to new customers (we are Ford, and want to set up an aerospace division. Why aren't government purchasers interested?)

The reason for setting forth the above is that it really helps clarify what any research is to do. Most executives can point to one of the above as being their concern. Any one of these can usually make for a satisfying research project. Once the above is in place the next step can be taken.

Step 3: *How* is the money being lost?

The barriers causing the problem can only occupy the TASK levels discussed earlier. It can be said with certainty that something about these levels will be the difficulty. The only question is, 'Which ones?' A rough idea of how to answer this question constitutes the next step.

Step 4: What is the *least worst* way to gather information?

In order to determine any answers, some sort of a plan will be required. The reason for stressing the words 'least worst' is to make a point underlying all post-modernist research. It can never be perfect. For any information gathered will (at best) be from the *present*, which becomes the *past* once known. And this information will be used to make *future-oriented* decisions. So from the very beginning some sort of compromise will be made. And anything uncovered may have to be taken with a 'grain of salt'.

What the options for forming such a plan may involve can be obtained from any market research book. One thing is certain. It will require consideration of at least two sources for the information needed: secondary and primary.

Secondary resources

Often called 'desk research', these are already-published sources of information such as books, periodicals, research papers, census information and so on, like those of the MIS. They are always consulted first because they are cheaper than primary research. And there is the hope they may be enough. If for any reason these resources cannot address the issues, there is only one other option.

Primary resources

This is information that the researcher goes out and gathers for him- or herself. It can be very expensive.

Whatever the mix between these two resources, a next step is essential.

Step 5: Is this research going to be worth doing?

Does the planned research look like it will be capable of uncovering enough barriers to pay for itself? This requires two 'guesstimates'. One is what the research may cost. (This is largely determined by how much can be found without primary research.) The other is what it may be worth. Both of these can be hard to pin down. But if some sort of *reasonable* educated guess says 'do it', the research can proceed. And (hopefully) this will provide answers to the last important stage.

Step 6: What should we do?

Answering this question requires assembling and interpreting all the patterns uncovered by the research. Knowing exactly how to gather and interpret information—while still avoiding the two errors found in 'bad' decisions—can be greatly aided by Figure 12.2.

The research plan flow chart

Figure 12.2 shows a step-by-step process for conducting post-modernist market research.

On one sheet of paper this summarises all the information that should be gathered in a logical fashion. Major section areas for any formal written report are provided, as well as their best sequence. Whether or not the research requires a formal report, the process sketched out by this figure will still be useful.

As shown by this figure, all research looks pretty much like an hourglass which narrows the focus down to the 'itchy' feeling already discussed, gathers information to support/deny this feeling, and then suggests what to do about it. In order to show how this works, an actual piece of research shall be followed through this flow chart.

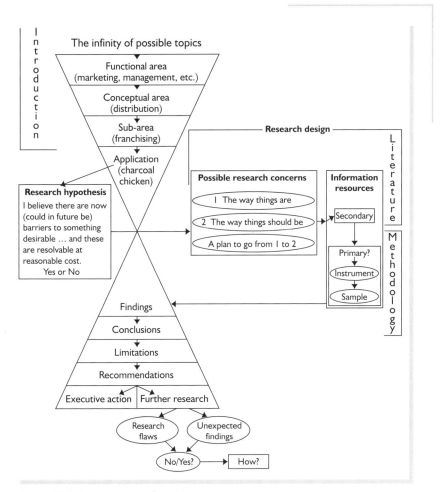

Figure 12.2 The research plan flow chart

A food-service executive did the research. He wanted to find out if there was a market for a Charcoal Chicken franchise outlet in a certain city.

Introduction

In this section the focus goes from any one of an infinite number of topics to one zeroing in on marketing in the distribution (availability) area as it involves a franchise operation selling Charcoal Chicken. This leads to the 'research hypothesis' which is just a fancy way of saying what this person's 'itchy feeling' was. Writing this down would have gone this way:

I believe there are barriers to making money represented by the lack of a Charcoal Chicken outlet in my city. And these can be resolved at a reasonable cost (yes or no).

Once this is expressed it becomes obvious that it will be necessary to gather information in order to answer the 'yes or no' question. This leads to the next section.

Research design

This section sets forth what is the least worst way to gather the needed answers. This may involve finding out *the way things are* for providers (e.g. are there any competitors? What would be my costs?), *the way things should be* in the minds of consumers (Do customers like Charcoal Chicken? What would they pay for one? What size?), or some sort of *process* consumers use for going from 'the way things are' to 'the way things should be' (often studied in a field called 'buyer behaviour'). Perhaps all three will be needed. From this point onward, carrying out market research is pretty much 'fill in the blanks'. And one starts looking for sources of information—the cheaper ones first.

Literature review

Of course, this will require looking through secondary information in what is called the literature review. (In this case the student did find a franchise plan suggesting both operating and set-up costs.) And what isn't found here will have to be found through *primary research*.

Methodology

How primary information will be gathered is called the *methodology*. It has two separate pieces. One is an instrument (questionnaire, personal interview, phone interview, etc.) used to gather the information. The second part is a group of people to whom this instrument is applied, called a *sample*.

In this situation the student devised a personal interview supported by a questionnaire to determine what people would pay for a certain-sized chicken. His sample consisted of standing outside of several supermarkets on weekends to ask people to answer his questions. Once a reasonable amount of information is present, the next step follows pretty logically.

Findings

These are the actual responses to the questions asked. In this case they were the business plan turned up by the literature review, and the responses (by size) as to what people would pay for a chicken. At this point it is necessary to think about how to put together what may be somewhat unrelated bits of information, and reach the next step.

Conclusion

What must happen here is to integrate the information in a *reasonable* (that word again) way to reach a conclusion that seems supported by the facts. This may be a largely intuitive process. In this example the student decided that—based on his findings—there probably was a market for a Charcoal Chicken franchise, but it wouldn't make much money.

But because all of the preceding may be full of 'holes' (remember, it *is* 'least worst'!), some sort of warning may be in order for any written report.

Limitations

Here, if necessary, the researcher 'comes clean' about everything in the research that was less than perfect, so nobody else (a reviewer) will think it was overlooked. Anyone who spots a flaw must be convinced that either 'somebody might *think* this was a problem—but it *really* isn't (here's why)' or 'it could be a problem, but was unavoidable'. In this case the student admitted that his primary research was pretty limited (about 30 interviews taken in three locations), but that was all the time the project could allow. Following this 'cigarettes may be hazardous to your health' type of warning, the really important part can follow.

Recommendations

This section answers the question, 'So what?' It has two parts. The *executive action* area tells managers what to do in light of the research. (In this case, it was, 'Don't start up a Charcoal Chicken Shop'.) The *further research* area covers work that may need to follow.

This will either be to remove *research flaws* (e.g. take a bigger sample), or to explore *unexpected findings* that usually 'fall out' of any research quite unexpectedly. (Several people said they didn't want Charcoal Chicken, but wished they could buy sushi.) Finally, for future researchers it may be useful to say whether or not this looks worth pursuing (the student thought not), and how (not needed).

In this case all the market research showed was, 'Don't do that'. Although disappointing, this could have saved thousands by avoiding entering into a market with too many barriers. Alternatively, had this research—or any of the other techniques discussed—discovered something more promising, the organisation would be at the same point as those using the 'whispers' in Chapter 10. Whatever the case, this leads to the next question.

We found a barrier/some barriers. What do we do with it/them?

This will be covered in the following chapter.

ACTION SUMMARY

A post-modernist approach can not only utilise classical marketing tools—it makes understanding their use much easier.

The use of classical tools is a good way to avoid the only two errors faced by decision-makers: failure to consider information, and a breakdown in logic. Since most people likely to review marketing decisions will come from a classical background, it is important this area not be overlooked, regardless of whether the marketer is a post-modernist or not.

The 'core' at the centre of both post-modernist and classical marketing is the same.

Both approaches depend on some type of pattern. Post-modernists use this to provide the 'logic' their 'avoiding bad decisions' paradigm demands; classical marketers may see it as a lasting foundation from which to make decisions. The only real difference between these two is how long they think this pattern lasts (the classical marketers suggest some are timeless— the postmodernists know they can't be, but believe they do last long enough to be better than nothing).

Marketing is a *historical* discipline.

Since no pattern can be enduring, marketers are mostly historians who record what has happened in the present (which becomes the past as soon as it happens) in the hope this can be used to make future decisions. As such, most marketing inputs are 'footprints in the snow of time' which show where people have come from, and hopefully where they (and their needs) will be in the future. These can suggest barriers. The 'footprints' studied (very briefly) in this chapter take four forms, and are used to show how to combine post-modernist and classical approaches.

Micro/macro environments study 'what's happening'.

Marketing decisions are not carried out in a vacuum, so it is crucial to know what might affect their chances of success. The micro-environment contains those elements (employees, suppliers, employee families, banks) closest to the producer. The macro-environment is concerned with the changes happening in the PESTs (political, economic/environmental, social and technological factors).

Demographics are the 'footprints' found in statistics.

These statistics are usually provided by governments and include elements such as age, marital status, wealth, income, and anything else easily recorded by numbers. As with most marketing measures, they are often most useful when compared over time. This is certainly true for the 'pig in the python', which is a name given to the rapid ageing of the population in most western cultures.

Market research is more aggressive.

Use of the above elements tends to be through a monitoring process which may not be all that focused. Market research is usually more problem-centred. It looks for barriers either through an MIS (marketing information system)—which is sort of an 'early warning' radar—or through specific research aimed at either avoiding or solving some particular problem.

The post-modernist market research process

A post-modernist approach to research begins by assuming that (somewhere) money is being lost and tries to find out where/how so this can be stopped. It is mapped out in Figure 12.2. This shows how information is gathered in a step-by-step manner which narrows an inquiry down to those issues most likely to be causing difficulty, looks for information about those areas, and then assembles that information in a manner likely to resolve what will ultimately be barriers.

THE BOTTOM LINE

It would be a mistake to assume classical marketing has nothing to offer the post-modernist. Let classical marketing's 'footprints in the snow' lead you to your barriers.

ACTION EXERCISE 12.1

Keeping the PESTs from destroying our business

For: Employees at all levels   **Format:** Individuals or 4–8-person groups
Materials required: Pencils and instructions
Objective: To see where our PESTs' footprints lead us

Instructions

In this chapter we were shown some elements of what is called the macro-environment which were summed up as PESTs (political/economic-environmental/social/technological factors). It was said that if changes in these elements were followed they might show what are now barriers or could be barriers in the future. An item chosen from each of these areas—plus one more called the 'pig in the python' have been selected to serve at discussion-starters. Please look at the following choices:

- political (a change-over in the 'ruling political party' takes place);
- environmental (laws forbidding pollution are getting tougher);
- social (more and more families are suffering divorce);
- technological (the Internet is everywhere);
- 'pig in the python' (the population is ageing rapidly, and soon 25% will be over 65 years of age).

Consider the following either in groups or as an individual.

In the first 10 minutes:

Choose one of the above in which you think the change noted may have the greatest impact on 'the way things should be' for the consumers we serve.

In the next 15 minutes:

Once your group has made its choice, discuss the following:

- Is there anything about the problems my employer solves which could be related to this change?
- What will any noticeable changes mean for 'the way things should be' about the problems we solve? (In other words, what may have to be different about the solutions we offer, their availability, their price, and how we tell people about ourselves?)
- Are we making any of those changes?
- If not, why not?
- If yes, will these changes be better than those of competitors?
- How do we know this?
  Then be prepared to share your answers with us.

Conclusion

The world, it is a'changing! If we don't change with it, our chances of survival are not much greater than those of the dinosaurs. We must be prepared to see what is happening around us, and move with it. As change is happening so quickly today, this is likely to mean what we do as an employer, and as individuals within it, will be quite different in the future.

13

Barrier-based action plans

SURE-FIRE SUCCESS STRATEGIES FOR BUILDING YOUR BUSINESS

Although barriers have been pictured as a hindrance, once they are found, they can be used to work *for you* as part of a larger plan. Here is how to form your plan.

We've found a barrier—now what?

Whether through post-modernist 'whispers' or classical marketing, once a barrier is identified it is important to do *something* about it. However, before rushing off to do this, it is important to know what is—and isn't—important about barriers. One key issue has been discussed before.

Not all barriers *have* to be resolved.

As mentioned in Chapter 10, some barriers represent a bother which the customer doesn't like, but will put up with (mostly because they can get no better elsewhere). So they aren't costing any money and may be ignored—at least for now.

Some barriers can be saved for *later*.

A major difference between post-modernist and classical approaches to marketing has to do with what amounts to strategy. The classical people seem to suggest that, once what a consumer wants is known, they should be given everything. Bad idea! Remember, a successful marketer doesn't have to be 'the best'—all they must do is become 'the least worst'. Not only may such a 'give 'em everything' approach over-do it (the customer *might* be satisfied with less), but also it doesn't leave much for 'the next round'.

The only thing that makes for unusual profit is the stupidity (reaction time) of competitors. If your employer 'makes its play' all at once, it lays out an easy action plan for competitors (e.g. just copy what they offer). Assuming a barrier is not costing anything because competitors don't know about it, a better strategy may be to 'drip-feed' improvements a bit at a time, in order to stay one step ahead of the competition.

This was certainly true for Daimler Chrysler when it introduced a radically retro car called 'the PT Cruiser'. Every auto magazine that tested the car raved about it, but noted it had a very small engine and lacked the power to match its appearances.

At the time of the writing of this book, this is simply conjecture, but want to bet that—once competitors start catching up and all the people who want one have one—Chrysler starts putting in a larger engine—then a turbo charger—then a V-eight, then offers it in a convertible?

Some barriers *shouldn't* be dealt with.

Recall the post-modernist approach to micro-marketing which puts all the emphasis on marketing tools being used to advance a *marketer's* career. Anything that will be personally harmful won't (and probably shouldn't) be done.

For that reason one issue that must be considered for any barrier is the likely payback period. This is how long it will take for any revenue generated by taking out a barrier to be greater than the costs of removing it.

The payback period for dealing with any barrier must be shorter than the 'period of patience'.

The 'period of patience' is the length of time for which key decision makers (e.g. owners) are willing to put up with lack of noticeable results before they do something about it. For most western cultures this is about a year to 18 months. (For some Asian cultures it may be considerably longer.) If nothing seems to be happening by the end of the 'period of patience' they are likely to 'throw the bums out', starting with whomever in marketing has spent a great deal of money that seems to be getting little in the way of results.

It is often hard to guess exactly what a 'payback' period may be. But in this situation all that can be done is to make a guess and say, 'Would a *reasonable* person agree with the marketer's estimate?' Having covered the basics, let's look at what's *most important* about barriers.

What's most important about barriers is *what's not important* about them—blame!

Conventional wisdom has it that if a barrier is found, the 'guilty one' should be hunted down and punished immediately. This is a bad idea. Doing so is only slightly less stupid than blaming the loss of a football game on the last player to miss a tackle.

The two situations have a lot in common. In both cases one person is made to 'take the rap' for something a lot of others had a hand in. For as in football, most organisations are so complex that it is almost impossible for any one individual (or area) to be solely responsible for a barrier.

So persecuting one individual or area will represent an injustice, and will almost always be counterproductive to everyone involved. People will know what is happening is unfair and resent it, whether it happens to them or not.

Beyond this, if the objective is to create an environment in which *all* employees guard against barriers, punishing one for his or her barrier will cause all the others to clam up. They won't want to 'blow the whistle' on a friend or suffer the same fate the next time. This is so true that it is one way to tell a sick management culture from a healthy one.

Signals sent by a sick management team

When presented with signs of a barrier, a weak management team will first try to deny the message by attacking the messenger, often by the 'perception versus truth' approach mentioned in the first chapter (e.g. 'Our last customer service survey said we didn't have an adequate display. How dare they say this, of course we had one. It was just in the back room [where nobody goes]'!).

When this doesn't work, the next words will be, 'Who did it?' (so they can be punished!) There is a much better way.

How to spot a strong management team

A strong management team will welcome any information about barriers as an opportunity to make more money (e.g. 'Just look at how well we shall do when we fix things'). The whole emphasis will be on getting the problem corrected to the point it doesn't happen again. Any punishment will be a last resort.

There *is* a limit.

There does come a time when something *must* be done if the barrier keeps repeating. But the first time is not that time. The only way to be successful is to create a workplace in which employees believe no one will be punished (initially) for a barrier, and those who find one may be rewarded. Then everybody wins.

Once this environment is established, the employer can set about dealing with his or her barriers. When this is done, the key to success is simple.

What *is* important about barriers? The system set up to deal with them.

'System' here means some sort of process which will (more or less automatically) keep barriers from being created, or deal with them when they are. Whatever system is created will depend on the situation. But the key parts are 'the three Rs'.

Recognising barriers is the first step.

Employees need to know the forms barriers take and be able to identify them. Raising their sensitivity to them through training in the whole post-modernist/barrier approach (including classical marketing elements) can do this. Then they need to take action.

Responsibility must be taken.

What this means is that seeing barriers is not enough. Someone must *do* something about them, if possible. This is very much like one of the first laws of first aid. If someone has been hit by a truck and is still breathing, one of the critical factors that will decide their fate is whether somebody on the scene takes responsibility for the situation and starts doing something. Otherwise people just mill around and nothing happens.

Employers are the same. If an employee sees a barrier they must take responsibility for it by doing two things. One is trying to fix the immediate problem as they see it happen (even if this is not the employee's job), and then alerting the rest of the organisation to the situation (so a more permanent fix can be made). This leads to the last and most important issue.

Reacting to barriers has to be done in the right way.

An effective response to barriers will require three basic elements:

1 resources;
2 visibility; and
3 consequences.

Resources are the tangible tools needed to get some job done. One important thing to understand is that barriers generally cannot be 'talked away'. If they could, they probably would have been dealt with years before. No, somebody is going to have to spend money on some sort of resources to put them right.

These resources may be extra staff, training or equipment (or some combination of all three). If these are not provided, the employee may feel quite justified in any failure to do what is needed (e.g. 'So why should I do anything?—they won't even give me the tools I need.').

Visibility means that it must be clear whether or not any process used to handle a barrier is being worked on—and is successful. It pays not to depend upon the 'nobility' of employees to do this for you. Sooner or later even the most 'noble' wear down and 'forget' to get the job done.

Whenever somebody does or doesn't do the job they have the *resources* to do, and this becomes *visible*, then the third factor of success—*consequences*—becomes important. What this means is that good performances must be rewarded (preferably) or bad ones punished (reluctantly)—sometimes both. People *are* selfish. If they are confident nothing will happen to them when creating a barrier, some will keep on doing it no matter how many resources they have, or how visible their failures may be.

A way to see all three elements of barrier resolution can be learned from two different hotel chains' approaches to a common problem. In this case the problem was centred in their housekeeping staff.

A good example of a bad approach

In one five-star hotel, said to be 'the best in the country', a guest happened to remain in the room when the maid came in. She offered to help this housekeeper with the chores, but the maid politely refused. The maid then stripped the bed and threw the pillowcases on the floor. 'Not to worry,' thought the guest, 'They do wash them'.

The maid then took the pillowcases into the bathroom and used one to clean the toilet. 'I hope they wash them very well,' thought the guest. The maid then used the *same* pillowcase to clean the bathroom vanity. By now the guest was feeling ill, but thought the worst was over. It wasn't.

This same maid then turned her attention to the two small glasses 'sanitised for your use' which are always present in hotel bathrooms. She used the *same* pillowcase to wash out these glasses.

(Lest you think this an isolated event, next time you are staying in rented accommodation, look for the housekeeping cart on the morning you check out. See if there are clean glasses on it. If there are, they may have come up from the kitchen dishwasher and may be all right. If there are not, ask yourself, 'How *do* they get those little glasses clean?'—and I bet you never drink from one again as long as you live!)

At first the guest decided not to tell the hotel what she had seen, as she didn't want to get the maid in trouble. However, concerns about a possible health hazard prevailed, and she wrote to the hotel manager about it—but was insistent the employee not be punished. To show her insistence she refused to name the maid concerned, or even tell the date on which the incident happened.

She got a very nice letter back saying how sorry the hotel was. It *also* said:

We have run your name through our reservations system and determined the last time you were here. We then cross-referenced this against our housekeeping roster to find the person concerned. [Notice all the effort going into attaching blame.] The maid involved has been given a very stern dressing down. I know she will never do it again.

Want to bet she (or somebody else) won't do it again? Of course *somebody* will. They will because management has not come up with an adequate *process* for dealing with the problem.

One deficiency is that *adequate resources* have not been made available. This is actually a common problem for hotels/motels. There is no easy place to wash those glasses.

A second shortcoming is that the process adopted was not *visible*. Glasses washed in the toilet and glasses washed some other way will look the same. Unless a manager is present every moment, they will never know how (or if) the glasses have been washed.

In addition, because the process was not visible, there can be no employee *consequences* from choosing to follow or ignore it. The only real consequences would be an outbreak of hepatitis A or something else, and the hotel being shut down by the Health Department. This seems a rather hard way to be alerted to process failure!

Contrast this approach with another one involving the same situation. A hotel chain with about two stars fewer *does* have the problem licked.

A better way to handle barriers

What they do is send up sanitised glasses from the dishwashers downstairs. They place these on the housekeeping cart, and identify them with plastic wrap pre-shrunk around them. The maids simply take the dirty ones and replace them with clean ones in every room. This solution has everything going for it.

Adequate *resources* have been provided in the form of the clean glasses. Having the plastic wrap around them ensures *visibility*. This lets both managers and staff see if they are being used. Process *consequences* can then be implemented if needed.

In fact, at least one of the consequences works automatically. Because the pre-cleaned glasses are easier for staff to handle than the ones that must be washed, they are bound to use them. So success seems certain. A similar approach will work with most barriers. But taking out your own barriers is only one side of the post-modernist tool kit.

Post-modernist marketers have two ways to go.

Remember Chapter 8? The other side of post-modernist marketing is to make barriers for a competitor by seeming to be willing or able to do something the competitor doesn't. There are two major strategies for doing this: segmentation and program differentiation. Both of these work using the same principle—in different ways. A simple way to understand this principle is to examine what happens in the most important purchase people ever make—marriage!

What can be learned about barriers from 'the most important purchase people ever make'

Some might wish to argue that marriage (or in today's world a long-term commitment) is not *really* a purchase. But it is. When one either makes or accepts a proposal of marriage, one is entering into a very long-term purchase with very poor return privileges and—face it—not much of a residual trade-in value!

Beyond that, if the initial 'shopping' was done on a beach, some element of 'packaging and display' will have come into play—or 'Wonder Bras' and gym memberships wouldn't sell as well as they do. Finally, after the purchase is consummated both parties will probably find there has been a tremendous amount of false advertising!

So marriage probably *is* a good way to make a basic point about purchases. In order to see what that point is, ask yourself (if appropriate), 'Why did I do that?' The longer ago it happened—particularly if you have done this more than once—the harder it may be to remember. But something most will agree with is that, at the time they did it, they chose someone they thought was 'special'.

The alternative is to admit that you decided to commit the rest of your life to someone who stood in front of you and said, 'Well, I'm no worse than the rest of them—and I'm breathing!' (You would have to be either crazy or desperate to do that!) At any rate, if one pulls apart the meaning of the word 'special' as used here, it loses some of its romantic lustre.

Special means being 'different'—in a good way.

What 'being special' means for a marriage prospect—as well as all purchases—is that something about some alternative is seen as different in a desirable way. And it is *thought* this will make things better for the purchaser than would otherwise be the case. The underlying notion is to establish in the mind of the 'customer' the idea that one is unique. This thought is what gives marketing strategies that use such an approach their name.

The unique selling proposition (USP)—how are providers 'special'?

Obviously, being uniquely special would present an advantage to all providers. The way each competitor's unique appeal is presented to consumers is sometimes called their unique selling proposition (USP). What this means is, 'How are we different—in a good way?' The answer to this question will provide a theme around which all efforts must revolve if consumers are to see anyone as having fewer barriers than do competitors.

There are at least two separate ways for marketers to achieve this situation: segmentation and differentiation. They have a great deal in common, for they both have to do with creating a USP based on differences between their offerings.

Segmentation and program differentiation—making organisations 'special'

How all of this works can be understood by turning to Figure 13.1.

Although classical marketers often treat segmentation and differentiation as totally different strategies, they probably aren't, for they both use the same principle of 'differences', but use them in dissimilar ways, related to the conditions facing the marketer. Let's see what they are.

Segmentation tries to serve some 'little corner of the world' competitors have ignored. Those who wish to segment try to find some group of consumers (called a 'segment') within a market who for some reason have very similar needs (which are not the same as everybody else's needs in the market). It is thought these needs are unsatisfied.

Market segmentation	Program differentiation
Relatively small no. of consumers	Relatively large no. of consumers
with	with
similar needs = segment	dissimilar needs
Exact fit	Average fit
No substitutes	We need a 'plus'—a differentiating factor

Figure 13.1 Two ways to produce differences

Because the people within this segment want pretty much the same thing, it is possible for a marketer to tailor a marketing program exactly to their problems.

What is hoped is that *nobody else will see this opportunity*, so there will be no substitutes for the marketer's offering. This means the marketer will have (as long as nobody else copies them) what amounts to a monopoly. Such situations usually pay big dollars, for there is nobody around to cut prices.

Example

There are a number of retailers around the world who specialise in merchandise for people who are left-handed. It seems that many items like scissors, golf clubs and appliances are made for the majority of people, who are right-handed. If one is not a part of this majority, life can be difficult (watch somebody who is left-handed trying to use a standard pair of scissors). So there are manufacturers who make—and shops that sell—unique, left-handed merchandise for this segment. People who are a part of this segment will go 'to the ends of the earth' to find these suppliers.

Generally, for a segment to be worth serving, a huge market from which to draw what is usually a rather small piece (which will still be big enough to support a producer serving it) is required. Those not having this happy situation must go to the other extreme by offering pretty much what everybody else does, but distinguish their offerings with some relatively minor difference.

Differentiation looks for a *small* difference that makes *all* the difference.

How this works is that a marketer starts out by looking at a huge market with so many people that it is not likely much will be found that is exactly common to them all. So, using the types of tools offered by classical marketing, the marketer figures out the average need of the average person in this group using the thoughts of the statistician who said, 'I have my head in the refrigerator and my feet in the oven—on the *average* I feel just fine!' Whatever this 'average' turns out to be, a product or service is made that reflects it—and is marketed.

However, this causes another problem, one that is easier to see if one imagines an example. Suppose a huge market, like that for motor vehicles. Both Ford and GM hire their marketers from the same universities ... that teach the same tools (except for those using this book—which give their students a real advantage!) ... and produce the same 'thermometers' stuck into the same mass of people. One side takes its results, makes it into a product, and calls this a 'Ford' (US) or a 'Falcon' (Australia/New Zealand). The other side takes its results, makes it into a product, and calls the product a 'Chevrolet' (US) or 'Commodore' (Australia/New Zealand).

Given this process, what is likely to be true of the two offerings, compared to each other? Are they likely to be similar or different? Of course, they will probably be *almost* identical. This is so much the case that, before Daimler Chrysler decided to drop the brand, it was said:

Put a Ford and a Chevrolet in a garage overnight—9 months later you get a Plymouth!

In this case, what will be the difference making each product 'special'? The answer is some *minor* difference that the marketers think will make *all* the difference to their customers. Marketers call this minor difference a *differentiating* factor. If it is successful, the lack of something similar for competitors will represent a barrier.

Example

A case of this in the Australian auto market was safety—which GM got to first by making a driver's air bag standard equipment. This beat Ford for a while— then they offered one. GM continued to follow this tack by then staying one step ahead with first a passenger air bag, and now side air bags. One wonders how long this 'can you top this' 'poker game' of competition can go on. (One European automaker offers 37 air bags as standard in one of its models!)

Another example you may remember from an earlier chapter is Joe CarNut, and the little rubbish bin on the keypad operating the car wash. This one little barrier (or the lack thereof) made all the difference to him. It doesn't *seem* a lot, but as noted in Chapter 8, it *doesn't take* a lot. Still, are there any differences which are better than others?

What makes for a great USP?

Not all differences are created equal—and some are better than others. Those which are the most powerful will generally score well on any measures of tangibility, competitor access, attractiveness and credibility.

Being *tangible* indicates a USP can be seen, felt, smelled, heard or otherwise measured. Don't rely on saying your major difference is *our staff*—unless you can prove it with external measures (e.g. numbers of staff, qualifications). For most people hearing this claim otherwise won't believe it, but will instead think, ' ... aw, let's all fall down, eat grass, and touch each other!'—or something else out of the 'feely/touchy' sixties.

Competitor access means, 'Can competitors claim the same thing?' If they can, your USP won't be unique for long, as competitors will run all over you. Try to find something that really sets you apart (e.g. 'Our tomato plants grow 20% bigger tomatoes than our competitors' do').

Attractiveness indicates your difference is something people really want. As shall be discussed, being 'different' can result in being either wonderful or weird. Make sure it's something consumers will *think* is wonderful. For instance, a 'hillbilly' restaurant in the Ozarks offers 'throwed' rolls. What this means is they bake all their muffins on the premises and people dressed up in hillbilly garb throw them to customers who then spread honey and butter on them. The line leading into the restaurant stretches out onto the road.

Credibility refers to whether your claim of being different will be believed—or greeted with laughter. For instance, it was once recommended that New Zealand beekeepers advertise their honey by stating, 'Our honey—from nuclear-free NZ—won't glow in the dark!' (This was suggested when the Chernobyl disaster put radiation into most of the competitor bees in Europe!) Since New Zealand had long beaten its breast about its nuclear-free status, people would probably have figured this was true. Russia would have had a hard time with a similar claim.

Whatever your particular case, whether what is needed is a 'one-off' removal of a barrier, or a complicated strategy making one for others through a USP, getting *something* to happen is the key. In an organisation of any size, that will be easier if there is some blueprint to follow.

You've got to have a plan! The post-modernist 'barrier-busting' flow chart

As can be seen by referring to Figure 13.2, what the flow chart does is to expand upon the above process.

231

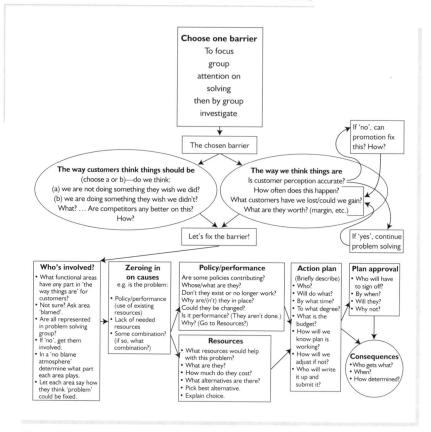

Figure 13.2 The post-modernist 'barrier-busting' flow chart

Although it was made for organisations of a large size and complexity, it can be scaled down to fit any employer. It also assumes a group of employees may be working on the situation together (see action exercise 13.2).

How barriers begin

The plan begins by assuming that (somehow) a barrier has been spotted. It then goes on to explore the thinking required to fix *all* barriers. The starting point is the reality that all barriers start out from a situation in which producers *suspect* customers are not totally satisfied with what is happening. (We can never be sure, for we are not in customers' heads—but something causes us to suspect they are not as happy as they could be.) Usually we assume that either we *are* doing something they wish we didn't (e.g. charging too much), or *are not* doing something they wish we did (e.g. not showing up on time).

For the purposes of illustration we will assume that the problem appears to be that some of the firm's orders are taking too long to process—and taking forever to receive. In other words, we are not doing what the customer thinks should be done. We shall follow this one through the flow chart just to show how it works.

Is it real?

The next thing to do is to see if that perception is accurate (e.g. customers could have it wrong). In our case this would require comparing our records for the customer's order-processing time to what they seem to think it is, and deciding if customer expectations are unreasonable (e.g. what are competitor order-processing times?).

If the customer is not correct, it may be possible to fix this perception with some form of promotion (e.g. advertising/salesmanship telling customers what the real situation may be). If not, one moves on to a decision of whether or not to fix the problem.

Is the barrier worth fixing?

This requires figuring out what the barrier may be costing, either with existing customers or those we don't service but would like to. And some estimate will have to be made about the costs of making a change. Of course, until a final plan is 'nailed down' this may be hard to do. But as long as a *reasonable* person would think the situation *may* hold promise, one can move to the next step.

Who's involved?

In a 'no blame' environment it is important to nail down who must be a part of any solution. One way to do this is to track the problem through *paperwork* (e.g. where did/could the customer's written details—order, request—go) or through *physical contact* (e.g. what areas of the firm either directly or indirectly had/could have anything to do with the customers and situation of concern?).

Finally, a good way to make sure all parts are present is to ask the area/person who would have otherwise been 'blamed' for any shortcoming (in this case it might be the warehouse manager), 'Who besides you could have a part of this?' This is usually quite productive, for they may be more than happy to sing like a bird!

They might identify the sales area who took the order, the clerical area who processed it, the people in information technology who maintain the order-processing systems, and even the delivery people who took it to the customer. All of these areas must be represented in any solution, and should be a part of the group seeking it.

What's the cause?

Barriers are the result of one or more of three deficiencies. Sometimes the problem is a policy. For instance, the firm may never have thought of having a minimum order-processing time. Or it can be a lack of some resource (e.g. they need a computer to track an order through the system). Finally, it might be a lack of performance. In other words there is a policy setting an order-processing time limit, but people are not performing to it.

At this stage all the possibilities are explored, and the best way to proceed is determined. This decision will highlight the resources that may be necessary to undertake any plan.

Resources will be needed.

As mentioned earlier, these resources may include staff, training, equipment, or some combination of all three. Getting approval for them will be easier if they can be presented as a part of a well-thought-out plan.

A 'barrier-busting' action plan

Once decisions as to causes and the 'best' cures are reached, it becomes possible to develop an action plan that tells who will have to do what, when, to what degree, and so on. A key part of the success of this plan will be any consequences that may flow from it.

Consequences

As emphasised earlier, people are selfish. Why should they go to any extra effort if they don't see something in it for them? It will be important to nail down in great detail that rewards will flow if the plan is successful; who will get 'what' if the plan is successful; and how this 'success' will be measured.

This last section will not only make people more likely to make any changes required by the plan, but also ensure that they monitor and (perhaps) nurture it once it is implemented. Otherwise, a marvellous plan may be made, but will become only a dusty document in some filing cabinet. At this point enough information should be available to make the final costs/benefits assessment required to get management approval.

Plan approval

This must come not only from top-level management, but also from managers of each area touched on in the plan. (For some reason getting this in writing seems to produce more powerful results.) Assuming permission from all parties is received, the plan should be implemented, and the monitoring device built into it should be the source of any rewards.

Rewards

At this point it is worth mentioning something that might seem obvious. It is crucial that the promised consequences—whatever they may be—*do* happen if the plan works. If it doesn't, the same may have to be said about any punishments promised for lack of performance.

If the plan *does* work, don't let some short-sighted manager think much money could be saved if the rewards were siphoned elsewhere, for this only has to happen once. If it does no similar plan will ever happen in the future. The same often can be said of threatened negative outcomes that don't take place when merited.

However, even if good things (or bad things) may seem likely to come from such a plan, this doesn't necessarily mean it *will* happen.

Gaining total cooperation

Remember the words of Chapter 1. Any improvement in customer service will always require that some employee somewhere do something different (and possibly more) than they have in the past. Why should they? This will be explored in the next chapter.

ACTION SUMMARY

We've found a barrier—now what?

Regardless of how barriers are found, it is important to *do something* about them. However, what is done may vary from case to case for not all barriers *have* to be resolved due to competitor issues—some can be *saved* for later, and some *shouldn't* be dealt with for financial reasons.

What is—and isn't—important about barriers

The most important thing about barriers is the *least important* issue concerning them—blame. Trying to affix blame for any barrier is usually unfair, the sign of weak management, and likely to impede future progress. What *is* important about barriers is the system set up to deal with them.

The key elements of a good 'barrier-busting' system

A good system for correcting barriers will contain the 'three Rs'. These are *recognising* them through increased employee sensitivity, inspiring employees to take responsibility for them, and reacting to the barriers in the right way. This third element requires any system set up to deal with barriers to offer resources for taking care of them, *visibility* to determine their effective/ineffective handling, and *consequences* for appropriate/ inappropriate action. There are two different strategies for using barriers to build business, both of which work towards the same goal.

The 'unique selling proposition' (USP)—being different in a good way

The ultimate goal of dealing with barriers is to have fewer of them (in total) in the mind of one's consumers than one's competitors do. Consumers would describe this condition as being 'special'. And marketers describe this as a 'unique selling proposition' around which all marketing activity must revolve. There are two ways to achieve this unique status: segmentation and program differentiation.

Segmentation serves some 'little corner of the world' (hopefully) forgotten by others.

Segmentation zeroes in on consumers within some larger market who have enough similarity to make it worth mounting a campaign of knowledge/ solutions/availability/transfer *uniquely* appropriate to them. It is hoped no competitors do something similar.

Differentiation looks for a *small* difference that makes *all* the difference.

Differentiation is a strategy used when there are no segments unique or big enough to be worth serving, so all competitors offer pretty much the same thing. But in order to produce a condition of having fewer barriers, some relatively small difference is introduced.

You've got to have a plan.

Whether a one-off removal of an annoying barrier, or part of a larger strategy, it is important to have a plan for removing barriers. This will start with a suspicion that customers think producers either *aren't* doing something for them that consumers wish they did, or *are* doing something consumers wish producers wouldn't do.

Once this behaviour is identified, it becomes necessary to see whether consumers are correct in their thoughts (if not, promotion might be helpful). If consumers are spot on, it is necessary to see if the barrier is worth fixing, and who should be a part of any correction plan.

Any barrier-correcting plan will require a change in resources, policies or performance (perhaps all three). Once the best plan is known, a cost-benefits analysis can determine whether it should be implemented. If so, managerial approval must be obtained, the plan put into practice, and consequences meted out for performance/lack of performance.

The 'best laid' plans ...

Despite all this effort, even an excellent plan will fail if the people asked to carry it out do not cooperate. How to secure this cooperation will be discussed in the next chapter.

THE BOTTOM LINE
Barriers can do a great deal to build your 'business'. Make sure they are handled appropriately.

ACTION EXERCISE 13.1
So what makes us different?

For: Employees at all levels and all areas (manager level is best)
Format: 4–8-person groups
Materials required: Pencils and instructions
Objective: To enable workers to see whether their employment rests on a sound basis, and whether that basis could be made even stronger

Instructions
In this chapter it was said to be very important for an employer to offer something to its consumers which is distinctly different from the offerings of its competitors. Today we shall explore whether or not this is the case for us—and how it could be made better.

Form into groups ... then:
- Discuss who our three biggest competitors are. (*Hint:* Be sure to name specific firms, groups, products, etc.)
- Is there anything different about what we offer our customers to that offered by our competitors? (*Hint:* Think about our solutions to customer problems, availability, price, and promotion.)
- List our two biggest differences and discuss whether we seem to be segmenting (if so to whom?) or differentiating ourselves (how?).

- How would the differences listed above fare when judged against their tangibility, competitor access, attractiveness and credibility? Are you sure?
- Is there anything more we could do to make ourselves unique? What?

Conclusion

Our salaries all rest on our ability to be both different and better than our competitors. We must be constantly looking for ways to achieve this.

ACTION EXERCISE 13.2

The great barrier-busting binge

For: Employees at all levels/areas—particularly managers
Format: 4–8 groups from all functional areas (and it may be a good idea to set up several competing groups)
Materials required: Pencils and instructions
Objective: To enable employees working as part of teams to develop a plan for dealing with apparent barriers—possibly in a competition

Instructions

Following on from the great reception given the 'barrier approach to business' instruction, it was decided it would be a shame not to carry it forward by letting people follow through by actually working on one of their barriers. How to do this is summed up in Figure 13.2. Some useful expansion of this material follows.

Step 1: Form your groups.

It may be useful here to form groups that have members likely to be part of some problem in which you are interested. If these individuals are not all in your geographic location, it might be desirable to get in touch by e-mail.

Step 2: Pick out a barrier on which to focus.

There are four possible choices here, one of which would introduce a time lapse which may not be desirable or necessary. One approach is to use an existing customer satisfaction survey (if you have one) to isolate key barriers in a problem area. A second would be to let group members choose one barrier on which they would most like to focus. The third would be construct your own customer satisfaction survey, send it out to customers asking, 'How do we do on this?', and pick a problem from their responses. Finally, you may wish to conduct some market research, or have it done for you.

At any rate, it is essential that your group somehow picks out a barrier on which it wishes to focus. (*Hint*: The simplest, most straightforward, easiest-to-solve barrier would be a desirable strategic choice.)

Step 3: Investigate the chosen barrier.

Barriers usually happen whenever some competitor is solving some part of a customer's problem less completely than others are. A good way to think of this is to compare how (for the chosen barrier) customers think 'things' (e.g. elements relating to their barrier) 'should be' (for maximum satisfaction) to how your firm thinks things really are.

How customers think things should be

Whenever a barrier is present it is usually easiest to sum it up in one of two ways. Either customers think we are doing something to them that they wish we wouldn't, or we aren't doing something for them they wish we would. An example of the first would be a case where a firm selling gas appliances required customers to pay for both the appliance and its installation before receiving them in order to receive a cash discount. Small wonder that nobody did.

An example of a supplier not doing something customers wish they did would be those who don't accept (for instance) certain major credit cards that get customers frequent flyer points.

In order to simplify your task it is easiest to choose one of the preceding and then state in simple words (from the customer's point of view) what the problem may be. At this point it might be well to ask whether any competitors do better on this. If they don't, one could wonder whether the barrier is worth fixing.

On the other hand, if competitors really do better on this it might be useful to ask, 'Which ones?' Once you find out, go and see how they do it (it may be easiest to copy them).

The way we think things are

Although customer perceptions are all important, they are not always accurate. So it is good to check out from an internal perspective how the firm really performs on the key issue. A case of this was a brewery that found it wasn't selling as much beer at football games as it thought it should. A survey of customers revealed that they weren't going to the refreshment stands because they thought the wait in line was 15 minutes (and they might miss something). A company check revealed it was only five.

If it is found that customer perceptions are inaccurate, it may be useful to see if some sort of promotion (e.g. advertising, salesmanship or public relations) might convince them of their error. This is likely to take a very long time if it works at all, but is worth checking. However, if customers are either right about the issue or stubborn about their incorrect attitudes the next question becomes whether the problem is worth fixing.

There are times when the cost of fixing a problem may well exceed the value of so doing to the firm. So it is useful to see what real lost revenues have been traced to the barrier. Don't just look at a one-time sale. But if a customer has been/may be lost due to an issue, multiply his/her normal average purchases per year times 10 years (the average shelf life of a customer). And consider what we may be losing from those customers we have never served (perhaps because of this barrier), but would like to. If the problem now seems worth fixing, go on to the next section.

Step 4: Determine who's involved.

As discussed in the book, it is rare that any one person or functional area can single-handedly be responsible for a barrier. So it is important to determine all possible influences (no matter how small). One way to do this is to ask what functional areas have any direct or indirect part in 'the way things are' for customers. A good way to do this is to track physical movement of the product through the firm or to track the paperwork attached to the sale of a product or service through the firm. If a product or service has either moved physically or had paperwork which passed through a functional area, it is a fair bet that area may have some influence on a situation.

Another good way is to see what person or functional area would normally be 'blamed' for the barrier (in the absence of other input). Ask them who else has a hand in the situation. They will frequently be quite anxious to share information.

Once all parts of the firm who could have any direct or indirect responsibility are isolated, see if they are all included on your team. If not, make sure they are. Then ask each area to discuss in a 'no blame' atmosphere what they think would be a good fix.

Step 5: Zero in on causes.

Generally, when a firm is not getting things to the point where customers think they should be, either policy, performance or resources (perhaps some combination) is responsible.

Policy/performance

At this point track through the system whether things are not happening because some policy is wrong or non-existent, or whether existing policies are not being carried out. A case of the first was seen when a policy requiring a purchase order was keeping orders from moving through dispatch. Dispatch got blamed, when it was actually the accounting department that made this policy. A case of a non-existent policy was a petrol station which got complaints that staff seemed cold or unfriendly. It turned out nobody had told them they were to talk to customers.

A good example of a 'performance' problem was a graduate school that started receiving complaints about the quality of its teaching materials..It turned out that there was a policy setting standards, but staff weren't carrying it out.

Often it may be that a 'people' issue is present—for instance, somebody isn't doing their job to their own area's standards. Even though this could be true, it is probably less inflammatory to call it a 'performance' problem and let the functional area concerned deal with the problem.

However, before pointing any fingers, precisely document specific times when a policy was not carried out. It makes a much more powerful case to say that, 'On June 3, 8, 11 and 16 orders left late in violation of our policy' than to say 'Orders never leave on time'. Should you use the latter approach—and somebody show occasions when they left on time—your credibility will be gone. Game over!

If the problem is an existing policy that seems wrong, it is useful to find out whose it is, why it is there and whether it can be changed. On the other hand, if there seems to be no policy existing, find out whose functional area is involved, and what would be needed to fix the situation. Are they willing to do this? Why/why not?

Resources
Finally, there may be additional resources required (whether policies exist or not). A resource can be anything which costs money. It may be a training program, a physical item like equipment, or even staff. Normally there are lots of things which could help. Find out all the alternatives and determine which is the best (least worst) combination.

By this point a clear pattern should be emerging. Try to get group consensus on what it is. Then start writing it up into some sort of action plan.

Step 6: Write up an action plan.
In this plan your group will need to summarise who will do what by what time and to what degree (e.g. how far will they go in producing results? For example, do you want a 1-day order turn around, a 2-day, and so forth?). As discussed in the book, an important part of any plan will be monitoring to make sure it works. Be sure to explain how you will do this, and what you will adjust if things aren't working as planned. Also be sure to nail down 'what's in it for us?' if the plan works.

Step 7: Consequences
A wise person once said, 'If somebody doesn't get paid for doing something, they generally stop doing it'. Suppose your plan works. How will you make sure some reward gets to those who have helped it to do so? Does this reward sound enough? How will you determine who gets it? Good luck on this one!

Step 8: Costs
By this point a cost-benefit analysis should be possible. Would a reasonable person think the plan will pay for itself quickly enough?

If so, choose somebody to write it up and submit it.

Step 9: Plan approval
Often a number of different people will need to agree to your plan, particularly if it involves establishing/altering policy in a number of areas or requires serious money. Find out whose cooperation will be necessary, and determine how and when you will get it.

Assuming approval is given ...

Step 10: Rewards

If the plan is successful, make sure any promised rewards happen. Or, if people let the side down, it may be necessary to make sure promised negative outcomes occur. If they don't, no future plan is likely to be made, or to be implemented if it is.

14

Steps to staff survival and success

TIME-TESTED TIPS FOR TAKING THE MESSAGE TO THE TROOPS

Employees do self-destructive things because they don't know why they *shouldn't*. So all of the insights of this book are useless unless some way is found to get them to *every* staff member. In this chapter a quarter of a century's experience in reconstructing cultures in customer-centred directions will be outlined, so your employer can do the same.

Getting the process right

The seminar on which this book is based has been given some 500 times over the last 25 years. From this experience it has been found that there are a number of different levels of knowledge that must be communicated—and some approaches seem to work better than others for so doing.

For smaller firms some of the steps can be combined, but an approach covering each of these for larger employers will be outlined so that every phase is understood. Tips for making each step work more smoothly will be provided, as well as some at the end that will apply to the entire process.

Step 1 (optional): Establish the need for a change.

Some customer service training is set off by a noticeable problem (e.g. horrible results on a customer survey, media disaster, loss of major customers). If so management buy-in is probably assured.

If not, it is common for executives and staff to refuse to accept that *their* employees could *ever* give bad customer service. This optimism is usually misplaced!

One way to show how badly needed any training and change may be is to conduct a 'mystery shop'. What this means is that a form to evaluate the quality of sales/customer service is developed and someone pretending to be a very desirable customer drops by several outlets and records/reports what happened. This works particularly well if some provider is represented at several locations, and can offer even more insights if competitors are *also* shopped.

Executives are usually shocked by what is discovered. For it normally suggests not only that customer service is worse or varies much more than was expected, but also may point out specific areas where a provider is deficient in terms of the TASK barriers.

Tip: Be careful about how mystery shopping is done.

It is *not* a good idea to use some existing employee as a mystery shopper. There are much better ways (private firms, friends, etc.) to do a mystery shop. Any employee who does it (in the mistaken belief it will save money) will be known forever more as 'the corporate spy/snoop/fink'. Beyond that, it *is* a good idea to make sure the CEO has given permission for any mystery shopping before it takes place. Otherwise, managers for the areas shopped may be very angry. (On the other hand it may not be a good idea to let lower level managers know what's happening before the shop takes place—corporate 'jungle drums' beat very quickly!)

Tip: Report mystery shop results very carefully.

Because of the way mystery shopping is done, it represents rather a 'snap shot' of any given outlet on any given day, and the mystery shopper may be able to visit only a relatively small number of the total outlets. There is no way this can be treated as typical for either that particular outlet or the employer in general, and one may expect staff to defend themselves by pointing this out.

It is a better idea to summarise the data and treat what is found as an 'early warning' of *possible* trouble. (Classical market researchers are fussy about getting a 'statistically random sample', but it still must be said that the total number of observations doesn't need to be particularly great. Unless something is awfully unusual about a sample, after seven or eight visits the mystery shopper knows 'where all the bodies are buried'. And the numbers stay the same from then on.)

Finally, it is generally a bad idea to release any individual outlet's findings to them, rather than just summarising the data. Though they may say they want to 'see where we went wrong', what they generally do is to try to channel the findings through the 'reality versus perception' argument outlined in the last chapter—and dispute them. This undermines the credibility of the whole process and does little good.

Tip: Don't punish anybody this time.

This is linked to the preceding thoughts. One observation at one point in time without any prior training is bound to get gross results. So it would be unfair to punish anyone at this point. However, it doesn't hurt to intimate that the mystery shopping *may* go on, and future failure to produce results *will* cause action to be taken. This establishes the essential 'visibility' section of a barrier-fighting system.

Step 2: The basics

The foundation of every customer-centred culture is employer-wide understanding of why such a focus is *personally* good for every employee, each of whom will have a role in achieving it. This requires making sure every single employee understands the following:

- The minute anyone works for an organisation their personal fortunes are wound up with that of their employer. (They don't work *for* their employer ... they *are* their employer.)
- All employers will be judged by *financial* terms, the benchmarks for which are beyond any employer's control.
- If these financials are not 'right' everything that happens to employees *will* be painful (e.g. going out of business, being merged/taken over, being the subject of undue cost-cutting).
- The best way to produce healthy financials is marketing, which builds revenue instead of cutting (employee) costs.
- Marketing doesn't make people buy things/be satisfied; all it does is take away the things called barriers that keep people from buying/being satisfied.
- Whoever has the fewest barriers wins.
- There is no *necessary* employee who cannot produce a barrier.
- *Everybody is a part of marketing/customer service.*

Tip: Keep the objective of the 'basics' in mind.

The purpose of all the preceding education is to get *every* employee to make the one personal commitment essential to marketing/customer centred success:

I agree to give up my 'God-given' rights to control what I do,
as much as my conscience allows.

What each section of this commitment means will next be explored.

... 'God-given' rights to control ...

When any employee has held any job for any length of time they begin to believe they have a 'God-given' right to keep on doing the same job in the same way, under the same circumstances *forever*. If every employee believes that, do you know what can be said of the outfit they *all* work for?—they're doomed!

Employers are the sum total of what *each* of their employees is willing to do as an individual. If none of these individuals is willing to change what *they* do, *their employer* can't change what it does. And when 'customers' *do* change their minds about what they want done, the employer will fail. This cannot be allowed to continue either for working-level staff or for people at the highest reaches of authority.

... what I do ...

This is comprised of all the details that make up each employee's job. The objective of education contained within 'the basics' is to turn attitudes around until each staff member would agree with the following:

I will do whatever I must do to get the 'business'.

Doing whatever must be done to get the 'business' will always involve one (or more) of three things suggested by the 'personal commitment'. They are:
- doing a different job;
- doing the same job in a different manner; or
- doing the same job in the same manner under different conditions (or some combination of the three).

Doing a *different job* may mean giving up a life-long career and starting out on something new. This was certainly true for one person growing up on a working ranch in the American West. It turned out that there wasn't much of a demand for the cowboy skills he had. So off he went to hotel school and learned how the hospitality industry works.

If he had been allowed to stay in his old job, the ranch would probably have gone under. As it is, he now manages one of the most successful 'dude ranch-resorts' in America.

Doing the *same job in a different manner* has struck almost everybody. A good example is the advent of laser surgery to correct eye problems. If patients now

246

demand the advantages offered by a surgical fix for their vision, eye doctors have a choice of complying or watching (!) their jobs disappear.

Doing the *same job in the same manner under different circumstances* is no easier. Some staff within a number of universities are learning they can no longer teach only Monday to Thursday during the middle of the day. If students want lectures at nights and weekends, or in remote locations, teachers will have to offer them or watch their ivory towers be pulled down, brick by brick.

Although flexibility is a fine thing, there is a limit to how far along this path any employee should go. And it is important that any education indicate what this is.

Tip: Make ethical issues a part of any training.

... as much as my conscience allows ...

Returning to the *personal* customer service commitment, what this section signals is that there *must always be a limit* to change, beyond which some employees cannot—and should not—go. What creates a need for this limit is the reality that, when marketing through minimising barriers to a consumer whose *selfishness is insatiable*, there *does* come a point one should not go beyond.

This happens when what started out as an economic employer issue becomes a highly personal one, because some employee is asked to carry it out, but can't. A good way to see how this could occur is through constructing an extreme case.

Imagine that some consumer walked into your organisation who, by throwing their 'business' to your employer (whatever that means for you), could double that employer's total revenue for the year.

(With apologies to Dr. Seuss's *Green Eggs and Ham*) *Would you/could you* give them a good sales pitch? Most would, but some would say, 'Oh, but don't ask *me* to do it. I don't like meeting the public'.

Would you/could you take them out to dinner at the close of the business day?—a normal business expectation. Most would, but some would say, 'Oh no, I've got to get home to my family'.

Would you/could you not only 'dine' them, but also wine them and dine them with large amounts of liquor, until the wee small hours of the morning? Most would, but some would say, 'Oh no, on a moral or personal choice basis I couldn't do that'.

Would you/could you do all of the above and find this client companionship of the preferred sex of a paid nature (if you catch my drift!) in the wee small hours of the morning? Some would, but others would say, 'Oh no, on a moral or personal choice basis I could never do that'.

Would you/could you lie, bribe, steal, commit murder, etc.?

Tip: There are limits!

It seems pretty clear that somewhere along this spectrum of drinking/lying/murder most would get off somewhere. And we would find out how committed to one's employer that employee really was!

It is not the intent of this book to determine for others where they should 'get off this train'. But it is important to realise that sometimes one must refuse change—or the job connected with it.

Certainly some workers have seen this. One student refused employment with a company that sold trailers to cross-country truckers. He was told he would be expected to take these people out drinking, but was a teetotaller Christian who knew he couldn't.

Churches struggle with this one too. Some Christian churches realise that the behaviours expected of their members can be barriers to increasing membership. But not requiring these behaviours (e.g. 'it's okay to sin'—see Chapter 8) demands moral compromise that they cannot accept.

Government employees and politicians can't get off the hook, either. How far they can go towards increasing their appeal to voters must often be limited by their own sense of right and wrong. There are no easy answers.

Tip: Personal ethics are not just 'warm fuzzies'.

If any employee goes beyond the 'point of no return' for him or her, that employee has a good chance of becoming a suicidal employee. So if an employee can't do something required by the job, they may have to request re-assignment or go elsewhere rather than becoming worthless to themselves and/or the employer. Fortunately, such a radical move is seldom necessary.

Tip: Seldom are ethical issues the real source of resistance.

Despite protests to the contrary, most employee resistance to what is asked tends not to be based upon ethical considerations but rather the issues already discussed (e.g. extra work, reluctance to change). It is just such issues that this book is intended to counter.

Only when these issues *have* been countered—and employees are willing to do whatever they must do to get the 'business' for their own good—can a lasting platform providing survival be present. At this point it is possible to go on to step 3.

Step 3: Build employee sensitivity to barriers.

Once 'the hearts and minds' of employees are won, it becomes essential to channel their enthusiasm in a positive direction. Some may be able to understand the idea of barriers for themselves. Others may need some help.

One approach is to let staff read this book and work through action exercise 10.1. Another approach is for managers to discuss with staff in some work area the sort of barriers most frequently causing trouble.

Tip: *Let staff visualise barriers.*

It is said 'a picture is worth a thousand words'. One way to provide staff with pictures of typical barriers is to let employees play the role of customers in a little skit designed to show the frustrations that come from poor customer service, then discuss it. Still another is to use an excellent video entitled, *Who Killed the Customer?* This may be available from a video supply firm.

What this video does is to offer a professionally acted performance of a firm full of well-meaning employees who—barrier by barrier—drive away a good customer. No employee who watches it can stop squirming, for they see themselves on the screen. Using the 'whispers' listed in action exercise 10.1 (and asking staff to identify them) with this video can highlight the forms most barriers take. (Almost every 'whisper' is portrayed on the video.) Once staff understand barriers, it is important to let them act on their knowledge.

Step 4: Let employees save themselves.

Employees are not fools! Once they understand how destructive barriers are to *their own* welfare, they can be expected to respond—and they will! Make sure your employer doesn't stop this healthy process.

Tip: *Quiet is bad.*

One way to tell whether a 'barrier-receptive' environment has been set up is to see what happens following any barrier-based training. If things stay quiet, something is wrong. Nobody is so good that *none* of their staff knows of *anything* that could be done better. Something is holding them back. Here are typical problems.

Tip: *Get rid of the notion that employees who report barriers are trouble-makers.*

Barriers always involve situations in which somebody has made mistakes. Having this pointed out is usually threatening. It is therefore important to make clear that the reporting of barriers is a *helpful process* essential to all. A receptive management attitude to staff that report barriers will be critical. At a minimum this will require the courtesy of thanking people who go to the effort of telling somebody about what they see as a barrier. Better still would be some sort of reward.

Tip: *Make sure no barriers reported by staff result in punishing another employee.*

249

As has already been discussed, punishing someone for a barrier the first time it is found is a very bad idea. Fear of this will really keep people from coming forward. A better way is to take an educational approach. An educational approach implies that people cannot be held accountable for any mistakes made *before* receiving training related to any barrier. This is much easier for everyone to take.

The completion of such education also sets a *firm starting point* for no longer tolerating behaviours that threaten the employer. And it introduces a new term, barriers, to be used when describing these behaviours.

In fact, that is one of the main strengths of the barrier approach. For it seems much less threatening to have someone ask:

Friends, why are we allowing this barrier that threatens all of us?

than:

Why is 'so-and-so' messing up? Boy, are they in trouble!

Tip: Set up a system for employees to report barriers.

One way to get staff to report barriers is to hold a work-group meeting (seven to ten employees works well) following any barrier-based training. And simply ask this group, 'Well, we all now know what barriers are. What keeps you from delivering great customer service?' (Then shut up and listen!) It pays to have a non-threatening member of management present (someone from human resources/personnel is a good choice) to record what is said.

Another is for managers to encourage people who feel they face barriers in their work to come and see them personally. As one owner of a motorcycle shop reported:

My door swung off the hinges. I was amazed at how many barriers we had. And my employees were more than willing to report them.

Of course, getting employees to report barriers is only a first step. Something must then be done about them.

Tip: Set up a system for using employee inputs.

How to deal with a barrier has been discussed in general terms in the previous chapter. However, equally important as what is done about any *single* barrier is the establishment of a system for responding to *all* barriers. Employees who go to the effort of reporting barriers will soon stop coming if they think nothing is going to be done. Two approaches work well to solve this problem.

A government employer who used the work-group system for reporting barriers created one. He required the person who recorded the group inputs to set up a four-column sheet of paper (running lengthwise) in line-item format. One column was the barrier, a second was the manager in charge of the area responsible for it, the third was a date by which that area was to have taken action—either by reporting how it was resolved or why it couldn't be eliminated—and a final column showing what action had been taken. This was updated regularly.

This really worked. Done in this way the employer produced 10 pages of line items. As reported by the CEO:

What was spooky about this is that most of these were really good stuff—and we didn't know about them ... but they did.

This technique was so effective that surveys of employee job satisfaction went from 'so-so' to 'This is a *great* place to work' in one calendar year. And the employer was also named 'the most effective government operation' in the state in which it was located.

A chain of over 100 rest homes tried another technique. They set up what they called a 'matrix' form of management. After receiving barrier-based training, this chain established a policy whereby staff could report a barrier to their immediate manager. If they felt nothing seemed to be happening, they had the phone number (and right to call) their manager's manager. If this didn't satisfy them they could call the next manager up the chain of command ... eventually leading all the way to the CEO.

The CEO reported that rarely did a staff member have to go all the way to his office. And when they did, it usually needed his attention. A case of this occurred when some minimum wage-caregiver phoned him to inquire, 'Why the heck can't we get some clean towels in Milwaukee?'

This caused him to look into the situation and say to a lower level manager, 'Well, why don't we have clean towels in Milwaukee?' And they got those clean towels.

The reason this didn't happen often was that managers all the way through the chain knew their superiors would hear about it if they didn't respond correctly the first time. So they usually did! This chain set profit records following the adoption of such a system. Still, nothing lasts forever.

Step 5: Begin to initiate consequences.

Once all of the preceding has been done, it is important to begin monitoring customer service performance, and to respond accordingly. The best way to do this is through rewards for noticeably good customer performance, but this may not always be enough.

Tip: Not everybody will respond.

Experience suggests that, following some sort of customer service program, staff will probably respond with actions that place them in one of three groups (which may not be equal in size).

One group will take everything that is said, run with it, and begin generating marketing/customer service thoughts of their own. For this reason one can usually expect an immediate improvement as this bunch begins to deliver the sort of service they (probably) always wanted to. What happens here is that the program gives them both permission and encouragement so to do.

A second group are more sleepy. They will say, 'Wasn't that great?' and then wait for somebody to tell them what to do. Formal programs of action borrowed from the first troupe may help with this bunch.

Finally, there will usually be a third group who will not only reject the message, but actually fight tooth-and-nail doing anything related to it. This opposition may be hidden or visible. If visible, it probably means the person doing it thinks they are 'above' marketing or customer service—and are invulnerable. If this opinion is not changed, others will copy it.

Tip: Sometimes one has little choice but to do something drastic.

I wish I had something more encouraging to say. But my own experience suggests that, if a customer service program accompanied by counselling and personal attention doesn't change a negative attitude, the only way to keep it from infecting the entire employer is to start monitoring everybody's customer service, focus on the worst/most visible cases of defiance, and terminate their employment. Those who thought the same way this person (or persons) did may suddenly change. However, apathy and opposition are not the only enemies of a customer service culture.

Step 6: Follow-up programs

It is true that all people do tend to 'run down' over time. And nowhere is this more apparent than in the area of customer service. It is essential that the topic be brought up with lower level staff at least every 3 months. People at the middle management level or higher generally benefit from workshops held at least once a year.

In such a setting functional areas that almost never see each other—let alone talk to each other—can be forced to both work and play together. This generally benefits everybody, and it is not particularly expensive.

If all of the preceding are done at each step, it may be expected that strong results will be produced. However, over and above these individual suggestions, there are some ways to make the total process work better.

Ways to make barrier-based education work better

Tip: Provide visible top-level support.

Both managers and employees will take necessary messages on board more readily if they know people at the top are 100% behind the program—and will tolerate little opposition. Otherwise, it may take quite a while for anything to happen as people figure 'this will blow over'. A good way to keep this from happening is to encourage the CEO (if possible) to introduce the program and give a strong message of support for it.

Tip: Involve everybody.

As used here, 'everybody' includes *all* employees—owners, workers and managers—because there are no *necessary* employees who cannot directly or indirectly produce barriers. As a rule of thumb, if anybody at any level doesn't get to hear thoughts like those in this book, they are *exactly* the ones who *will* make a barrier.

Tip: Make sure all *levels* of *employees are* seen to be participating equally.

Don't ever assume *any* employee at *any* level is 'too knowledgeable', 'too high up', or 'too important' to be involved. The people at higher levels sometimes need to have this explained to them. The explanations I have found useful for this are as follows.

Explanation 1: The ideas of *When customers think we don't care* are based upon beliefs that tend to be new to all.

Since many of these post-modernist ideas would be 'new' even to marketing academics, it is unlikely that anyone, regardless of their education, will have heard *all* of them before.

Explanation 2: Managers and owners can be responsible for just as many barriers as workers.

Sometimes employees do stupid things because they have been told to do them by a management that doesn't know any better, or thinks it can somehow 'pull the wool' over workers' (or customers') eyes. This never works, and high-level managers need to know why.

Explanation 3: Employees take education about their employer more seriously if the management is also seen to be involved/supporting it.

To some extent this has already been discussed regarding the very top level (e.g. CEO support). But one additional thing I have noticed about 'barrier' education is: 'The troops take better notes when their managers are present'. From the front of the room I can usually tell whether or not the program is going to work. It *will* work if the managers (from the top down) are visibly receiving the same education as the workers—and are being affected by it. If this isn't the case, the employees don't seem to get very excited. How can workers take the program seriously if their leaders don't?

What this can mean is that some managers may sit through the program more than once. This is not necessarily bad. The all-time champion is one postal service manager who listened to the basic program eight times. By the end he was mouthing the punch lines to my jokes! He didn't seem to find this a waste of time, but instead reported:

Every time you sit through this program you hear something new. Repetition doesn't seem to hurt at all.

It is good that such repetition doesn't hurt, for the next tip often requires it.

Tip: *Make sure middle managers are motivated to send all their people.*

Since the education requires *everyone* to be involved, it is important that *all attend it*. This isn't easy to achieve. As discussed in earlier chapters, many managers see the program as being one on *classical* customer service or marketing *only*. Not having been told about post-modernist marketing, they assume *their* employees are not involved in either activity, so they won't send them. Top management can try to counter this by requiring attendance, but this seems at odds with any team spirit the program is trying to build.

But if lower level managers *have* seen the program, the following reaction is typical:

Golly, I wish 'old Charlie' could have seen this.

Every employer in the world seems to have an 'old Charlie' (or 'Charlene') who is their personal 'suicidal employee'. If managers have seen the program first, they can understand how it applies to all employees (including theirs). And they can get excited about what it might do *for them* with employees that are particularly difficult.

So the approach that seems to work best with larger organisations is to have top management review a summary of the program first. Then show it to middle managers, and finally ask lower level managers *and* employees to participate in it together.

Tip: Don't let anybody miss out—even indirectly.

If anybody is missed out in this process (those absent and new-hires), it helps if a way is found to them as well (see the video culture changing kit offered on page 287). For this means everybody starts out with the same foundation.

If all these steps are taken the employees should be ready to make the most of any education. The next tip suggests what this education should be like.

Tip: Make sure any education covers the basics in an engaging manner.

'Engaging' education is learning that encourages people to take part. This means it must:
- be impartial;
- be short;
- be 'fun';
- have some incentive for attendance; and
- be understandable by all.

Be impartial
If the program seems to take the management side too much it will be rejected as 'propaganda'. And if it takes the workers' side too much 'owners' and/or managers will not use it.

Be short
The education cannot take too long. Employee time is expensive when measured in financial terms (if done during working hours) or in personal ones (if done after-hours). This is why 'the basics' of this program was first done as a 3-hour seminar (including break).

Several of my clients have tried offering the basic program in split halves (e.g. half of the employees one day, and half the next), as it makes no sense to do a program on customer service and leave no one to actually attend to customers! The second 'half' is always bigger. The employees come to hear the jokes and see the show.

Or one could ask employees to read this book and then spread out the exercises over a number of weeks. This seems the maximum time employees and/or employers are willing to invest in *any* education.

Be fun
It helps if the program is 'funny' or 'fun' to listen to. This not only gentles over some of the harsh messages, it also encourages attendance. People won't sit and

listen to dull lectures. Being humorous is not the only way to offer an incentive for attendance. Another is to put on something like a free meal or drinks in conjunction with it.

In order to cut costs many clients have offered the program after working hours on a non-overtime basis. They either serve a buffet dinner (before) or drinks (afterwards)—sometimes both—to make up for this unpaid attendance. This seems to work.

Tip: *Find a qualified outsider to deliver the 'basics'.*

One of my clients once summed this one up by saying:

Rich, I don't know why it is. But you tell my employees the same kinds of things that I do, and they listen to you, but not to me.

This is not pointed out just to promote myself. If this book is successful there will soon be others doing the same thing (sigh!). Neither is it due to any special magic. Rather, it is because of a number of very good reasons for using a qualified outsider to get the job done.

Reason 1: Many of the messages are extremely threatening.

Employees have to be informed that if they allow too many barriers they are going to lose their jobs. When told this by a manager, workers may respond with actions ranging from anger to strikes.

An airline reservations manager found this out to her regret. She noticed her employees were all taking their breaks at the same time, thereby leaving the phones unanswered. To correct this she put up a big sign saying, 'Keep the phones answered ... No customers—no jobs'. She had a full-scale union uprising within the hour.

Having a qualified outsider deliver harsh messages seems to work without getting anybody annoyed. The basic program on which this book is based has already been delivered to over 40 000 employees in many industries that are characterised by aggressive unions. Not once has a union ever formally objected (so far!).

Reason 2: It avoids destructive rumours.

As the messages required *do* involve survival, having an outsider deliver them in a relatively standard format (some terms have to be tailored to different audiences) clearly signals they do not apply to the receiving employer *only*. Neither do they suggest this employer is in particularly desperate straits that require unusual action. Without this 'canned' approach such messages may cause more trouble than they are worth. For they can start off rumours in an organisation that usually had more than enough to begin with.

One auto firm found having managers even *suggest* the necessity of cutting costs had employees panicking. They all assumed the firm was about to go under and started looking for new jobs. In fact nothing of the sort was even likely, at least not until their best employees started leaving.

Reason 3: It establishes credibility.

If the presenter is just some average 'Joe' or 'Josephine', why should the employees believe him or her? Having some sort of credentials as an 'expert' *does* make the message seem truthful, as long as these and the presentation are not off-putting. One manager of a rubber products company found this out when he tried to tell his employees some basic facts about marketing. He practically got hooted off the stage.

Reason 4: It gives an air of impartiality.

As stated earlier, for the basic barrier message to be effective, it must be applied to *all* employees equally. If workers think the message is just 'some sort of company line', they will reject it as propaganda. Bringing in an outsider who *does* try to let any axes 'cut both ways' goes a long way to assuring people they are not being 'hustled'.

Tip: Think of all customer service education as a continuous process.

Although it is understandable that humans normally desire closure, customer service training doesn't work like that. One can never state with finality, 'Well, we got that one done. Now, what will we do next?' Rather, it can be expected that the process of staff customer service education can never end—unless the employer does.

This is well represented by Figure 14.1. Although this chart symbolises what is necessary for larger employers, the basic issues are the same for all. The only things that really change are the number of people concerned and the layers involved.

Figure 14.1 does a good job of summarising both this chapter and the ones that preceded it. It shows the step-by-step process necessary for effective change and an order of presentation for many of the exercises (already introduced) that makes sense. By being presented as a loop, it shows that this process is a continuous one which should go on forever.

Figure 14.1 also underscores a point made earlier. Effecting a complete customer-centred focus within any employer is best seen as a partnership between the employer and a skilled outsider, with each partner doing those sections which they can perform most efficiently. Those areas that a client can

257

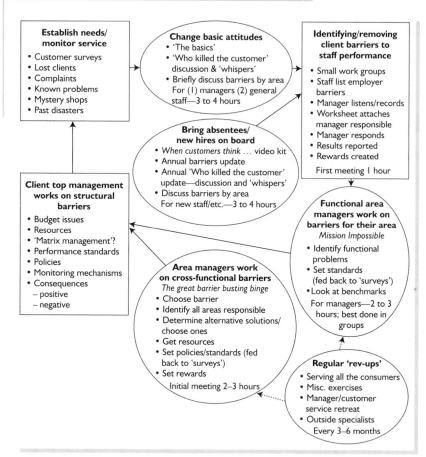

Figure 14.1 How to build better customer service—a step-by-step process

perform most effectively are within a square. Those best left to an outsider are within an ellipse. Those that could be shared have both of these.

If all of the preceding steps and tips are kept in mind, the messages delivered to staff should produce very positive results. That brings up one remaining question.

Why not get started?

An old Chinese proverb states, 'The longest journey begins with the first step'. That applies to changing the culture of your employer as well. However, sometimes taking that step can seem rather threatening—for the changes suggested are enormous. The next (and last) chapter will explore why these changes *will* work—and should be made.

ACTION SUMMARY

If barrier-based marketing is to work, an organisation must get *all* employees to 'pull' together for the benefit of all by using the insights of this book.

Education is the best way to do this. A quarter of a century's experience has shown that not only are a number of steps essential to this education process, but also that there are ways to make each of the steps within it more effective.

Step 1 (optional): Establish the need for a change.

Unless there has been evidence to the contrary, many managers and staff won't believe their customer service is other than perfect. One way to challenge this (usually) mistaken belief is through a process called 'mystery shopping' in which mock customers pay outlets a visit. This tool and its results must be handled very carefully to get the most value from it.

Step 2: The basics

Getting employees to commit to better customer service requires convincing them that their fortunes are wound up with that of their employer, who will be judged by financial standards which—if not 'right'— will result in personally painful outcomes. From an employee viewpoint, marketing is the best way to produce healthy financials, while a post-modernist/barrier-based approach to marketing shows that every staff member can produce a barrier and is, therefore, a part of marketing.

The objective of basic training is to encourage staff flexibility through a *personal* commitment to do whatever is required for the welfare of their employer, until ethical considerations indicate that they shouldn't.

Step 3: Build employee sensitivity to barriers.

Employees must be able to respond to barriers when they occur through general staff sensitivity to the forms they take. There are a number of ways to produce this sensitivity.

Step 4: Let employees save themselves.

Once employees understand how important self-destructive barriers are to their personal welfare, and the forms they take, they *should* respond. Employers can encourage this response by refusing to punish for barriers not the object of prior training, altering perceptions that make reporting barriers the same as complaining, and setting up a system for reporting/acting on employee-suggested barriers.

259

Step 5: Begin to initiate consequences.

Following customer service training it is important to make sure that good performances are rewarded—and bad ones not ignored. Response to a program will break itself into three groups: (1) some will take everything said and run with it; (2) some will wait to be told what to do; and (3) some will either passively or visibly fight any change. Members of this last group can't be ignored, and the only way to change their attitude may be to change their employment.

Step 6: Follow-up programs

Without constant reinforcement a customer-centred focus is soon lost. It is important to make sure that an emphasis on this element is repeated with both management and staff.

Tips for improving all barrier-based education

The overall process for teaching employees what they need to know in order to survive can be made to work better by top-level support, involving every employee, making sure all levels of staff participate in training, implementing education from the top down, making sure all education is presented in an engaging manner, having a qualified outsider deliver basic messages, and viewing customer-service training as a continuous process.

THE BOTTOM LINE

Creating a customer-centred culture requires delivering the post-modernist, barrier-based message to staff in a suitable manner. If this is done the chances of both the message and your employer surviving increase dramatically.

ACTION EXERCISE 14.1

Who's a part of marketing?—everybody!

For: Employees at all levels   **Format:** Small groups
Materials required: Pencils and instructions
Objective: To show that all necessary employees are a part of marketing, as they can directly or indirectly produce barriers

Instructions

In this chapter—and earlier ones—it was said that there is no necessary employee who is *not* a part of marketing, because all such employees can directly or indirectly produce barriers. Today we will see how this works.

Form into groups ... then:

You will be assigned one of the following employee groups who normally might not be considered a part of marketing. In the first 15 minutes you are to discuss in your group what barriers these 'non-marketing' employees might produce and how. Some hints to start your thinking will be given. It is hoped you will expand on these and come up with a list of many more thoughts of your own.

The groups with which you are to work are as follows:

1 The accountants who do your organisation's financial statements. (*Hint*: Think about late billings, incorrect billings, unwillingness to grant credit, mistakes on payrolls, etc.)
2 'Coldly professional' nurses working in a health-care organisation. (*Hint*: Have you ever been treated by someone like this? Think about waking you up to take a sleeping pill, refusal to talk with the family, too rigid enforcement of rules, etc.)
3 Truck drivers who drive an organisation's (employer-identified) trucks. (*Hint*: Think about bad driving, causing accidents, refusing to move over on two-lane highways, etc.)
4 People who work on the loading docks shipping an organisation's materials. (*Hint*: Think about late deliveries, getting shipments 'wrong', packing goods so poorly they arrive damaged, etc.)
5 Members in the armed forces in uniform in town, or any employees whose uniform makes their employer obvious. (*Hint*: Think about drunken behaviour, looking sloppy, being discourteous, etc.)
6 Repair technicians working for the service department of some organisation. (*Hint*: Think about poor work that must be redone, failing to get things finished on time, bad attitudes in answering questions, etc.)

Then be prepared to share your answers.

Conclusion

Any necessary employee of *any* organisation can produce barriers that threaten his or her job. We all need to keep this in mind on a daily basis. All the 'marketing' in the world cannot save us from ourselves if we don't.

ACTION EXERCISE 14.2

Taking the mystery out of mystery shopping

For: Employees at all levels
Format: Small groups (at least 2 hours may be needed)
Materials required: Pencils and instructions
Objective: To devise a means of detecting our own barriers

Instructions

In this chapter a concept called 'mystery shopping' was discussed. What this means is developing a form to evaluate the quality of sales/customer service and having someone pretending to be a very desirable customer dropping by several outlets and recording/reporting what happened. Today we will see how this could be applied to us.

Form into groups of workers who are employed in one particular area.

1 Then for your own area (telephone receptionists will be used as an example) discuss what behaviours customers might consider to be barriers. Some typical items might include:
   - length of time taken to answer the phone;
   - coverage during breaks/noon hours;
   - telephone courtesy;
   - knowledge of the operator;
   - length of time on 'hold';
   - other items you might consider—be sure to come up with some.

2 Develop these behaviours into questions that could go on a questionnaire. For instance:
   - How many rings did it take to have the phone answered? (length of time in rings)
   - Is our coverage the same during noon hours and morning/afternoon breaks? (Yes/No)
   - How would you rate the courtesy of our operators? (Excellent/Good/Poor)

3 Then be prepared to share your answers, which could be combined with other work areas to produce a 'mystery shopper' form for your employer.

4 Discuss whether you think your employer should be 'mystery shopped'. (Why/Why not?)

5 How would you suggest this be done?

6 What should be done with any results?

Conclusion

We must all be constantly on the lookout for job-destroying barriers. Sometimes an outside viewpoint is a good way to see them. And when these are pointed out, the results should be helpful, not harmful.

15

Of confidence, costs and caring customer service

WHY AND HOW TO BECOME A POST-MODERNIST MARVEL

Permanently fixing customer service problems does not mean 'painting over them', but rather blowing up traditional structures and starting over. Because what is required is new, beginning the process can seem daunting. Here is why and how to do it.

It's different, but is it better?

Although a post-modernist can use all classical marketing/customer service concepts, the pieces are put together in a very different way. Those faced with so many new ideas may rightfully be concerned about whether it is worth doing. Normally, the way to settle such concerns is through a 'cost-benefits' analysis. Because the post-modernist approach has so much going for it, this approach will be turned around.

A 'benefits-cost' analysis

A good way to proceed is to examine each part of the post-modernist model picture in Figure 15.1 and highlight not only why it is different, but also summarise what benefits may come from adopting this unique viewpoint. Although these have mostly been covered before, it is not a bad idea to assemble them all in one place. We shall start at the bottom and work up.

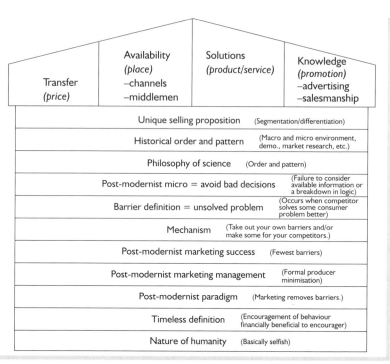

Figure 15.1 Rebuilding the House of Marketing/Customer Service—a post-modernist approach

Nature of humanity is selfish

Whether or not they wish to admit it (somehow, knowing post-modernists, I doubt they will!), a post-modernist approach implies a different answer to the question, 'What is basic human nature?' Though most other approaches assume universal human mobility, this one requires the opposite, though doesn't devalue humanity in any way by so doing. This produces a number of benefits and understandings not available in any other way (see Table 15.1).

Timeless definition of marketing— encouragement of behaviour financially beneficial to the encourager

Past definitions of marketing have often done more harm than good. They have focused on marketing as it was practised then, and thereby excluded people to whom the discipline would some day be offered. The timeless definition doesn't do this, and thereby offers these advantages:

Table 15.1 Benefits and understandings of the 'selfish human nature' approach

In general	For workers	For managers/owners
• Squares with reality. • Doesn't devalue humanity. • Fits into one of world's great religions. • Makes people more productive. • Makes for better decisions. • Provides more information. • Creates accepting atmosphere. • Encourages working together. • Prevents in-fighting. • Is an all-new approach!	• Allows *real* motives to be discussed. • Focuses attention on most important motivator (making a living). • Identifies workers with employer. • Shows true objective of HR. • Exposes suicidal employees. • Shows how to deal with these. • Makes employer financial motives more acceptable.	• Enables workers to be warned. • Exposes who's in charge. • Reveals profit motives. • Shows profit motives alike for all employers. • Shows moneymaking aims apply to workers. • Reveals penalties for poor financial performance. • Explains why new owners are no better. • Shows managers can't prevent penalties. • Focuses attention on 'a better way' (marketing).

- It shows the desired outcome of all marketing activity.
- The use of the word 'encouragement' doesn't suggest more than the discipline can do.
- It separates the discipline from other applied sciences.
- The inclusion of a financial 'string' will be useful for defeating the classic marketing paradigm.

This last point eventually leads to the creation of the post-modernist marketing paradigm.

Post-modernist paradigm of marketing— marketing doesn't make people buy things/be satisfied; all it does is take away the barriers that keep people from buying things/being satisfied

The 'Pepsi paradox', in which the ultimate power of the classical marketing paradigm is assumed to be true, shows why selfish competitor activity means that it can't be true. Rejection of this paradigm—and consideration of what remains when it is shown to be untrue—produces what has been called the post-modernist paradigm. This new paradigm and the thoughts leading to it have a number of advantages going for them (see Table 15.2).

Table 15.2 Advantages of the post-modernist marketing paradigm

In general	For non-marketers	For marketers
• Based on realistic view of human nature. • Is simple. • Easy for 'non-marketers' to internalise. • Makes no claims it can't back up. • Is culture-friendly.	• Shows that every producer markets. • Employers can only market 'well'. • Worries of 'what will people think?' are unfounded. • Removes one ethical problem. • Means marketing is not optional—unless jobs are.	• Makes explaining marketing concepts easy. • Explains why no guarantee is possible. • Explains some troubling issues. • Is 'cutting edge'. • Is comfortable with all known theories of marketing. • Suggests possibilities for other applied sciences.

Post-modernist marketing management— formal producer minimisation of important barriers to desirable consumer behaviour

Extending the post-modernist paradigm produces the above approach to marketing management. What makes this approach unique and desirable is:

- It indicates that much of marketing's 'power' simply comes from doing in a *planned* way that which always got done accidentally.
- It shows that anyone dependent on others is a part of—and must control— this process.
- The word 'important' states that not all barriers must be dealt with (e.g. 'bothers').
- It works equally well with 'de-marketing' undesirable behaviours.
- The expansion of 'consumer' to those that are 'rarely considered' increases the reach of marketing into many diverse areas in a search for competitive advantage.

Post-modernist marketing success—the 'winning' competitor in any market arena will be that one with the fewest barriers (e.g. the 'least worst')

Extending post-modernist marketing management to what should be its logical conclusion reveals how it is attained—through having fewer barriers than competitors do. Acceptance of this conclusion produces the following positive outcomes:

- Emphasis on being 'least worst' keeps complacency about being 'the best' from stifling obvious need for improvement/change.
- The competitive 'can you top this' search-for-barriers process soon pushes the domain of marketing far beyond its classical 'promotion' limits.
- Eventually, marketing becomes 'everything' (though employers reach this realisation in stages).
- Acknowledging that outside suppliers (such as carpet installers) are seen by consumers as being at one with the basic service provider (e.g. carpet retailer) expands the reach of marketing managers into outside organisations.
- Examination of 'what's a competitor?' (e.g. 'firm/form/financial/feeling') minimises the likelihood of disastrous 'marketing myopia'.
- Being 'least worst' means the classic strategy of giving consumers 'everything' may not be necessary or desirable.

Post-modernist marketing mechanism— taking out your own barriers, or making one for a competitor by being willing (able) to do something they don't.

Being somewhat mirror images of each other, these two approaches to having fewer barriers provide the driving force behind most marketing strategies. They offer the following to whomever wishes to accept them:

- They make what needs to be done (e.g. having fewer barriers) a constant focus of staff within existing operations.
- The need to make barriers for a competitor by doing something they don't reveals a never-ending necessity for competitor information.
- A desire to do something competitors don't provides a motivator for improvement and innovation.
- What is required for a good market result may not be very much.

Post-modernist barrier definition— unsolved problem

A barrier is anything which keeps consumers from doing what producers want. Further extension of this idea shows that a barrier is an unsolved consumer problem. This makes a number of marketing concerns easier to see:

- Money is a by-product! Competitors who solve consumer problems most completely *will* make it, and recognising this produces a better vision of what must be done.
- All unsolved problems mean is 'the way things are' for producers is not the 'way things should be' for consumers.
- Looking at what consumer problems may be and breaking them into their component parts reveals what might be potential barriers.
- The 'whispers of buried barriers' so essential to finding barriers within an employer are all elements of a problem not solved, or solved better by, some competitor.

Post-modernist micro-marketing— avoiding 'bad' decisions

Post-modernist micro-marketing uses the discipline to reach goals desirable both to some organisation *and* to the marketer making the decisions. Within limitations (imposed by the marketer's needs), this requires making 'the way things are' for the marketer's employer closer to 'the way things should be' for consumers than competitors do. The only way a micro-marketer can do this is to solve problems on some consumer's behalf better than others do. This doesn't mean making decisions that 'always work out well', for this is impossible due to the inability to control competitor activity and consumer tastes.

All a post-modernist micro-marketer can do is avoid 'bad' decisions. As used here a 'bad' decision is one that fails to *consider information* one could reasonably have been expected to consider or has a *breakdown in logic* either in how information was gathered or what was done in light of it. Use of this different approach to micro-marketing leads to several useful ends:

- Admitting that marketers will not do anything they feel is 'hazardous to their health' is useful to understanding what they will/will not do.
- The only barriers that will be dealt with by a post-modernist micro-marketer are those whose payback is less than 'the period of patience' for his/her employer, which is usually culture bound.
- The standards for a 'bad' decision are those used by most professionals.

- These standards are 'all that can really be done'.
- The standards for a 'bad' decision are easy to remember and understand.
- This approach to micro-marketing is culturally inclusive.
- This approach is time-sensitive.
- The issue of 'logic' enables post-modernism to bridge back into classical marketing tools.

Post-modernist use of the philosophy of science—order-and-pattern

The basic foundation of both classical and *useful* post-modernist approaches to marketing is that there is 'order-and-pattern' beneath all human behaviour. Knowledge of this pattern enables better decisions to be reached than would otherwise be the case.

Classical marketers tend to suggest that their patterns—and the tools leading from them—are timeless. Post-modernists know this can't be true, but will sometimes admit that the ideas of classical marketing do suggest a logic useful for avoiding bad decisions either by gathering information or suggesting what to do in light of it. Recognition of this produces some desirable outcomes:

- Marketing concepts are primarily historical in that they record what was once thought true.
- The 'historical' nature of classical marketing order-and-pattern requires that caution be used when using the tools related to it.
- The recognition that marketing patterns are historical indicates a never-ending need to conduct new marketing research once it is suspected this pattern has reached its 'use-by' date.
- The admission by a post-modernist that there may be *any* kind of useful pattern (not all would!) makes understanding classical marketing easier. For everything contained within classical approaches is (1) a discussion of 'how', 'why' and 'where' various bits of information should be gathered; (2) an analysis of how to use it; or (3) suggestions about what to do once it is gathered.

Post-modernist sources of historical order and pattern—the marketing environments, demographics and market research

Linking the preceding to the micro-marketer's need to make decisions produces a useful basic understanding. This is that there are a number of ways to 'get a handle' on the history represented by classical marketing sources of order-and-pattern. What have been called the 'macro/micro' environments are generally used to suggest 'the way things should be' by looking at past experience. Demographics reveal similar patterns through statistics. Marketing research looks for these patterns either passively (through the MIS) or actively through formal market research. Keeping this perspective in mind leads to:

- understanding of how to use what otherwise can be fairly vague concepts (particularly in the case of macro/micro environments);
- the notion of managers having an 'itchy feeling' that something is keeping their employer from making money because 'the way things are' (for them) is not 'the way things should be' (for consumers) greatly clarifies the marketing research process.

Post-modernist approach to achieving a USP—segmentation/differentiation

A post-modernist has a very clear idea about how to achieve what classical marketers call a 'unique selling proposition' (USP). Keeping in mind that barrier-based success is achieved by having the fewest barriers, either by taking out one's own or making one for others, proves very compatible with classical concepts of segmentation and differentiation. Both of these are simply strategies working towards the same goal.

The way to choose between the two strategies is through using historical patterns to see which of them classical marketing suggests will be most appropriate. The post-modernist doing this enjoys the following:

- Seeing that these are *not* different strategies but rather points on a spectrum of market conditions may aid choice as to which seems best suited to the market situation.
- Understanding that the key driving factor of segmentation is to eliminate competitors by serving a market otherwise forgotten makes understanding it easier.
- Visualising what may be a good differentiating factor is helped by the notion of 'unsolved problems' associated with a barrier.

Post-modernist approach to 'the four Ps'— transfer/availability/solutions/knowledge (TASK)

It would be hard to find a classical marketing concept more beloved than the 'four Ps'. The post-modernist doesn't have to leave them behind. All they represent is different places in which barriers may be driving customers away. Admitting this to be the case (and renaming them) leads to:

- easy visualisation of what marketing is doing;
- understanding of how to link marketing patterns to 'the way things should be' for customers in each of these areas;
- suggestions where problems may be happening;
- expansion of the 'four Ps' in ways not easy to see with their original names;
- reinforcement of the notion of a barrier being an unsolved problem.

Although the preceding list of benefits seems impressive, it must be admitted that there can be some downsides to a post-modernist approach.

Clinkers, lumps and limitations—the costs of a post-modernist approach

A quarter of a century's experience in developing the preceding has shown that a post-modernist view is not without some hazards. They are as follows.

Classical marketing academics are very hostile.

They see this approach as too simple and not *scientific* enough. They would rather grind away with research that never proves lasting, is made difficult to understand and almost impossible to use rather than admit their basic paradigm is wrong. Since these people control most of the journals, getting anything published suggesting 'the emperor has no clothes' is not easy.

Classical marketing practitioners don't like what the post-modernist paradigm suggests about their 'powers'.

Although there *are* practitioner benefits from this approach (see the above sections), it does cut directly through a fog of complexity and 'magic' with which marketers have always earned their living. They don't give up easily.

'Non-marketers' trying to learn about marketing can be panicked by classical practitioners.

This isn't always the case, for 'non-marketers' (in the sense of 'professionals') frequently like the approach and the ethical 'hooks' it avoids. But for some others, the opposite is true. How this works is that 'non-marketers' frequently take business education because they are worried about the very thing that makes for a 'bad' decision in a post-modernist sense. They are afraid they will be 'caught out' in a bad decision through failing to know something.

Classical marketers can prey on this fear if these 'non-marketers' can be made to think that (somehow) they are missing something through learning via a post-modernist approach (as it supposedly means less time to learn about *real* marketing). Since these 'non-marketers' have little means for comparison, they do scare easily!

There is little that can be done about either of the preceding shortcomings. All one can do is wait until the benefits of post-modernism become too numerous for either group to ignore. Then both will latch on to it with a passion.

A post-modernist approach opens up a new ethical concern.

How this happens is made easier to understand by recalling the 'poker chip' approach to competition. As each competitor 'raises' by doing something more than the others, the goal posts shift. Whatever now 'works' becomes the minimum standard for survival.

What ultimately drives marketing's domain beyond the promotional area (that everybody is *already* doing everything that can be done) eventually begins to be true for *all* areas. When this happens what it means is predictable—and of concern.

All competitors are 'marketing' like mad, gaining no additional revenue, but can't stop! For a marketing academic or practitioner there is something depressing about admitting that all the money spent on the discipline ultimately turns out to be self-cancelling, but impossible to stop without some sort of collusion (i.e., if anybody stops advertising on their own without substituting something else, they will lose their shirt!).

A good proof of this was the tobacco industry in the US. When the American government forced it to stop advertising on television, that was the greatest favour it ever had. For sales remained relatively constant, but all their profits *went up* because a big expense item was no longer there.

One way to feel better about this (inevitable) deficiency is to recognise that all this competition probably *does* result in more consumer choice and, because a post-modernist approach is so new, your adoption of it will probably allow you to stay ahead of competitors long enough to last your foreseeable career!

After 25 years of working with this approach, the preceding are the only major deficiencies that I have encountered, or that you are likely to. This leads to another interesting question.

So, what's your 'benefits-costs' analysis say?

Let's apply the 'micro-marketing' test. Would a reasonable person say that adopting a post-modernist approach (tied in with classical marketing tools) would seem a good idea? If not, stop here (actually, I doubt you would have made it this far were that the case). If it does seem a reasonable move, let's look at a simplified way to implement it.

How to be a post-modernist marketer in '10 easy steps'—or five hard ones!

Let's assume all of the training implied by this book has been done, the troops seem with us, and we want to become a post-modernist marketing marvel. The actual process of doing this is relatively simple. Readers of this book, whether they are a part of a 'marketing' organisation or not, may find it has a decidedly familiar ring to it. The reason for this feeling of *déjà vu* is that the barrier-based process of marketing is the one which all successful organisations have always had to follow if they were to survive.

Step 1: Set goals.

This must always be the first step in any plan. No attempt will be made to reproduce all the work others have done in this area; it will simply be assumed that reasonable goals, and strategies to accomplish them, have been decided upon.

What sets post-modernist marketing apart is that it does not assume employees (particularly workers, and to some extent managers) are robots who can be relied upon to carry out strategies to accomplish goals having selfish appeal only to 'owners'.

Thus, something new must be added to strategic planning—seeing how getting to goals can be made rewarding to employee interests. Most frequently this can mean money, but not always.

Other issues, such as job enrichment, personal development and most tools of human resource management, can come into play here, but what must be made clear is that moving towards employee goals is *conditional* upon employer performance—not passed out from Santa Claus.

Step 2: Determine the groups whose behaviours are of interest to employers.

Although it sounds awfully greedy, the only groups whose behaviours are of interest to employers are all those who affect the money stream that feeds employee/owner goals.

What this definition does is to sum up a group of items (over and above 'customers' in the classical sense) that many texts spend countless chapters discussing under various headings. Mostly what all these chapters do is show what has already been discussed—that these 'rarely considered consumer' groups can be dangerous if they hit barriers produced by employees.

What the post-modernist approach does is take these groups and directly 'translate' them into influences on income that feed *employee* interests. In more traditional approaches this linkage is almost never made.

Step 3: Determine if the number of 'customers' is large enough to feed the interests of all employees.

This is a step common to most marketing plans. In most marketing approaches all it does is make sure an employer doesn't go 'charging off' in a direction which is a 'dry hole' to begin with.

What is different here is that post-modernist marketing suggests planning should begin with an emphasis not just on providing for 'owner' desires, but also for employee needs. All this really does is raise the minimum-planning threshold required.

Classical approaches hold it will be enough to provide a return on owner-invested funds equal to that of other alternatives. What this can do is produce some decisions that may be awfully marginal when it comes to feeding 'all the little piggies lined up at the employer trough'.

Once the owners are fed, there may be enough left for only the most minimal treatment of workers and managers. In such a case who could blame these employees for feeling uninspired to protect an employer not really thinking of them from the beginning?

In the long run it would seem to everyone's advantage if all planning started with an assumption of supplying better-than-average returns for owners *and* employees. The worst that can come of this is that the employer will have a built-in 'safety-margin' should times get tough. The best that can come of it is results that reward and inspire everybody.

If this approach is followed, there should be increased employee interest in step 4.

Step 4: Determine the behaviours of the groups in step 2 of interest to employers.

Again it seems greedy but the only 'consumer' behaviours of interest to any employer are those which produce and/or threaten the income stream which currently feeds *employee* interests.

In more 'classical' approaches to marketing, a field called 'consumer behaviour' attempts to answer the age-old riddle of why people buy things. In a barrier-based approach the marketer doesn't really care why anybody buys anything. All they care about is that they keep on doing it! Or as one famous movie star put it:

I don't care what you call me—but call me often! (Mae West)

Similarly, it's really a great deal easier (and useful) to take the mystery out of marketing by saying, 'I don't care *why* they do anything—I just want them to give me money by doing it'. And then the marketer can go on from there.

For most businesses this is determined by somebody buying something. For charities, government departments and non-profits, the same sort of thing is taking place; it just may be harder to see. Some digging will bring it into the open. Nobody in this selfish world ever gets a living for nothing.

Once *how* the money gets to an organisation is known, finding out *who* controls the process gets easier. Usually all this requires is tracking some sort of paper trail backwards until one finds a decision maker and his or her influencers. For the moment this is all anybody needs to know, or will know for certain. But once this is known, the next step can be taken.

Step 5: Determine all the barriers in the world.

This may seem a very difficult task. It really isn't. Every classical marketing book in the world is simply a collection of information about barriers.

As has already been discussed, this is the point where the post-modernist approach is united with other schools of marketing thought. Once one understands barriers it is relatively easy to recast most marketing textbooks as a collection of information about the following:

- Who are the *types* of people with whom barriers might become a problem (macro- and micro-environments)?
- How might one see what could constitute a barrier (some consumer behaviour, demographics and marketing research)?
- What tools can be used to move from information about consumers to the construction of a marketing program which will minimise barriers (product differentiation and market segmentation)?
- What are the various forms that market-program barriers and efforts to minimise them might take ('TASK', etc.)?

Whatever the specifics of any marketing tool, the objective is to come up with a 'laundry list' of ideas concerning barriers that seem to 'improve the odds'. As shall be seen, these 'better odds' have a great deal to do with accomplishing the following steps involving barrier-based marketing.

Step 6: Discard those barriers not relevant to the situation.

Obviously, once one has produced a 'laundry list' of possible barriers, the next step is to start zeroing in on those that will be the focus of any plan. And the first step in this process is to get rid of those which don't apply to a situation.

This is not as easy as it seems. I assign my MBA students a task of producing a list like this suitable for use with their own employers. (How to do this—and use it—is a part of this chapter's action exercise.)

They tend to struggle with two basic problems in doing this assignment:

1 a refusal to see how the majority of options could apply to their organisation; or

2 a tendency to try to use tools which are inappropriate for their employer.

The first problem is caused either by a fundamental lack of creativity, or some blind assumption that an organisation will never be attacked. This is almost never true.

The second extreme, that of using inappropriate tools, can be just as bad, although it is less common. This error sees people trying to 'drive a nail with a saw' and getting nowhere. Clearly, some middle ground is in order—and finding it is not easy.

Once again the way to avoid either type of error is by asking oneself whether a 'reasonable person' would agree that what was done would be considered logical and complete. This is always in the mind of the reviewer, but a positive assessment is more likely to be produced by marketers who use a number of measures to judge the usefulness of their information.

In roughly descending order of respectability (the most respected first), the major justifications from which one can choose for taking any action are:

1 Competitors do/don't do this successfully.

2 Customers have directly or indirectly requested/ignored this.

3 Specific marketing research suggests this barrier is/is not relevant.

4 General marketing theory indicates this is/is not a barrier worth considering.

5 Prior decision-maker experience hints that this barrier should/should not be worked on.

6 Intuition (e.g. it seemed like a good idea at the time!).

At any rate, once some process has sorted out promising barriers from ones that don't apply, it becomes possible to go on to the next step.

Step 7: Identify all competitors and study them carefully.

What this means is marketers must:

1 determine who their competitors are (e.g. firm, form, fiscal and feeling); and then

2 learn all they can about what each of these is doing.

Once again this step is not totally at odds with classical approaches to marketing. However, in these non-barrier approaches the way to achieve success is pictured as follows:

1 Start out with a blank sheet of paper.
2 Isolate some consumers to serve.
3 Find the needs of these consumers.
4 Serve these needs as completely as possible.

Only after this has been done are competitors brought up, and in some books this seems almost an afterthought. Not only is this seldom the way it works in 'real life', but also this approach can waste some real opportunities. Post-modernist marketing does just the opposite.

Remember that the most important element of marketing success is not 'customer' satisfaction alone. Rather it is the level of 'customer' satisfaction for one employer *as opposed to its competitors*.

Because of this there are two reasons for emphasising competitors rather than ignoring them until the end. One is to determine the level of barriers they have so that it can be bettered (e.g. how can we know we are 'less worse' than they unless we know what they are up to?).

The second reason is to learn ideas from them. The cheapest (and best) market research in the world is always a successful competitor.

The reason analysing successful competitors is often more useful than normal market research is that market research is always one step behind—and one step from reality. 'One step behind' relates to the historical nature of marketing.

Being 'one step from reality' means that market research often involves some sort of information-gathering which may, or may not, be representative of the marketplace. For instance, getting customers to fill out a questionnaire indicating what they *may buy* is often a far cry from what they *do buy*. Beyond this, even the most unsuccessful competitor may have something to offer. As one popular joke puts it:

Even a broken watch is right twice a day!

If a competitor is doing well enough to survive (i.e. to be a 'competitor'), it is rare that they are not doing something better than those with whom they compete. If this is known, it can be copied or bettered.

How to gain this information about competitors can be learned from any standard textbook (also see *Marketing intelligence* in Chapter 12 and the material on mystery shopping). Once all competitors are known as well as one knows one's own employer, the next step can be taken.

Step 8: Eliminate all barriers with a minimal cost.

As stated in Chapter 10, not all barriers cost something to remove or minimise. Sometimes updating a system (for instance) actually reduces cost. And some barriers are the result of an oversight—or outright stupidity. Seeing what textbooks suggest and what competitors are doing reveals a lot of these. Getting rid of them generally costs little or nothing.

It therefore makes sense to work on these relatively cost-free and risk-free actions first. A good rule-of-thumb for identifying them is as follows:

Minimal cost barriers are those whose removal causes so little additional expense that they don't require higher management approval.

This decision-rule should be communicated to all employees, no matter how far down the pyramid they may be. It gives them a guide for correcting situations they might not otherwise bother with.

For instance, the phone is ringing and you are a janitor. It is not your job to answer phones, but no one else is around, and you have been told this rule. Does it cost anything for you to at least try to take a message? No! So, answer that phone!

Unfortunately, one tends to run out of these low-cost options very quickly. Then it is time to go on to the next step.

Step 9: By market arena, evaluate all remaining barriers on a line item and total basis compared with the competition, to get even.

As used here 'market arena' means a focus consisting of any group of competitors (including the subject employer) who seem separate from other groupings. Most textbooks will have any number of ways of grouping (see for example 'Defining a market'), including these categories:

- geographical (e.g. those competitors in the same town);
- product/service (e.g. those making/doing the same thing);
- client type (e.g. those serving the same types of 'customers');
  ... and so on ... and so on ... and so on.

Whatever the focus chosen, the barrier-based approach may use it in a different manner from other marketing frameworks. What makes it different is that the barrier approach does not insist on a 'one-size-fits-all' mentality.

A lock-step approach can be produced by marketers insisting that total consumer satisfaction is the goal. Once some formula to achieve this is found it tends to be applied uniformly, meaning that all markets will be treated the same.

Unless some sort of management savings is involved, this just doesn't make sense. For instance, I had a travel agent client who represented a chain of locations ranging from huge cities with many competitors to no-competitor 'bumps in the road' consisting of the agent, a post office, and a Coca-Cola™ machine! It would have been crazy to insist the city operators *had* to attack the same barriers in the same way as their country cousins. It is much wiser to deal with each separate market individually, doing just enough to stay ahead of competitors in that market.

The term 'line item' implies that barriers will first be compared on a unit-by-unit basis. For instance, whether you need a 'flashy' brochure/location/salesperson may be indicated by whether your competitor has one. However, this is one indication only.

This item-by-item comparison must also be part of a 'total impression' comparison done at the same time. Clearly, some barriers *are* more important than others. Also, sometimes synergy—in which the sum is greater (or less) than the total of its parts—does happen, so one must *also* somehow take a measure of each competitor's total position.

A good way to do this is to (truthfully) answer the following question:

> *Would a reasonable person agree that we are at least equal to our competitors? And, if not, why not?*

The objective of all this is to find those areas where an employer seems to be worse off (have more barriers) than its competitors. Or we might create one for a competitor by doing something different from them. But it is not necessary to work on each and every one of these barriers in order to get even.

Every employer will have some natural advantages which cancel out barriers in other areas (e.g. *they* have a better brochure, but *we* have better advertising). Furthermore, some barriers will be more important than others.

What will be required is a balancing act that tries to at least bring the employer to a point of equality (or better) with its competitors. Once this is done it is possible to go to the final (and most important) step.

Step 10: Very carefully minimise a few more barriers.

The reason this must be done *very carefully* is that getting to the same level as competitors means most easy options for taking out barriers will have been tried already (particularly in a market which has been around awhile). As one Chinese proverb put it:

> *The longer two enemies fight the more they begin to resemble each other.*

There may be a few clear barriers 'left over' from the earlier analysis which didn't need attention just to get even. Doing something about these may give an employer a temporary advantage with minimal risk, but sooner or later the advantages will no longer be apparent and everybody will look alike.

The next step will generally be into uncharted territory, for which there is probably little history indicating the right way to go. There can only be three main reasons why the 'opportunity' to do this exists:

1 Somebody has tried it before, but it *didn't work*.

2 Nobody has tried it before, and it *won't work*.

3 Everybody has overlooked it, and it *will work*.

Unfortunately, this analysis looks very much like the way one footballer described both a thrown ball and affairs of the heart:

> *There are* three *things that can happen—and* two *of them are bad.*

The odds seem to favour doing nothing, but nothing ventured, nothing gained. One can't keep on copying competitors forever. Sooner or later one has to 'boldly go where no one has gone before'. And the outcome of taking out a new barrier can produce one of only two extremes: wonderful or weird.

After an untried barrier is removed, 'customers' *may* think the employer is wonderful because they wanted it gone. The already mentioned 'PT Cruiser' is an example of this. Chrysler removed a barrier by producing a product nobody else knew anybody wanted. They made a fortune.

On the other hand, after 'the smoke settles', a great deal of money may have been spent on something not bothering anybody. And the customer may then think the employer is just plain weird. This is not at all wonderful because it means the marketer has chosen poorly, and spent money with no return. This will probably lead to a later price barrier in order to get it back.

A classic example of this was the 'effervescent Edsel', *New Coke*. Coke marketing research suggested that people preferred their cola to be slightly sweeter, so it changed the basic formula. Although at first successful, Coke drinkers eventually were outraged. They felt something that was a real part of their heritage, the 'Old Coke', had been taken from them. Sales plummeted. Coke eventually had to admit that, despite the millions spent on market research, what it had produced was 'weird' and nobody wanted it. Coke reintroduced the old product and sales shot back up.

Of course, one item which must be added to this package is one involving costs. Remember, marketers should deal only with barriers for which the payback period is less than the 'period of patience' for their employer.

Obviously, estimating the payback period for a barrier of unknown importance is not easy, and figuring out how long those in decision-making capacities will wait for results is no easier. It involves both objective (e.g. interest rates, goals) and subjective (e.g. personalities, prior experience) variables which are hard to estimate. But unless this factor is at least taken into consideration some really dumb things can happen.

When all is said and done, there can be no guarantees. Because of this it may be important to recall what one general said about all strategy:

If it works you're a hero. If it doesn't you're a bum!

Although this is probably the truth, let us quickly proceed to some more comforting thoughts related to this entire process. The most important of these is the following.

If one adopts a post-modernist approach, who is in charge of your survival? You are!

If one truly believes in barrier-based 'business', one conclusion is inescapable— what happens to your organisation does *not* depend on strangers. Whether your employer lives or dies is not really up to competitors, governments or anybody outside of it.

These 'outsiders' are not in control of the barriers your employer produces. The ones in control of these barriers—and your future—are *you and your fellow employees*. The only way your source of economic survival can perish is if you collectively or individually cause it to happen by producing barriers that push your 'business' elsewhere.

To a large extent whether this happens or not will depend upon the answer both employer and employees provide through actions—not words—to the most important question regarding this book, and your employer.

The most important question of economic survival—'Will anything change?'

What is meant here is whether, after reading this book, you will *do* anything about it. Will you make sure *all* in the business understand everything it says? And will someone make sure this understanding causes things to be done in a different way than before? For your sake, I hope so.

A post-modernist approach certainly seems likely to offer better chances than other more classical ones, particularly if these aren't working especially well for you. Any reasonable person would probably say that. And the consequences of failing to follow through on that assessment may be horrendous.

For if nothing changes you can't be better off—no fewer barriers are present than there were before. You aren't even 'equal-off'. The reason is that this exposure had to have some cost associated with it. And, if nothing changes, the only ways to get this cost back are through reduced 'profit' or increased 'prices'. Either way makes for more barriers to success, and you would therefore be worse off than if you had never heard of it at all.

So you see, whether you and those with whom you work sink or swim must be ultimately up to you, your fellow employees, and your answer to the most important question for any organisation:

Will anything change?

ACTION SUMMARY

A permanent fix for customer service problems doesn't mean painting over them, but rather blowing up traditional structures and starting over.

An important issue is whether this post-modernist approach is actually better. A 'benefits-cost' analysis may help with such an assessment. Let's see what is different/better.

A post-modernist approach assumes universal selfishness.

This produces many benefits, mostly by allowing people to be open and so work together for the common good.

Defining marketing as encouragement of behaviour financially beneficial to the encourager

This definition is broad enough to be timeless, but narrow enough to separate marketing from other disciplines, while providing the 'string' which controls how it works.

Accepting a paradigm that marketing doesn't make people buy things—it takes away barriers

This is both truthful and solves problems for marketers and 'non-marketers'.

Defining marketing management as 'formal producer minimisation of important barriers to desirable consumer behaviour' applies the paradigm to the real world.

The post-modernist mechanism of taking away barriers/making them for others simplifies understanding marketing.

Explaining that a barrier is an unsolved problem

This shows how to use the mechanism.

Micro-marketing by a post-modernist avoids 'bad' decisions.

'Bad' decisions are most often caused by ignoring information.

Classical and post-modernist approaches rely on order-and-pattern.

This is something they have in common.

Classical marketing tools are historical and lead to creation of a USP through segmentation/differentiation.

Both segmentation and differentiation minimise barriers in different ways.

The post-modernist uses the 'four Ps' but broadens them ('TASK').

TASK stands for transfer, availability, solutions and knowledge.

There are few limitations to using a post-modernist approach.

What there are relate to classical marketer resistance and an ethical problem produced by realising *all* marketing effort is eventually *self-cancelling*.

Implementing a post-modernist approach is easy.

It requires (1) setting goals, (2) determining consumers, (3) deciding if markets are large enough, (4) determining the behaviours of interest, (5) identifying all barriers, (6) discarding those not relevant, (7) identifying/studying competitors, (8) eliminating low-cost barriers, (9) establishing competitive equality, and (10) carefully taking out one more barrier.

Implementing a post-modernist approach makes sense.

It offers many new advantages while losing none of the benefits of classical marketing.

Who is in control? You are!

Job-destroying barriers are not created by outsiders. They track back to you and your co-workers. Whether you sink or swim will be up to the most important question asked by this book:

Will anything change?

THE BOTTOM LINE

A post-modernist/barrier-based approach to marketing and customer service offers overwhelming benefits. How long will you threaten your own survival by not using it?

ACTION EXERCISE 15.1

Building a barrier-based marketing manual

For: Mid/upper management, employees   **Format:** Individual/group
Materials required: Quite a lot of time and any good 'principles of marketing' text (e.g. try any edition of McCarthy, Kotler or Stanton). Later on, a management conference will be needed.
Objective: To look at items which might be barriers to your organisation with an eye to their eventual removal in order to gain advantage over competitors

Step 1: Construct a barrier-based marketing 'manual'.

The purpose of this exercise is not to immediately provide you with answers to your employer's marketing problems. Such a detailed treatment will require effort on the part of more people than yourselves (see step 2). Rather, it is the focus of this exercise to get your employer to consider areas of marketing that could serve as the basis for removing barriers to your customers, or making them for a competitor.

The end-result of this could easily comprise a marketing manual that will be user-specific to your employer.

In order to carry out this exercise it will be necessary for you to do the following:

1   Choose the most important product or service (or group of products/services) your employer 'sells' and describe it (them).
2   Determine the major competitors your employer faces in this market (e.g. firm, form, fiscal and feeling), and describe who they are.
3   Read your chosen textbook lightly. As you do, ask yourself if there is any way in which the topic being discussed could be of interest to your employer. If 'yes', you may wish to highlight it. If 'no', be sure ... then read on.
4   Once you have done this, go back over the highlighted items. Assume at some point that you will have at your disposal a workforce of people who will try to answer these questions for you.
5   For each topic you think *could* apply to your employer (*hint:* do some creative thinking):
    - List the topic area (e.g. demographics).
    - Follow this with a discussion of how the topic works in general,
    - Explain how it relates to your employer's activity (e.g. what do we do regarding this, have we ignored it?)
    - Construct questions or orders you would wish your employees to carry out to see whether the subject area would be worth further attention or not (e.g. is the ageing of the population going to affect the market for pogo sticks—and how?).

Try to be as detailed as possible. Give specifics. If you don't know where to find an item, then ask somebody to find it. In all cases, what you are doing will be to find out if a topic area could contain in it thoughts which could lead to barriers present in your organisation or a competitor—barriers which if known could be used for marketing success.

You are to develop a format for presenting your work which makes sense to you. The most difficult question will be, 'How far shall I go in asking questions?' This is up to you, but the more specifics there are, the more your employer can learn.

If well done, this manual may ask some questions so interesting you won't be able to resist trying to answer them. And, more importantly, they may serve as a 'jumping off' point for the next step.

Step 2: Put the manual created to work.

Knowledge of barriers is useless without *doing* something about them. The best way to do something is by organising some sort of weekend management strategy conference. It will be most useful if the people at this conference have some job-related issue in common (e.g. they all are in the accounting area, all have something to do with shipping, and so on).

Before this conference, sort out those questions that seem to have the most to do with this target group. Then use your manual as a basis for stimulating discussion about areas in which your employer could either:

- minimise its own barriers (by stopping the doing of something foolish); or
- make a barrier for a competitor (by doing something better than it does).

It will be best if the emphasis is placed on these questions:

- What is involved with this barrier?
- How do our competitors handle this issue?
- What better ways exist for handling it?
- How could we put this knowledge to work?

Throughout this discussion keep in mind the three-step requirements of any process involving barriers:

1. What resources which we don't now have are needed to do the job? (And would their cost be justified by increased 'sales' within the 'period of patience'?)
2. How can we make sure that any processes of dealing with this barrier (both the process required to make sure somebody initially does something about it, as well as that required for keeping at it into the future) are visible?
3. What consequences (positive or negative) will attach to both of these processes?

Conclusion

If this process is faithfully carried out it should help your employer isolate areas in which it could gain a competitive advantage. Finding out what these areas are—and doing something about them—is essential to ensuring your employer's survival.

Endnote

Those of my students who have undertaken this assignment have frequently sold it back to their employer for as much as $25 000. The reason for this high value is due to its constantly challenging the status quo (the way things are) of any employer with the most 'cutting edge' knowledge of the way things 'should be'.

These manuals seem to be used for years and years, with some organisations getting them out once a year, choosing some chapter, assembling the executives responsible for that chapter's functional areas, and then conducting what most say is 'the most beneficial strategic planning session in the history of the employer'.

Appendix

The contents of this book are offered in both a number of seminars (presented by the author personally) and in a six-module video *Customer-centred Culture Kit*. These fast-moving, critically acclaimed presentations can teach your staff how to fight 'the enemy within' and produce meaningful changes in your workforce.

We also can help you source the *Who Killed the Customer?* video mentioned in Chapter 14.

If you would like further information regarding any of these tools, we can be reached 24 hours a day using the following contact details:

Richard W. Buchanan, PhD
Buchanan and Associates
12 Mountain View Road
Palmerston North
New Zealand
Tel: +64–6–354–0033
Fax: +64-6-350-5577
E-mail R.W.Buchanan@massey.ac.nz

About the author

Dr Richard Buchanan is uniquely qualified to shake business thinking to its core. Prior to becoming Massey University's first Professor of Marketing Education, he worked as a gardener, a truck driver, and on assembly lines. This gave him a viewpoint unique among marketing gurus—that of the common working person asked to carry out marketing/customer service actions, with no reason for so doing ... *until this book appeared!*

His formal education included completing three degrees at some of the finest business schools in the United States of America, as well as teaching at four others. He has corporate experience at firms as diverse as Merrell Dow and Ford Motor Company. He also ran his own nationwide consulting firm before immigrating to New Zealand in 1986 to accept a post at Massey University. His responsibilities there have included the required marketing content of the Massey executive MBA program (recently named as the best MBA program in New Zealand).

Hailed as 'the most sought after business speaker in New Zealand', Dr Buchanan is a frequent speaker to groups and conferences in New Zealand, Australia, Asia, the United States, Canada and Britain. His clients have included General Motors Holden, AMP Life Insurance, Caltex Oil, Mobil Oil, ICI Pharmaceutical, Telecom, NZ Post, Hewlett-Packard, Westpac Bank, Mack Truck, Suzuki, the New Zealand Department of Energy, Presbyterian Social Services and many more.

He was the only Australasian business academic asked to address the prestigious American Young President's Organisation, and was the only New Zealander ever invited to give a keynote presentation to the International Group of Agencies and Bureaus.

His last book was an international bestseller translated into German, Spanish, and Chinese, and has been sold in more than 30 countries. In this book he 'pushes the envelope' even further by doing something no one has ever done before—operationalising the 'cutting edge' world of post-modernist marketing into something everyone can understand and use.